Secularization in Contemporary Religious Radicalism

Theological Seminar
Series
5

ISSN 1566-2098

Deo Publishing

SECULARIZATION *in* CONTEMPORARY RELIGIOUS RADICALISM

An Introduction

Corneliu C. Simuţ

BLANDFORD FORUM

Theological Seminar Series, 5

ISSN 1566-2098

Copyright © 2013 Deo Publishing
P.O. Box 6284, Blandford Forum, Dorset DT11 1AQ, UK

All rights reserved. No part of this publication may be reproduced, translated, stored in a retrieval system, or transmitted in any form or by any means, electronic, mechanical, photocopying, recording or otherwise, without prior written permission from the publisher.

Printed by Henry Ling Ltd, at the Dorset Press, Dorchester, DT1 1HD, UK

British Library Cataloguing-in-Publication data
A catalogue record for this book is available from the British Library

ISBN 978-1-905679-23-2

Dedicated to

Professor Dr. Nagy V. Endre
and
Associate Professor Dr. Juhász Ferenc

*in recognition of their exemplary medical competence
and warm personal character*

Contents

    Foreword ix
    Acknowledgments xii
    Introduction 1

1. **Setting Things on Their Feet: Ernst Bloch**
   Sobriety and Enthusiasm 15
   Hope and Matter 17
   Teleology and the Reality of This World 21

2. **Destroying the Values of the Past: Herbert Marcuse**
   Desacralization and Industrialization 25
   History and Metaphysics 28
   The Use of Reason and Pacified Existence 31

3. **Dismissing the Otherworldliness of God: Karl Rahner**
   Secularization and Demythologization 34
   Incarnation and Creation 36
   Man's Self-Transcendence and God's Self-Communication 40

4. **Stripping Nature of Sacred Meanings: Mircea Eliade**
   Desacralization and Rationalization 43
   The Acknowledgment of the Sacred 46
   Consciousness and Unconsciousness 48

5. **Lessening the Importance of God: Edward Schillebeeckx**
   The Lessening of God 52
   The Move Away from the Church 54
   Critical Thinking about God 57

6. **Keeping God at a Distance: John Hick**
   The Christological Confusion 60
   Mythology and the Image of Christ 62
   Global Religion and Freedom 65

7. **Growing Responsible towards the World: Paul van Buren**
   Spiritualization and the Totality of Reality 68
   The Death of Jesus and the Value of Life 71
   Hope and the Notion of Messiah 74

8. **Reducing Religion to a Human Phenomenon: William Hamilton**
   Radical Theology and Language 77
   The Death of God and Monotheism 80
   The Post-Historical Jesus 83

9. **Being Aware of Temporality and Finitude: Gabriel Vahanian**
   Secularity and Secularism 86
   Christology and Anthropology 89
   Faith and the Dead God 92

10. **Accepting God as Dead: Thomas J.J. Altizer**
    De-Christianization and Re-Christianization 95
    Criticism against Christianity 98
    The Death of the Christian God 100

11. **Turning to Humanity: Hans Küng**
    The World, Religion, and Theology 104
    Emancipation, Equalization, and Autonomy 106
    Openness, Social Awareness, and Freedom 109

12. **Seeing Reality as It Is: Harvey Cox**
    Nature and Faith 112
    Politics and History 115
    Ethical Values and the World 117

13. **Putting an End to Religion: John Shelby Spong**
    Religion and Interiority 121
    God and Man's Reality 123
    Experience and Objectivity 126

14. **Absorbing the Sacred into the Profane: Don Cupitt**
    Religion and Humanism 129
    The Church and the World 132
    Rationality, Mythology, and Meaning 135

15. **Recognizing the Indispensability of Religion: Mark C. Taylor**
    The Power of Religion 138
    Immanence and Transcendence 141
    The Necessity of Cyclicality 144

16. **Cultivating a Civil Religion: Vito Mancuso**
    The Reevaluation of Atheism 147
    The Reconsideration of Incarnation 150
    The Redefinition of the Trinity 152

Viewing Secularization Today: A Synthetic Conclusion 156

Bibliography 187
Index of Subjects 202

Foreword

It is difficult to find two people who understand secularization in the same way. As a historical process it is also very complicated. Its roots have ramifications far back into history and even today most people interpret it differently. As for myself, I generally try to perceive secularization as a social phenomenon which originates in a civilized world related to or influenced by Christianity. From this Christian spirituality secularization has radiated out into other religious societies. That is why Christian thinkers have to make an attempt to clarify conceptually the reality of this fact having penetrated deeply into the life of mankind. One of these Christian scholars, Professor Corneliu C. Simuṭ from Emanuel University of Oradea, has tried to shed light on this phenomenon in a special way. He hit upon an idea, he discovered a clue, and by following in its tracks he now points to the meaning and origin of secularization in modern European history referring to the fact that, to some extent, it has a relationship with Christian thought. I realize that anyone who tries to explain it is not able to neglect its Christian roots, because consciously or unconsciously everyone is in touch with Christian culture or with the history of the church. Because of its Jewish-Christian background, secularization in its basic form is closely related to European spirituality. This fact inspires us to read this book with a high degree of interest.

Professor Simuṭ also proposes to investigate the idea of secularization as a fundamental phenomenon which accompanies contemporary assessments of religion. He presents the various understandings of secularization as seen through the eyes of sixteen modern thinkers. He starts with Ernst Bloch and the Marxist philosophy according to which secularization is an attempt to demystify religion in order to make it acceptable for the modern man. Then great figures of the intellectual life of Europe and America tell us what they think about this topic. Herbert Marcuse understood it as desacralization and industrialization. Karl Rahner argued that this process originated within Christianity itself. Mircea Eliade claimed that secularization was both desacralization and rationalization through the nullification of transcendence. Edward Schillebeeckx's notion of secularization implies one's active movement away from the church, something which is no longer relevant for today's lay consciousness of our secularized society. John Hick showed that secularization was a process aiming at a reconstruction of Christology for man's contemporary consciousness. Paul van Buren, despite significant changes in his own views throughout his career, does not offer any significant place for metaphysics in his hermeneutics. William Hamilton's thought is a radical theology, trying to see the human being as something absolutely autonomous from any traditional religious and Christian norms. Gabriel Vahanian makes a sharp distinction between secularity and secularization, the former being a necessary result of traditional Christianity, while the latter is an unfortunate development, replacing the rigorism of traditional religion with the tyranny of nonreligious convictions. Thomas J.J. Altizer's dualist approach to secularization is based on the dichotomy between spirit and flesh. Hans Küng sees secularization as a process which causes the boundaries between the church and the world to be a fluid reality. Harvey Cox approaches secularization from the perspectives of nature (demystification), politics (desacralization) and values (deconsecration). John Shelby Spong's secularizing program is the end of religion as man knows it. Don Cupitt sees secularization as a shift from traditional religion to a humanist perspective on God. Mark C. Taylor argues that secularization neither attempts to restrict the influence of religion, nor seeks to abandon it in any way whatever. Finally, Vito Mancuso defines secularization as a process of rethinking fundamental concepts such as atheism, incarnation, and trinity.

The vivid as well as intriguing presentation of all sixteen thinkers reveals not only that Professor Simuţ has deeply immersed himself in the modern literature of systematic theology, but also that he is well acquainted with contemporary philosophical notions as well as with the specific fields and areas of religious studies. The helpful titles and subtitles throughout the work betray an inherent familiarity with the themes and thinkers he has set out to present. The scientific method of parallel analytic presentations is combined with a refined synthetic vision showing how diverse the interpretation of the idea of secularization has become both within and outside Christian theology. The reader of this book really feels the extent of the tension which exists between the *saeculum* and the *aeternum*. A solution can always be found in the dialectic perception of the temporal world and the timeless being of God. As the author states after a thoroughgoing conclusion at the end of his work: "secularization happens when our lay consciousness understands that God must exist within humanity. ... God cannot be cancelled by humanity; it can only be brought to the level of humanity."

This work is certainly a laudable attempt to provide the reader with an overall presentation of this complex and multifaceted phenomenon with a keen eye focused on important details which may often contain some of the most significant clues to the future changes and possible developments in Christian mission.

Prof. Dr. Habil. Botond Gaál, PhD, DSc
Professor of Systematic Theology
Debrecen Reformed Theological University
Debrecen, Hungary

January 2nd, 2012

Acknowledgments

My personal history has recently intersected with those of just a few people whom I should thank for intervening in my life in such a way that the publication of this book became possible: Dr. Ionuț Popescu, lecturer in philosophy at the Greek-Catholic Faculty of Theology within the Babeș-Bolyai University of Cluj-Napoca (the Oradea Department), who – in a very brief conversation with me which he chaired at an academic conference on secularization back in 2010 – gave me the idea to expand an paper into a whole book; Dr. David E. Orton, who not only graciously accepted the original manuscript for publication, but also generously put a huge amount of work into copy-editing and typesetting it; Professor Dr. Nagy V. Endre, an exquisite endocrinologist, as well as Associate Professor Dr. Juhász Ferenc, a highly competent endocrine surgeon (both working and teaching at the Faculty of Medicine within the University of Debrecen) without whose prompt actions this book would have never seen the light of day (and to whom my work is dedicated), and Professor Dr. Gaál Botond, Chair of the Doctoral and Habilitation Committee at the Reformed Theological University of Debrecen, who in addition to supervising and accepting my book as a Habilitation thesis, decided to take upon himself the rather complex and time-consuming process which eventually led to my being awarded the *venia legendi* at Debrecen's old Protestant university. To all of them I am truly and wholeheartedly grateful.

Corneliu C. Simuț

Introduction

This volume investigates the idea of secularization as a fundamental phenomenon of contemporary approaches to religion. Regardless of whether secularization is discussed from within or from outside the sphere of practical religion itself – based on various writings produced over the last hundred years by historians and philosophers of religion, as well as by theologians of different persuasions – the main focus of that research is on eliminating the supernatural content of religious ideas, a focus which I call "religious radicalism". Set in contrast with religious traditionalism, religious radicalism not only seeks to present religion in purely historical terms, but it also attempts to translate supra-historical concepts of divinity into notions with a merely human content. From this perspective, my work presents the idea of secularization as it emerges from the writings of sixteen scholars, who are all concerned with presenting religion – or theology as a particularization thereof – from the conviction that religion is only a human phenomenon whose concept of God has nothing to do with references to the ontologically real existence of a transcendent being in charge of the whole universe. Quite *au contraire*, religious radicalism accepts God exclusively as a concept which may or may not present a certain degree of significance for the human being and his wide range of religious manifestations.

Organized in a historical fashion, my book unfolds – at an introductory level – the development of the idea of secularization during the last century in the main works of representative contemporary religious thinkers, while deliberately resisting systematic categorizations such as history and philosophy of religion, "death-of-God" theology, and Catholic or Protestant liberalism so as to organize the material based on each author's adherence to certain academic "schools" of thought. These are certainly not ignored when authors and their products are analyzed throughout the book, but they are not instrumental for the organizing principle of my work, which is predominantly historical and follows a timeline built on the course of each author's life.

Thus, in Chapter 1, *Ernst Bloch* (1885-1977) discusses the issue of secularization from the perspective of Marxist philosophy and sees it as a process which, although reaching its apex in modernity, has its origin in religion itself. Secularization is an attempt to demystify religion in order for it to make sense to modern man.[1] Thus, the hope of traditional religion in an ontologically real and metaphysical God is stripped of its mythological layer and is then presented as a human hope in man's own historical, and specifically human, future. If secularization is to take place effectively, Bloch shows that man needs sobriety and enthusiasm, which are methodological instruments for deciphering the past and the future. Man, then, must set his imagination in action, then activate his militant optimism in order to see that, once the past has been demystified, the future presents itself as a sum of real possibilities awaiting to be actualized in the reality of the world. Man, thus, must have hope in himself and the possibilities which he has in his own future within the reality of the physical world. This is to say that man's hope must always be directed towards what exists in the world and what is possible in the world. Although traditional religion is robbed of its belief in a transcendent God, this does not mean that the idea of purpose is eliminated. Bloch still believes in teleology, but this must never be detached from the reality of this world. As a result of his Marxist idea of secularization, the notion of God is altered to the point that it is presented as an ideal of humanity, totally demystified and dissolved in anthropology. Consequently, the idea of God as understood through the lens of secularization must provide man with an image of himself, which is scientific, true, and dialectical-critical. This is, according to Bloch, the only way modern man is able to find hope for his own existence, namely by understanding himself within the only reality which exists in nature, the reality of the physical world beyond which there is no God, but in which man reigns supreme.

For *Herbert Marcuse* (1898-1979), discussed in Chapter 2, secularization as the desacralization and industrialization of agrarian societies belongs to his view of the critical social theory that sees the demystification of pre-industrialized values and customs as a condition for the achievement of liberalism and democracy. From this perspective, secularization is viewed as an attempt to fulfil man's basic needs through the mediation of industrialization which happens within capitalism and communism. Consequently, secularization appears as a step towards progress, although the realization of progress itself is not the guarantee of the total demystification of unseen human beliefs and customs. The invisible constituents of human existence continue to be interpreted in

---

[1] The term "man" is used in its inclusive sense as shorthand for humanity, male and female.

ways which are irrational or spiritual in the midst of industrialized societies. This is why there is an acute need for industrialization to be accomplished by means of reason; the use of reason, though, must educate the human being to the point that he believes in the uniqueness of his physical reality as the only environment for his existence. The use of reason does not preclude philosophy from working with concepts like transcendence and metaphysics but they must be restricted to and defined in accordance with the physical reality of the world. Any mythology must be detached from concepts, so references to transcendence or metaphysics should be confined to a rational rationality, which is the only means to achieve progress. Irrational rationalities can disrupt progress, produce violence, and even cause destruction, so the process of secularization must take this into account if freedom and pacification are to be attained for man's existence in the world. The sensible use of reason within the larger project of secularization is supposed to avoid any mythological perspectives within society, regardless of whether they refer to pre-industrialized ideas or post-industrialized technology. Unseen beliefs as well as visible things must be understood through the lens of reason. Thus, reason is supposed to regulate man's perspective on the visible things of reality, while art – defined within the all-encompassing presence of reason in industrialized societies – is meant to deal with the invisible side of man's existence. Nevertheless, both reason and art should present man with a historicist understanding of his existence in the physical world, which sees religion in terms of oppression and exploitation.

In *Karl Rahner* (1904-1984) secularization is presented as a process which – as shown in Chapter 3 – originates within Christianity itself, so its doctrines have the capacity to be understood in a way which is consonant with the modern discoveries of science and technology. This is not supposed to mean that Christianity should wane in order to let science and technology lead humanity towards progress; it means, though, that the traditional dichotomy between spirit and matter should be understood as pointing not to two distinct realities, but rather to one, unique reality. Secularization, therefore, should be applied to doctrine and the most evident example of a secularized dogmatics is seen in Christology. The means whereby secularization can be applied to doctrines is a demythologization which deprives Jesus of his traditional ontological and metaphysical divinity in order to transfer it into the existence and experience of all human beings. The immediate result of such an exercise is the modification of the traditional content of other doctrines, such as creation and incarnation. While in traditional theology, creation and incarnation refer to the acts of a transcendent and ontologically real God, in Rahner's secularized thought they point to realities pertaining to human experience. Thus, creation indicates man's belief in the unity and uniqueness of the material world (traditionally called "creation"), while incarnation refers to man's ability to see the materiality of the world in spiritual terms. In other words, the traditional features of God, but also those of Jesus Christ, are transferred to the human being. As a result of this, Rahner's idea of God's self-communication no longer points to the God of traditional theology, but rather to man's self-transcendence, which is his innate ability to relate to himself and the world in a spiritual way. Rahner's secularized theology produces a Christology which does not deal primarily with Jesus Christ, but with man in general, seen as a natural embodiment of the hypostatic union, namely a natural blend of materiality and spirituality within the space, time, and history of the universe.

In Chapter 4, *Mircea Eliade* (1907-1986) sketches a perspective on secularization which is predominantly described as desacralization and rationalization through the nullification of transcendence, the acceptance of relativity with reference to reality, and the promotion of doubt in connection with man's existential meaning. While secularization tries to eliminate religion or at least its influence in the world as a result of scientific and technological progress through the demystification of religious symbols, Eliade stresses that it cannot completely extract the sacred from the profane. The very structure of human beings from ancient times has been oriented towards consciously interpreting religious beliefs as myths and secularization cannot put an end to this state of affairs. It can seriously alter it, but religion cannot be extracted from the existential reality of the human individual. This is why Eliade points out that religious manifestations remain within the sphere of modern man's existence and experience in the world, so the acknowledgment of the sacred is a key aspect of secularization. In modern society, secularization managed to demystify fundamental events in man's existence – such as birth, marriage, and death – but though stripped of their ritualistic component, they still remained an essential part of man's experience and, given man's innate propensity for a religious interpretation of the world, secularization will most likely be incapable of producing a completely areligious person.

Secularization therefore will continue to advance within modern society but, in doing so, it will also embrace some hidden manifestations of religious behaviour, which will continue to characterize humanity in our heavily industrialized world. Eliade shows that these hidden manifestations of religion are, as a matter of fact, unconscious attempts by human beings to reconnect with their religious past. This is why profoundly secularized patterns of thought like Marxism and psychoanalysis unconsciously promote the myth of the saviour and the ritual of initiation, so characteristic to religion in general.

Eliade admits that the ideal of secularization, which is the emergence of a totally areligious or nonreligious man, is for now a merely theoretical construction. As Eliade emphasizes, empirical reality proves that, despite all efforts to secularize society by pushing religion aside, religion continues to manifest itself both consciously and unconsciously as an attempt to solve the existential crisis of the modern man in a meaningful way.

As evident in Chapter 5, the concept of secularization in *Edward Schillebeeckx* (1914-2009) starts from an image of God which is dramatically decreased in importance as compared to the traditional doctrine of God. Schillebeeckx portrays God only as a human reality, which needs to be set against the view that sees God as present, and different from man. In Schillebeeckx's secularized thought, God is not different from man, at least not from the reality of man's existence in the world, so he is seen as absent. The classical theistic doctrine of God, but also of man, gives way to Schillebeeckx's new perspective on God seen as absent from the world and from man's life. Both God and man should no longer be accepted in theistic terms, but rather from an atheistic perspective. The waning of God from theism to atheism and from a real presence to a real absence means that he is silent as far as humanity is concerned, so he no longer speaks to humanity through the church. Consequently, secularization also implies man's active movement away from the church, which is no longer relevant for today's lay consciousness of our secularized society.

Then, Schillebeeckx moves forward with an explanation of the need to think critically of God; this means that, in addition to seeing God as absent and silent, he should be seen as total freedom. Traditional religion can therefore be abandoned because God is not a presence any longer. He is rather the sum of possibilities which exist for the human race in the future, so God is now the temporal future of humanity. Secularization therefore drafts a picture of God whose characteristics are absence and silence; he can be known through atheism and agnosticism, and then should be constantly pictured as man's total freedom that can only be unveiled in the future, which seems to hold the key for man's unprecedented progress in science and technology.

In Chapter 6, *John Hick* (b. 1922) proves that secularization is a process which aims at a reconstruction of Christology for man's contemporary consciousness based on three distinct stages. First, secularization starts from the need to evaluate contemporary Christianity and especially the doctrine of Christ from the perspective of a specific awareness that sees a sheer confusion when it comes to understanding who Christ was. What Hick hopes to achieve by attaching confusion to traditional Christology is a break between the image of Christ as God and the historical existence of Jesus of Nazareth because today's secularized consciousness is not willing to accept that God can be connected with a single human being as representative for all men and women in the world. The image of Jesus as saviour of the world should be secularized and, thus, Jesus is detached from the Christ of God, the Logos, and the Son of God.

When this happens, the second stage becomes evident in portraying Christ as a mythological figure. The myth of Christ who becomes incarnate in the human person of Jesus of Nazareth is a necessity for the church because claiming that Christ is the saviour of the world is not offensive to other religions since Christ is only a myth, but saying that Jesus is the saviour – and Jesus is also the Christ – can be understood as an expression of Western imperialism and the utter contempt for the beliefs of other religions. This is why Christianity as a religion must turn into a mere religion amongst others; the traditional conviction that Christianity is the only true belief in the world as based on the connection between the Jesus of history and the Christ of faith proves to be utterly irrelevant within today's pluralistic society.

Consequently, Jesus – not Christ – should be proclaimed to the world, because his humanity is common ground with the humanity of other religious founders. Jesus cannot touch God in the sense that he is already God; what he can do is show how God can be made accessible to humanity. God is available to all human beings and to all religions because Jesus is only an example of man's desire to meet God. Only Jesus – not Christ – is therefore able to speak to man's secularized consciousness in a way which discloses man's expectation to meet God sometime in the future, when man's ability to understand God in a better way becomes a reality for all religions.

As demonstrated in Chapter 7, the idea of secularization in *Paul van Buren* (1924-1998) underwent significant changes over his long career from being seen as an interest in the world and its affairs based on a non-metaphysical understanding of the gospel, to being placed in opposition to spiritualization; in the latter case, both secularization and spiritualization were dismissed as extreme perspectives on the world which elude the compulsoriness of human responsibility to the world and to God. Although in his later writings van Buren does not advocate secularization as a must for the world, it is evident that his thought is thoroughly influenced by it. Van Buren may have attempted to detach himself from his earlier views on secularization, but his later thought did not become less secular. This is evident when he expresses his conviction that patterns of thought – old and new – must be approached in freedom and with criticism. It is indeed obvious that he follows his own advice, so the criticism he applies to the gospel and the Bible leads to the sheer cancellation of metaphysics in his hermeneutics. He continues to speak about God, Jesus Christ, redemption, and hope; his discourse, however – although overtly biblical in content – is not traditional at all.

Lacking any metaphysical connotations, van Buren's theology uses biblical information to convey the idea that, faced with the reality of death, humanity is forced to see its existence in the world in terms of hope. To be more precise, hope informs humanity of the possibility that death can be faced; indeed it can be faced successfully, which means that the idea as well as the prospect of death assists humanity in seeing its experience in the world as meaningful and good. Consequently, life and death can be considered good, which is shown by Jesus' own life and death.

What van Buren seeks to gain is proof that all human beings are engaged in walking the same Way and – despite the wide range of approaches to the Way – what unites humanity in its pursuit of meaning is the reality of hope and the concept of God. The two do not necessarily overlap since in van Buren the concept of God may be renounced and may even disappear; nevertheless, hope is what remains forever as a dominant feature of the Way, namely of man's quest for meaning as he explores his existence and experience in the world.

In Chapter 8, *William Hamilton's* (b. 1924) theology is defined as a radical attempt to see Christianity in a different way through the results of the process of secularization which has been dramatically affecting Western society since the Industrial Revolution. This is why his thought is described as radical theology, an attempt to see the human being in terms of its absolute autonomy from any traditional religious, and specifically Christian, norms. Radical theology approaches the problem of traditional theology not from the perspective of ontology, but from the angle of language. Consequently, God is no longer accepted as a being supernatural and transcendent, but as a concept which can be deciphered in linguistic terms.

In Hamilton, the traditional God of Christian ontology is seen as dead and, as contemporary society still needs God for the purposes of maintaining its foundation of morality, the idea of a dead God is preached as more relevant than the traditional doctrine of a living God. The switch from the living God of traditional Christianity to the dead God of contemporary secularization turns Hamilton's radical theology into an advocate of pluralism, but not a defender of atheism or modern polytheism. Religion needs to decrease its influence in today's secular world; this, however, does not mean that the role of religion in morality is to be cancelled. For as long as religion makes sense for the individual experience of the secular man, Hamilton has nothing against it. Christianity, as a specific manifestation of religion, must be seen as equally valid amongst the rest of the world's religions, and this should be true also for other monotheistic faiths as Islam and Judaism. The monotheistic God of Christianity, Islam, and Judaism is dead to contemporary society, but he is alive to the secularized mind of today's people as a metaphor.

As a direct consequence of this belief, traditional Christology becomes an investigation of the relevance of Jesus for contemporary society. Hamilton is convinced that Jesus, the man from Nazareth, cannot be known through the instruments of history, so he must be accepted today as a post-historical figure. To be sure, this does not cancel the historicity of Jesus; it only presents Jesus, the historical man from Palestine, in terms which avoid history but favour language, literature, and literary devices. Thus, Jesus is a literary figure, God is a metaphor, and the Gospels are fiction in Hamilton's radical theology as informed by contemporary process of secularization.

Chapter 9 shows that *Gabriel Vahanian's* (b. 1927) notion of secularization is based on the sharp distinction between secularity and secularization. While the former is seen as the necessary result of traditional Christianity as an interest in the affairs of the world, the former is considered an unfortunate development which replaced the rigorism of traditional religion with the tyranny of non-religious convictions. Secularization must exclude secularism and embrace secularity as an attempt to prove that the uniqueness of man's reality is confined to the material boundaries of the natural world. The sacred and the profane are to coexist in one single human reality, but in order for this to happen, secularization must take into consideration a dramatic alteration of traditional Christology. Thus, the values represented by the traditional Christ of God and his redemptive works should no longer point to a supernatural and transcendent reality; what they should do is characterize the present state of man's existence in the world. This means that the traditional understanding of redemption should not be based on a transcendent Christ and a redeemed existence beyond this world, but rather on the meaningfulness that the human being is able to find within this world. This is why Vahanian's secularization brings Christianity into the middle of world religions; Christianity is no longer presented as the only or the best religion in the world, but merely as a religion like many others. Secularization, in this respect, redefines the concept of God from its traditional otherworldliness to a contemporary immanence. To be sure, in Vahanian, secularization is the process which does not describe God as a living being any longer; on the contrary, God is believed to be dead, immanent, and soaked in man's immanence, materiality, and naturalness. From this perspective, secularization presents contemporary society with the awareness that humanity has moved into a new stage, which is able to see Christianity as a matter of the past, as well as accept that the human being lives today in a post-Christian environment.

Swaying between de-Christianization and re-Christianization, *Thomas J.J. Altizer's* (b. 1927) notion of secularization is presented in Chapter 10 as an attempt to rid religion of its influence in the contemporary world, but also to recognize that the idea of religion can still be meaningful for man's existence within the same setting. This is why secularization by de-Christianization tries to prove that the traditional concept of God as a supernatural being is no longer relevant, while the other facet of secularization – this time through re-Christianization – seeks to demonstrate that spirituality has not totally lost its spiritual and existential significance for humanity. Altizer's dualist approach of secularization is based on the dichotomy between spirit and flesh, which he sees in Christian theology as a hindrance from a relevant understanding of the idea of the Word of God.

In Altizer, the Word can be embraced in a meaningful way only when the spirit and the flesh become one, as in Jesus Christ, but his divinity should not be connected with that of a supernatural being. When detached from transcendence, divinity remains in the humanity of Jesus, and the traditional God of Christianity is dead. This is why, in Altizer, the death of God does not refer to the death of the gods of all religions; on the contrary, he specifically mentions that it is only the God of Christianity who should be considered dead for having turned Christianity into an existentially meaningless religion. Devoid of his traditional transcendence, the God of Christianity dies away in the humanity of Jesus, which conjoins the spirit with the flesh, with the reality of matter, so that humanity may be able once again to reclaim the content of the Word in a meaningful way.

Altizer's criticism of Christianity suggests that Christianity itself should be deprived of its religious character; once turned into a non-religious phenomenon which promotes a radical – specifically atheistic – theology, Christianity gives up its traditional understanding of sin, guilt, alienness, distance, and oppressiveness. Its Christology reveals the self-negation of God in Christ, which is also the final confirmation that the essence of secularization – namely the death of the Christian God – will have accomplished its purpose.

As revealed in Chapter 11, in *Hans Küng* (b. 1928) secularization is a process as well as a characteristic which should define contemporary Christianity, not only today's society. There is a symbiosis between the church and the world in Küng which makes the boundaries between the two institutions a fluid reality. The church is supposed to move towards the world in order to embrace the latter's values, so the church must become not only acquainted but also cooperative with the world. In order to do so, Christians must redefine whatever they mean by the world, religion, and theology. All three concepts, and their corresponding realities, have to undergo a process of laicization, in the sense that traditional values should be excluded or transformed into the mundane expectations of today's society. As Küng explains, man must turn to the world, as must the ordinary Christian in order to see the world, religion, and theology from the perspective of the world, not from the perspective of God as in past times. The same perspective, which is essentially human, not divine, needs to be applied to how the human being is perceived as part of today's society. Man must emancipate himself from the traditionalism of the past which promotes the ontological reality of God in order to see himself as part of the world. Ideas such as equalization and autonomy are the natural consequences of secularization seen as emancipation. Man's preoccupations are mainly social, material, and concrete; the progress of science, technology, and culture must serve this main purpose even when this involves the research of the physical macrocosm or the investigation of the psychological microcosm.

Today's Christian must learn above all how to be a man, a man of this world, a person who is open to society, socially aware, and free from any constraints whatsoever. Being a Christian today is living as a secular person of today's society dominated by our contemporary lay consciousness.

Chapter 12 is dedicated to *Harvey Cox* (b. 1929), who approaches secularization from a threefold perspective: nature, politics, and values. When it comes to nature, secularization produces a demystification of nature, in the sense that the natural realm is emptied of any references to divinity. Nature should be seen as it exists in reality, so what needs to be done in order for secularization to work in today's society is that natural religions should lose their capacity to see God or gods in the elements of nature. The origin of secularization in this particular respect is the Bible itself, which speaks about a God that is totally detached from nature. An equally important aspect consists of the fact that man is also presented as separate from nature in terms of his origin. This is why, in the Bible, nature appears in light of its sheer reality, without references to God as being ontologically present in nature. In other words, secularization promotes the separation between the sacred and the natural.

A second aspect of secularization is the detachment of the sacred not only from nature, but also from politics. If natural religions are secularized as a result of keeping God away from nature, the attempts to separate the sacred from politics affect the religion of Christendom. With a long history of cooperation between the secular state and the institutions of the church, Christianity must be kept away from secular politics, which means that politics needs to be desacralized. When nature is disenchanted and politics desacralized, secularization should proceed with the deconsecration of values; in other words, traditional values should no longer be accepted as making absolute claims to truthfulness. Ethics should be relativized, and God should not be seen as the ultimate source for morality and human behavior. The moral quality of persons and things is to be established by man, not by God, which eventually leads to the promotion of an idea of God that is not characterized by metaphysics.

As a result, Cox sees secularization as a process which is both irreversible and beneficial – an enterprise which leads to progress, freedom, and pluralism as based on man's non-religious maturity and responsibility.

In Chapter 13, the end of religion as man knows it seems to be the main slogan of *John Shelby Spong's* (b. 1931) secularizing program. Whatever religion has meant for centuries and even millennia is no longer valid given the freedom of today's man to use his reason in a way which also compels the heart to follow in its footsteps. For secularization to take place in an effective manner, Spong delineates three main aspects which constitute the very essence of his attempt to take humanity beyond traditional religion. First, he points to the internalization of religion, which means that religion should no longer be seen as a reality external to humanity. In our secularized society, religion – seen as an external dogmatic system – is utterly incapable of dictating man's life as it used to in the past. Contemporary society believes in the possibility of promoting man's innermost expectations and desires as the core of what can be termed "religion".

This brings Spong to the second aspect of secularization, which is the lowering of God to the level of humanity. God does not exist as a supernatural being in a reality which lies beyond the materiality of the universe; God lives in humanity, in human individuals, which means that humanity takes God's place in the new secularized religion. As a matter of fact, man does not only replace God, man becomes the God of today's secularized society and its internalized religion. The internalization of religion not only leads to the lowering of God; it also generates the third element of Spong's program of secularization, which is the investigation of human experience. Fathoming experience is thus man's attempt to find meaning in his own existence in the world with a view to fighting against the deep sense of alienation which comes from his realization that a supernatural God no longer satisfies the rationality of our secularized society. This is why everything religion has taught so far and especially the idea of God must be brought down from the non-real domain of transcendence to the reality of the material world.

The subject of Chapter 14, *Don Cupitt* (b. 1934), presents secularization as a shift from traditional religion to a humanist perspective on God and eventually to a non-realist connotation of the same concept. Modern society and especially the critical thinking of today's philosophy have led to the widespread conviction that traditional theology and religion no longer serve their initial purpose. The promises of religion which attempt to bring the divine into the reality of nature and matter cannot be supported on objective grounds. Consequently, religion needs to reinvent itself by re-branding its most fundamental concepts.

Cupitt predominantly discusses the doctrines of revelation and incarnation, which should not be understood as attempts to present a supernatural God to humanity, but rather as ways to convey that man's traditional concept of divinity should be defined exclusively with reference to the human being. This is why, despite its interest in unmasking religion as superfluous for today's scientific perspective on the world, secularization can be ready to embrace the perpetuity of religion in contemporary society if religious concepts are disclosed as mythological. When myth is recognized as informing the tenets of all religions, then the concept of God becomes meaningful only as a non-realist construct. What is important in the end has nothing to do with whether religion continues to exist in today's world or not, but it has everything to do with the need that religion should be subject to contemporary secularist thought. This is why religious concepts, and especially the notion of God, must be interpreted through the lens of science as still existentially meaningful for today's people, provided their content is fundamentally non-realist.

Cupitt's secularization sees religion as a human effort to deal with natural reality in a meaningful way, but this understanding of religion is achievable today only when religion is brought under the control of science and critical thinking. Through secularization, religion and its doctrines become open to the world, an essential property of humanity, which has the right to impose whatever emerges as meaningful for one's individual existence on the actual content of religious terminology.

Chapter 15 discloses that in *Mark C. Taylor's* work (b. 1945) secularization is not discussed in the context of its traditionally negativistic approaches to religion. Thus, for Taylor, secularization neither attempts to restrict the influence of religion, nor seeks to put it off in any way possible. At the same time, Taylor is not interested in confining religion to certain interpretations based on contemporary definitions of its most fundamental concepts, such as the notion of God. Taylor takes exactly the opposite approach, which sees secularization as a means fully to recognize and promote religion. Stemming from Taylor's conviction that religion cannot be exterminated in our society simply because it is a basic manifestation of human culture, his perspective on secularization works with the fact that religion is a reality which is constantly present in the world. Thus, secularization is based on the recognition of the presence of religion in the world and, at the same time, is the constructive attempt to take the religious beyond the church into the scientifically informed culture of contemporary society.

In order for this understanding of secularization to be applied practically within society, one needs to approach religion as an essential human construct. When isolated to the realm and possibilities of humanity within the general context of the world, religion is seen in the same way as any other human manifestation. Thus, secularization embraces religion in human terms and tries to make sense of its ideology and history in a way which can be constructive for today's society.

Religion, therefore, is studied from the perspective of its ideas of God, and Taylor differentiates between monistic immanent religions (in which God is present in the world) and dualistic transcendent religions (in which God is absent from the world). The two types of religion are conflicting perspectives, so they manifest within the history of humanity in a cyclical way; this means that monistic immanent religions are replaced by dualistic transcendent religions and then the cycle is resumed over and over again because in both approaches God is perceived in terms of disappearance. God disappears in the world because he is seen as too present in monistic immanent religions and then he disappears from the world because he is viewed as too absent in dualistic transcendent religions. Either way, while God is embraced as "disappearance", the concept of God remains very much present in religion. When this awareness is appropriated, secularization can be said to have successfully provided contemporary society with a view of religion which is no longer confined to its traditional ecclesiastical background but available for use in politics, economics, and even science.

Chapter 16 shows that in *Vito Mancuso* (b. 1962) secularization is a process which involves rethinking fundamental concepts such as atheism, incarnation, and trinity. While atheism is not the denial of God, it is thinking of God in a way which goes beyond traditional theism. Atheism should never be aimed at cancelling the validity of God; on the contrary, God should continue to inform the spirituality of humanity but not as a transcendent being; God should be accepted as a concept which confers meaning to our material existence. This is why God should be seen as being; not a transcendent being but rather the immanent, material, and physical being of each man and woman in the world. God is therefore in humanity but he speaks conceptually of our divinity as beings that are capable of pursuing goodness and justice in love. This is why secularization is bringing God to the level of humanity in a way which places together human hope, life, and man's awareness of his existence as a concrete being. The concreteness of man's being calls for the redefinition of the incarnation, which points to the immediate availability of God based on the life of Jesus. Far from being the incarnate Son of God or the Logos as in traditional theology, Jesus is just a man who showed humanity that the idea of God can be grasped by anybody and be applied in this world.

Thus, secularization means that humanity should lose its traditional theological religion; religion and theology should be essentially civil or lay in nature and when this reality is achieved, a common ethics for all is no longer an impossibility. Ethics reveals that the application of such civil religion or lay theology is based on sincere and total commitment in active and truthful relationship. What explains the reality of such relationships to our contemporary secularized society is the concept of trinity, which affirms the primacy of relationship over identity. The trinity should no longer speak to humanity about God as Father, Son, and Holy Spirit; on the contrary, it should tell all human beings that the concept of God helps us cultivate sincere relationships that are meant to promote the practical application of love through goodness and justice.

1

Setting Things on Their Feet: Ernst Bloch

Sobriety and Enthusiasm

Ernst Bloch's theory of secularization is a defense of Marxist philosophy and especially of its view of the world as material nature. For Bloch, secularization is "the power of setting things on their feet" – a direct reference to Marx's conviction that the past or history should be set on its feet[1] – in order for contemporary society to discover what lies ahead of it. The past must be turned upside down, so that whatever is mystical within it be left behind and its "rational core" be rediscovered. In other words, secularization is a device which investigates the past in order to identify its mystical elements so that, once they are placed aside, what remains is rationality – the only aspect that is able to place the past on its feet and, in so doing, it also helps "things" (reality, as it were) to stand on their feet as well. This is to say that secularization is meant to help contemporary society to deal with its future in a rational way, unlike previous societies did with the past, which was understood in mystical terms. Secularization, therefore, is a reality which is supposed to take the human being "into fresh and strong air"; it is meant to provide man with a new perspective on life and reality. In this respect, Bloch's Marxist understanding of secularization is aimed at bringing down what lay in "a sacred space" with the clear intention of making it worldly in a way which can be defined as irreverent. This is indicative of Bloch's attempt to present man's existence as a reality which not only happens in the material reality of the world, but also needs to be grasped without the traditional reverence for mystical ideas.

Thus, secularization demystifies the reverence of the past in order for contemporary society to understand that the only reality for man's existence is the world of matter and nature. Bloch admits that secularization – as a historical reality – began in early modern Europe with the

---

[1] François Furet, *Marx and the French Revolution* (Chicago, IL: University of Chicago Press, 1988), 59.

transformation of church property and privileges into matters handled by the state.

All these dramatic changes, however, reflected not only a rethinking of human action — they were also a serious reconsideration of human thought. The traditional reverence for mythical ideas about another world gradually waned and turned into a modern irreverence which favored the concerns of this world, which for Bloch was a way of setting things on their feet. In Bloch, secularization is the attempt to offer the human being a new perspective on his existence in the world, which has to do both with his present and his future. Unlike the past traditional faith in another world, secularization gives man a rationalized understanding of this world, a blend between sobriety (which seems to investigate the present) and enthusiasm (which appears to look into the future). Marxist secularization, Bloch insists, is characterized by an anticipatory sense which replaces the "effusiveness and clouds" of past mystics.[2]

In other words, secularization develops a real preoccupation for this world; secularization sees the reality of the world with sobriety and enthusiasm. When the two are used in conjunction, the human being is able to understand what Bloch calls "the Real". Nevertheless, in order for the human being to understand "the Real" in a rational way, there must be a "constant oscillation" between sobriety and enthusiasm, which provides modern man with a "trained perspective" on the world, which for Bloch is the reality of this world.[3]

The combination of sobriety and enthusiasm as the methodology of secularization for seeing man's existence in the world between the past and the future cannot work properly without a rational and dialectical awareness.[4] This ingredient, though, is defined by Bloch through a sharp distinction which he draws between *common sense* and *bon sens*. While *common sense* makes reference to the non-dialectical understanding of the world based on prejudices, *bon sens* is the dialectical perspective on reality which does not exclude anything in advance.

According to Bloch, sobriety and enthusiasm cannot traditionally work together since they find themselves in some sort of "frozen solid antithesis". Marxism, however, brings the two together and makes them work together due to its understanding of secularization which is

---

[2] For details of Bloch's idea of mysticism, see Vincent Geoghegan, *Ernst Bloch* (London: Routledge, 1996), 93-94.

[3] Ernst Bloch, *The Principle of Hope*, vol. III (Cambridge, MA: The Massachusetts Institute of Technology Press, 1995), 1359-1368, originally published as Ernst Bloch, *Das Prinzip Hoffnung* (Frankfurt am Main: Suhrkamp Verlag, 1959).

[4] See also Benjamin M. Korstvedt, *Listening for Utopia in Ernst Bloch's Musical Philosophy* (Cambridge: Cambridge University Press, 2010), 29-30.

able to bring both sobriety and enthusiasm "to something New".⁵ The novelty of the juxtaposition between sobriety and enthusiasm in Bloch's understanding of secularization is based on his conviction that a correct understanding of reality – which is evidently provided by Marxism – must work with a broad perspective on the world that is coupled with "imagination in action". The key word here is "action" because it attempts to rid contemporary society of its traditionally contemplative philosophy, which reportedly comes with an equally ideological understanding of the world. When contemplation is eliminated, a concrete analysis of reality can be performed, which is then followed by a perspective that can be characterized as "instruction for action".

Secularization therefore is a process which offers man the chance to see the world in a brand new way. Thus, leaving behind a mystified past, man is enabled to see that his existence can be dialectically accepted as present reality as well as future imagination. What lies ahead of modern man is a reality that can be rationally understood in the present based on the conviction that this world is able to provide him with all the possibilities for progress and meaning which can be achieved within the material reality of this world. According to Bloch, secularization sets things on their feet and, in doing so, it also sets modern man on his feet by endowing him with a dialectical, critical sense of history which allows him to understand reality from the perspective of the present and the future. As long as the traditional reverence for mystics is avoided and man's abilities and needs are put forward, secularization will be able to explain Marxism as a philosophy of action for the benefit of both the individual and the society in which he exists as a person.⁶

Hope and Matter

If secularization sets things on their feet – a treatment from which even human beings are said to benefit extensively – then it means that the reality of humanity is this world, and this world is the totality of reality for the individual. In Bloch reality must be apprehended dialectically, and the dialectical process consists of three main elements: first, the *Front*; second, the *Novum*, and third, the *Matter*. According to Bloch, all three – *Front*, *Novum*, and *Matter* – are bound together by hope, which is "the

---

⁵ See also M. Keith Booker, *The Post-Utopian Imagination: American Culture in the Long 1950s* (Westport, CT: Greenwood Publishing, 2002), 6.
⁶ Bloch, *The Principle of Hope*, vol. III, 1368-1369.

most honorable human quality".[7] The three aspects of the dialectical process which defines secularization and man's modern understanding of the world seem to be a combination of time and space that place present and future within man's grasp with a view to a meaningful apprehension of the world. The *Front* is the "most advanced section of the age", which offers perspectives for the future. The *Novum* is the "real possibility" of what presents itself as not yet actualized consciously; it is a state characterized by the virtuality of becoming. *Matter*, Bloch explains, is not a "mechanical lump", so it is not to be equated with the physical reality of what exists in the world but rather with the reality of possibility which has the capacity to reveal itself in a historical way.

It is evident therefore that, in Bloch, the *Front*, the *Novum*, and *Matter* indicate concepts which speak of man's possibilities in the natural world.[8] They all point to how humanity is capable of shaping the world – first, in a theoretical, conceptualized, and dialectical way, then in a practical way. *Matter* is not seen in physical terms because that would not allow Bloch to perceive it in "living" terms. In order for modern man to understand the world in a meaningful way, the reality of life must be brought before his very eyes or rather before his very mind. The traditional understanding of life as originating in the other world, in the realm of God himself, is rendered useless by Bloch's Marxist secularization; this is why life needs to be presented as a real possibility even before it happens in its actuality.

Thus, the *Front*, the *Novum*, and *Matter* blend the reality of possibility with the virtuality of becoming; time and space are brought together in a way which is said to depend on the idea of *Matter* as the "real substratum" of what can exist "according to" as well as "in" possibility. This is why, in Bloch, *Matter* is seen as a living reality; it is not physical matter but rather theoretical matter which can be described as living, the *Matter* which exists in possibility and virtuality before being actualized within the practical reality of the world. In Bloch, *Matter* appears as "moved Being" and it is in this capacity that it mixes time and space, the present and the future together. *Matter* as Being can be perceived in the present, but as moved Being, *Matter* can only be understood from the perspective of the future. *Matter* is the substance in which the future is delivered, Bloch points out, which means that – at least theoretically and from the perspective of the present – *Matter* has not yet been delivered. This is why hope is absolutely necessary for Bloch's Marxist

---

[7] For details about Bloch's idea of hope, see Ruth Levitas, *The Concept of Utopia* (Bern: Peter Lang, 1990), 97-122.

[8] See also David J. Schmidt, "Circles-Hermeneutic and Otherwise: On Various Sense of the Future as "Not Yet'," 67-80, in David Wood (ed.), *Writing the Future* (London: Taylor & Francis, 1990): 74.

idea of secularization; it is only hope that can actualize the virtuality of the *Front*, the *Novum*, and *Matter* which together express the wide range of the real possibilities that have not yet been realized.[9]

The process of secularization, however, cannot be fully achieved without hope. While distinguishing quite sharply between subjective and objective hope – the former is *spes qua speratur* (hoping hope) and the latter is *spes quae speratur* (hoped hope) – Bloch explains that true hope is the hope which is delivered to society through mediation.[10] In this respect, he wants to point out that the real hope which can make sense of secularization is that kind of hope which is transmitted through history. This type of hope is not subjective, because it does not depend on the agency of the individual; it even contains the objective reality of hope in the world itself. True hope, Bloch contends, moves within the world, through the agency of the world itself, and becomes effectively implemented together with the process of the *Front*; in other words, hope is connected with what the world might look like in future. In short, real hope works with the possibilities contained within the reality of the future, so – in this respect – secularization is characterized by both hope and confidence in the future. To be sure, Bloch does not refer to a subjective understanding of either: hope and the future must be seen as realities which are nurtured and trusted by humanity as a whole.

What follows next is the *Novum* which speaks of real possibilities but, as Bloch points out, the goal of secularization – which is socialist humanization – can be seen from two distinct perspectives that are both connected with the *Novum*: first, a "dark" side (which speaks of the possibility that secularization could fail) and a "bright" side (which presents the possibility that secularization could prevail). This indicates that secularization lies within the realm of "objective-real decision". In other words, decisions influence the course of society towards either a "dark" end or a "bright" conclusion, which can take the hope in the future of the *Front* forward to the real possibilities presented to society by the *Novum*. In this respect, the hope of the *Front* should be coupled with the optimism of the *Novum* but, as secularization progresses, one should realize that such optimism is never certain. The most one can predict of optimism is that it could be presented to society as "militant optimism" in the real possibilities which are contained within the *Novum* and which, if directed towards the "bright" side, could result in

---

[9] Ernst Bloch, *The Principle of Hope*, vol. III, 1371.
[10] Olli-Pekka Moisio and Juha Suoranta, "Hope and Education in the Era of Globalization", 231-246, in Klas Roth and Ilan Gur-Zeév (eds.), *Education in the Era of Globalization* (Dordrecht: Springer, 2007): 239-240.

something beneficial for the world. Bloch emphasizes that the hope of the *Front* and the optimism of the *Novum* must be characterized by openness to history, but then openness, hope, and especially optimism must be accepted as something which is not certain; much too often the misery of the world presents certainty in optimism as "wicked" or "feeble-minded".

In Bloch, this is a critique of traditional metaphysics and, of course, of religions which believe in the otherworldliness of God, who is presented as Absolute, a fixed reality whose definition is clear and so real that nothing can change it. Certainty in optimism, which cannot be supported given the huge problems of the world, is specific to theism, whose metaphysical understanding of God exists in a "hypostatized other world". Bloch's secularization promotes the idea that another world does not exist because hope in and optimism concerning a God who lives in another world are not justified by the reality of this world. While admitting that human life can be characterized by something that exists beyond the realities of the world – perhaps a reference to the spirituality of the human being, which is termed "concrete-utopian" in Bloch – there is no transcendence in the traditional sense of the term, a transcendence which characterizes some "hypostatized other world" as home for a real, otherworldly, and absolute God. The only reality in which man can hope and towards which man can manifest a militant optimism is the material reality of nature. The reality of the material world proves that man's hope can only be directed towards the future which can be manifested as real possibility in this world.

Thus, Bloch speaks of the "immediate visibility" of the facts of this world which are the basis of man's hope and optimism, not the "mythological invisibility" of traditional theism and metaphysics. In other words, man should not place his hope in a God who is said to live in another world; on the contrary, man's hope should be connected with the real possibilities which are presented to him by his future in this world. Man's courage does not depend on the otherworldliness of a theistic and metaphysical essence called God; man's courage should venture towards the hope which exists in the *Front*, in his future in this world, which is fundamentally not guaranteed and uncertain. The process of secularization must help man realize that nothing can be guaranteed in future, but it is the fact of uncertainty that should prompt man towards hope and optimism concerning what lies ahead of him in the future. This is real authenticity in Bloch, namely man's trust in something which has not yet happened, which presents itself as a real possibility which awaits to become "founded" in the world. Thus, real authenticity is hope, that reality which helps modern man understand the idea of transcendence as part of this world, as spirituality which hopes for real possibilities to become a beneficial fact for humanity so that militant optimism is open to the *Novum* as something which is not "pre-ordered".[11]

Bloch's secularization is an attempt to explain that humanity is able to forge its own future (as sum of real possibilities which are not pre-ordered but open to history) based on its decisions which should be taken without any metaphysical or theistic constraints if hope is to be understood as capable of turning *Matter* (real possibilities that are capable of revealing themselves in history) into something good for humanity.[12]

Teleology and the Reality of This World

The fact that man is able dialectically to leap into the *Novum*, into the reality of new possibilities which have the capacity to become real facts as a result of "bright" decisions, reveals another basic feature of secularization, namely its purpose. The teleology of secularization is given by the "not-yet" character of its *Novum*, which presents itself as virtually real possibilities that have not yet become actualized in the physical reality of the world. Consequently, teleology and secularization cannot be detached, but – as Bloch points out – teleology should not be seen in the traditional sense of the word as a dogmatic proposition which is deciphered by means of the idea of providence. Since providence speaks of God as Absolute essence, Bloch's Marxist secularization cannot accept anything which is pre-ordained. Thus, Bloch's idea of teleology is not "mythologically guided from above".[13]

It is clear therefore that, in Bloch, teleology has nothing to do with transcendence, God as a fixed ontological reality belonging to another world, or any other traditional – and specifically supernatural – notion which can be interpreted in mythological terms. Teleology, however, must remain a crucial aspect of secularization because it brings with it not only concepts such as goal and purpose, but also the fundamental idea of meaning.

Bloch's Marxist teleology, though, is anything but static; it is, in fact, essentially dynamic in the sense that it cannot be "dogmatically settled once and for all". In other words, reality has a purpose or man can identify a wide range of goals which can be put together under the

---

[11] See also Tom Moylan, "Bloch against Bloch: The Theological Reception of *Das Prinzip Hoffnung* and the Liberation of the Utopian Function", 96-121, in Jamie O. Daniel and Tom Moylan (eds.), *Not Yet: Reconsidering Ernst Bloch* (London: Verso, 1997): 116.

[12] Bloch, *The Principle of Hope*, vol. III, 1372-1373.

[13] See also Celia Deane-Drummond, *Ecology in Jürgen Moltmann's Theology* (Lewiston, NY: Edwin Mellen Press, 1997), 248.

name of purpose, but this purpose should not be understood as having any connections with metaphysics, transcendence, and providence.[14] It is a purpose which derives from man's capacity to believe in his future, which presents itself to him as virtual real possibilities waiting to become real in the physicality of the world. When this happens, matter can be said to have been moulded into something which – from the perspective of the future – has a definite goal for humanity. This indicates that, in Bloch, teleology may not be characterized by a fixed dogmatic meaning, but it does have a feature which is always constant, and that is direction. Humanity may not be always able to decipher the goal which is concealed in its own future, but it is able to understand that it goes towards the future itself; humanity, as it were, has a direction regardless of whether or not it actually knows what its purpose is. Because humanity exists in history, Bloch is clear when he shows that this direction seems to be the "the only unchanging thing in history".

This direction, though, is very difficult to identify; even for Bloch, it appears as if it were a reality which simply occurs in time and space without special attention being drawn to it. Bloch himself describes this direction as something "which speaks for itself" but at the same time it remains silent. Actually, its silence points to its capacity to speak for itself, so direction is something which happens in the world, and it can be perceived as a reality, but it cannot be precisely identified as something distinctly clear.[15]

What is clear, however, about humanity's direction has to do with the fact that it is connected with hope. When man has hope he has direction, and whenever hope is open to the future, there is also a sense of direction that comes with it. In order for hope to have direction, man must be fully aware and conscious about the fact that the true horizon of his existence does not go beyond the knowledge of realities; in other words, the world as man perceives it, is the realm of his hope and direction. In Bloch's words, when man nurtures such hope in the world he knows "reality itself as one of the horizon"; such knowledge is informed by a hope that corresponds to reality, and by reality he means the reality of this world. Any hope which believes in a reality beyond this world, in a transcendent God, in a world characterized by otherworldliness, is uninformed, undirected, and will lead man in a wrong direction. Hope must remain within this world in order for it to make sense for Bloch's image of secularization as belief in man's capacity to see the meaning of his future within the boundaries of all the virtually real possibilities that can take shape in the physical world of nature.

[14] See Roland Boer, *Criticism of Heaven: On Marxism and Theology* (Leiden: Brill, 2007), 51-52.
[15] Bloch, *The Principle of Hope*, vol. III, 1374-1375.

It turns out that, in Bloch, the idea of the absolute still remains valid but not in connection with the traditional image of a transcendent otherworldly, and dogmatic God; on the contrary, what can be described as absolute in Bloch's Marxist notion of secularization is hope itself.[16] Hope points to a direction as well as to a goal; neither can be deciphered in totality. Man's goal and his direction in the world remain – to use Bloch's words – "unfound" and "opaque", but man's hope to see them becoming real is absolute. Hope and will are the two features of man which provide his existence with scope, purpose, and meaning because they point to an end (*terminus*) that can bring with it a beneficial reality for man's life, such as a new world as a result of humanity's capacity to create.[17] There is the possibility that man will be able to discover the true essence of his being in the future, so access to the reality of his being is his own hope and will, which are open to the future. The future is not known in its entirety, but what can be said for a fact about man's future is that it can be known as it unfolds within the reality of this world.

This is why, in Bloch, secularization is the process which leads to the awareness that the true origin of being – with reference to the human being – is to be found at the end, in the future which is constantly being awaited in hope. Humanity will eventually understand its true purpose, the meaning of its existence when – sometime in the future – its present hope will turn into a radical existence, which means that in the future man will have discovered the meaning of his roots.

Certainly, though, the rediscovery of man's roots as part of humanity's future is a constant activity which happens in the actuality of the present. Man must work in the world if he wants to see the root of history; man must be creative within the physical world if he wants to see his hopes taking shape in the future. The essence of Bloch's secularization consists of man's awareness that he has the capacity to shape and reshape the reality of "given facts", which can be found exclusively in the world perceived as "homeland". Man's home is this world, not the traditional world of a transcendent God who lives beyond history, time, and space. Bloch's Marxist idea of secularization underlines that, in order for man to find purpose and meaning in life, he must measure his hopes against the realities of this world to the point that this world

---

[16] See also Richard Kearney, *Modern Movements in European Philosophy: Phenomenology, Critical Theory, Structuralism* (2nd edn, Manchester: Manchester University Press, 1994), 190.

[17] See Antonio Negri, *The Labor of Job: The Biblical Text as a Parable of Human Labor*, trans. Matteo Mandarini, foreword by Michael Hardt, commentary by Roland Boer (Durham, NC: Duke University Press, 2009), 14-15.

– not a realm beyond it, not transcendence, and certainly not a God who preordains things – is accepted as his true home.[18]

---

[18] Bloch, *The Principle of Hope*, vol. III, 1375–1376.

2

Destroying the Values of the Past: Herbert Marcuse

Desacralization and Industrialization

Herbert Marcuse describes secularization as a process which attempts to destroy values and institutions. Although no particular identification is made concerning what kind of values and institutions he has in mind within the definition, it is clear that a parallel process of desacralization has already begun for the same institutions. This indicates that secularization goes hand in hand with desacralization: they are both directed against the values and institutions that appear to have existed previously as part of mankind's life in the world; at the same time, they are reflections of a certain kind of convictions that are not necessarily connected with the actuality of history.

This observation is confirmed by Marcuse's indication that secularization and desacralization represent a dramatic transformation of underdeveloped societies into communities which are characterized by a high degree of industrialization.[1] Consequently, secularization manifests itself as desacralization of pre-industrialized societies with the specific purpose of industrializing their existence in a particular historical setting.

The reference to history is important here because, as Marcuse points out, industrialization does not happen in a vacuum; industrialization takes place in history, which means that it is history as the reality of man's existence that not only offers the context for industrialization but also proves to be an incentive for a historical understanding of life in the world. When man understands that history is the environment of his existence and that he totally depends on a particular historical setting for his life, then he realizes that his entire view of the world, life, and experience must be formed in accordance with the reality of history.

---

[1] His convictions about the role of underdeveloped countries in the making of industrialized societies led to Marcuse's being place under surveillance by the Federal Bureau of Investigation. See Stephen Gennaro and Douglas Kellner, "Under Surveillance: Herbert Marcuse and the FBI", 283-314, in Harry Dahms (ed.), *Nature, Knowledge, and Negation* (Bingley: Emerald Group Publishing, 2009): 306.

Marcuse appears convinced that industrialization must happen in countries where the standard of living needs a serious upgrade since the basic needs of the population are not being satisfactorily met; in other words, each society with an agrarian, specifically pre-industrialized way of thinking (which is based on values characterized by sanctification and beliefs with meta-historical content) must find a way to produce goods and services in such quantity and quality that the needs of the populations are fulfilled.[2] When this happens, people begin to realize that satisfaction no longer comes from beliefs in meta-historical benefits, but from enjoying a standard of living which can be economically measured within the historical reality of his or her social setting. This is why, in Marcuse, industrialization is the evident result of secularization seen as desacralization because the pre-technological and – as Marcuse emphatically points out – even the pre-bourgeois customs of pre-industrialized experiences are seen as "dead weight". Such a perception of these customs leads to their abandonment in favor of a way of life which is no longer based on meta-historical ideas but rather on a wide range of experiences that are shaped by man's life in the actuality of history.

Given that pre-industrialized customs and beliefs cannot be rooted out easily since they manifest strong opposition to industrialized development, man must realize that he should choose between two authorities: on the one hand, the authority of pre-industrialized customs and beliefs and, on the other hand, the authority of an industrialized way of life. If the latter is chosen, man must be willing to submit himself to what Marcuse calls "a system of anonymous powers", which is supported by the mechanical process (as part of industrialization) seen as a social process.[3]

It is important to understand that, as far as Marcuse is concerned, industrialization only happened in capitalism and communism, seen as economic and social blocs which have managed to implement the mechanical process within their respective societies. This is indicative of the capacity of both capitalism and communism to crush the traditional resistance of pre-industrialized customs and beliefs in favor of advanced forms of thinking that are based on liberalism and democracy. Leaving aside Marcuse's hopelessly optimistic – as well as idealistic – perspective on communism as provider or even creator of democracy (which, at least as far as Eastern Europe was concerned, did not happen with the destruction of the Berlin Wall), it is crucial nevertheless to highlight his conviction that liberalism and democracy provide secularization with the means to desacralize society of its pre-industrial beliefs and customs. In

---

[2] See Edward Granter, *Critical Social Theory and the End of Work* (Farnham: Ashgate, 2009), 70.

[3] Herbert Marcuse, *One-Dimensional Man: Studies in the Ideology of Advanced Industrial Society* (Boston, MA: Beacon Press, 1964), 46.

other words, secularization can and should be implemented as desacralization through the imposition of the authority of liberalism and democracy as a means to promote advanced industrialized patters of thought and life.[4]

Despite his idealistic view of communism, Marcuse is quite realistic about the possibilities of liberalism and democracy to achieve a rapid transition from pre-industrialized to post-industrialized thinking in underdeveloped societies. The resistance of traditional ways of life is too strong for such a sudden move, so Marcuse proposes that societies which have not yet been industrialized through a natural occurrence, as well as development, of liberalism and democracy should eliminate what Marcuse calls "oppressive and exploitative forces". When it comes to these forces, however, Marcuse briefly defines them as material and religious, which can be a way of pointing to social, economic, and political oppression on the one hand, and to religion on the other hand. Suffice it to say for now that religion is seen as a hindrance, a barrier which prevents society and human existence in the end from moving towards liberalism and democracy.

Economic progress can be reached without industrialization in countries where natural resources are able to provide society with a decent degree of "human life", not only with subsistence, but in order for such development to be achieved without industrialization, something else must happen. In this respect, Marcuse points out that "social revolution, agrarian reform, and reduction of over-population" are compulsory conditions for development to take place, but industrialization will still be out of reach for such societies. In other words, economic development cannot reach its full potential without industrialization because only industrialization is able to make man aware of the historical character of his life and experience in the world, so it is only industrialization which can – in the end – provide man with liberalism and democracy as a necessary means to secularize man's agrarian belief and customs through desacralization.

Such a statement also points to Marcuse's conviction that in order for secularization to work efficiently, self-determination is crucial.[5] When self-determination is achieved, pre-industrial beliefs and customs – most notably religious patterns of thought and life – are abandoned in favor of an industrialized understanding of human experience as fundamentally historical. Self-determination though cannot be fully accomplished

---

[4] For details about the results of industrialization in Marcuse, see Carl Boggs, *The End of Politics: Corporate Power and the Decline of the Public Sphere* (New York, NY: Guilford Press, 2000), 247-248.

[5] See also George G. Brenkert, *Political Freedom* (London: Routledge, 1991), 102.

without industrialization — the only force which, in Marcuse, appears to be able to destroy all forms of neocolonialism and, in doing so, to abolish exploitation of any kind, mental, material, and evidently religious. Such a program requires what Marcuse calls "the rule of law", but the idea of law is connected with the reality of history. No law from above or beyond the law which works in history should be accepted if human progress and development is to be achieved in full. Quite obviously, since religion is based on laws promoted by entities that are said to exist beyond history, religion is a form of oppression which hinders man from reaching self-determination. This is why religion must be subject to secularization through the desacralization provided by liberalism and democracy as vehicles of industrialization.[6]

History and Metaphysics

Secularization as desacralization within the context of industrialization through liberalism and democracy cannot be achieved unless a certain philosophy is developed as part of the process. In order for pre-industrialized concepts, values, beliefs, and customs to be turned into an industrialized way of life, an entire mindset must be changed and this requires a philosophy which is able to explain the new realities of life based on the acknowledgment of the old ones as outdated. This is why Marcuse points out that philosophy has a specific historical function within the intellectual culture of industrialized society. His conviction about philosophy's historical awareness shows that industrialized beliefs are entirely based on man's perception of his life as a historical fact.

While acknowledging the historicity of man's life, one has to accept that aspects of human existence which cannot be seen as physical entities pertaining to the actuality of material history — such as the human mind, consciousness, will, soul, and self, which Marcuse terms "universals" — must be dealt with from the perspective of history.[7] Nevertheless, as they cannot be seen in the same way as other things which exist in history, explaining them as well as their relationship with the things that can be seen is a little more difficult. Universals are traditionally associated with what Marcuse sees as "myths" and "metaphysical 'ghosts'", because neither myths and metaphysics on the one hand, nor universals on the other are visible to man's physical eye. They all transcend the physicality of the human being, which explains their association in patterns of

---

[6] Marcuse, *One-Dimensional Man*, 47-51.

[7] See also Caren Irr, "One-Dimensional Symptoms: What Marcuse Offers a Critical Theory of Law", 169-186, in Jeffrey T. Nealon & Caren Irr (eds.), *Rethinking the Frankfurt School: Alternative Legacies of Cultural Critique* (Albany, NY: State University of New York Press, 2002): 179-180.

thought that promote beliefs in disaccord with an industrialized way of life. This is why secularization must deal with universals and their capacity to transcend the physical side of human existence in a way which shows that the whole totality of the human being – with its seen and unseen, physical and metaphysical aspects – are part of, and fundamentally belong to, the physical reality of material history.

Myths and metaphysics, Marcuse suggests, are difficult to exorcise, in the sense that they cannot be easily explained in terms which avoid poetry, which means that their connotations appear to be stronger than their denotations. In other words, although universals belong to the reality of man's bodily existence (as material being) in the world, what he means by them – with particular references to ideas which can have a "mythological" substratum – can oftentimes make reference to beliefs that are not supposed to be contained in the immediate historical reality. Consequently, in order for the universals to explain human existence as thoroughly historical, physical, and material, they need to be translated and – as Marcuse shows – such translation needs to be performed on the basis of human experience and the rejection of "supra-linguistic analysis". In other words, language must be "taken at face value", as Marcuse indicates, which means that denotations – rather than connotations – must be used to explain human reality and experience in the world. When this happens and metaphysical connotations are excluded, it is possible to translate the unseen human universals into visible "modes of behavior and dispositions" which are stripped of their mythological character. This means that the translation of universals into demythologized patterns of thought and experience must be done through a process of demystification, which indicates that secularization has to be embraced as a social process. Society, in other words, needs to have this translation realized in order for the members thereof to advance towards progress and development.

As an instrument of this social process, secularization demythologizes, demystifies, and historicizes the unseen universals of human thought into visible patterns of behavior. Myths must be dissolved into behavior, very much as the hypostatized universals need to be translated "into concreteness",[8] which indicates that there is no "mythical entity" behind universals; the only entity behind the reality of universals is man with his unseen humanity, who exists in history as a physical, material being with his visible and invisible constitutive aspects.[9]

---

[8] See also David Held, *Introduction to Critical Theory: Horkheimer to Habermas* (Berkeley, CA: University of California Press, 1980), 228.
[9] Marcuse, *One-Dimensional Man*, 203-207.

It is crucial to understand that Marcuse does not want to destroy the metaphysical aspect of universals; he only wants to translate it as pointing to material, concrete, and physical realities in the world. For instance, beauty as an abstract concept can only be experienced through the mediation of something concrete, which exists in a material form. Religion, to follow the same pattern of thought, must be understood as referring to mythological ideas which in turn must be accepted as mythological – not as real – given man's acknowledgment of history as his only existential reality. This is why, Marcuse shows, there must be an evolution from religion to mythology and from mythology to logic in the sense that when religion is understood as mythology, logic has already done its job. Religion, though, can only be understood in mythological terms if reality is confined to the materiality of nature.[10] There is nothing beyond it and nothing behind it; history as the totality of events that happen throughout the material universe must be accepted as the only true reality if universals are to be embraced as unseen realities which define human experience.

This is why, in Marcuse, secularization is a manifestation of what he calls "historicism", namely the perception of transcendence as part of history. In other words, philosophical concepts (with their metaphysical, poetic, or transcendent connotations) have an evident "internal historical character" for the very simple reason that philosophy is done in history and the philosopher speaks within a definite historical and social setting. Secularization shows that philosophy, concepts, or anything which is unseen from the perspective of the material world can have an objective validity; but firstly, this depends on the materiality of the subject who works with concepts and second, the subjects are understood to exists within the same realm of "natural conditions", namely within the same materiality of the world.

This means that the only aspect which defines concepts as objectively valid – which in Marcuse can be associated with the notion of "transcendent projects" – resides in the physicality of the natural world. For as long as the ideas of transcendence and conceptuality are explained against the reality of the natural world, they can be accepted as valid in an objective sense. This is why secularization translates the idea of transcendence as an aspect of humanity which must be "in accordance with the real possibilities" of culture as manifested intellectually and materially. Consequently, secularization is performed through the application of the

---

[10] This means that, traditionally, religion is characterized by duplicity, in the sense that it refers to man's unfulfilled ideals, since when understood as mythology, religion is seen through the lens of industrialized beliefs that speak about the fulfillment of man's needs. See also Richard Murphy, *Theorizing the Avant-Garde: Modernism, Expressionism, and the Problem of Postmodernity* (Cambridge: Cambridge University Press, 1998), 8.

notion of rationality, which means that, in Marcuse, the reality of nature and matter is accepted as the only reality for man's existence and experience.

At the same time, this means that truth cannot be detached from reason since they both define secularization as an attempt to find an objective ground for historical rationality.[11] In other words, man is free to believe anything as being transcendent and metaphysical as long as it does not go beyond (meaning that it is not conceived as dependent on a meta-historical entity accepted as ontologically real) the truth established by his rationality which is defined by, and exists and manifests itself in, the reality of material history.[12]

The Use of Reason and Pacified Existence

When secularization is applied in industrial societies, metaphysics becomes physics in a dramatic transformation which speaks of the rationalization of the irrational, the latter being equalled in Marcuse with the spiritual.[13] This means that human values are transformed into needs, which happens when material satisfaction is achieved through the development of needs based on satisfaction. One can easily see that the burden of the entire process rests on the reality of human need which is visible in the actuality of history. The reality of need, however, is fulfilled only when the values which are supposed to inform and supply it with meaning become rationalized in order for them to be translated into reality. In practical terms, the values of justice and freedom for instance must be applied in truth and good conscience if the human need for existence is to be met effectively. Human existence, however, must be characterized by peace in order for it to be properly defined as fulfilled from the perspective of the translation of values into needs.

This is why Marcuse speaks of a "pacified existence", which is the final goal of secularization through the implementation of science and technology.[14] Marcuse, though, warns against the fact that technology should never be considered capable of supplying human existence with all the needs it craves. Thus, the technological man is not omnipotent; for all it's worth, technology is able to provide man with power while, at

---

[11] For a position which makes a clear connection between Marcuse's idea of historical rationality and Edmund Burke's thought, see Ian Ward, *Shakespeare and the Legal Imagination* (Cambridge: Cambridge University Press, 1999), 25-26.

[12] Marcuse, *The One-Dimensional Man*, 218-220.

[13] Jean E. Petrolle, *Religious without Belief: Contemporary Allegory and the Search for Postmodern Faith* (Albany, NY: State University of New York Press, 2008), 30.

[14] See also Douglas Kellner, *Herbert Marcuse and the Crisis of Marxism* (Berkeley, CA: University of California Press, 1984), 333.

the same time, make him weak and utterly vulnerable. Belief in the technological supremacy of science is a mystification in itself, which must be secularized and demystified like any other mythological belief that hinders human progress.

The idea of pacification must become a reality if secularization is to be considered efficient, but pacification – as Marcuse shows – is based on the fact that nature is mastered by the human being which, at the end of the day, is in utter need of pacification. The reality of mastering nature can be ambivalent, in the sense that there is a positive and a negative attitude when it comes to actually subjecting nature with a view to exerting control over it. The positive control of nature is liberating while the negative control of nature is enslaving. The former produces peace, the former results in conflict. Man must be fully aware that he must seek the liberating control of nature which leads to pacification, otherwise he will never be able to master nature "in the light of freedom"; in other words, nature must go through the process of civilization and, in so doing, forsakes its quality of being nature and becomes, in turn, history.

This is why, in Marcuse, history is defined as having the capacity to negate nature because man is capable of transforming nature into history through the application of reason. This is why the main purpose of secularization is to use reason in such a way that the matter of nature is subject to a set of rational "standards and aims". Reason, as it were, sets a standard for the transformation of nature, a standard which is considered sufficient for the actual turning of metaphysics into physics in order for man to find a pacified existence. When this rational standard is met, man's existence is said to be rational. On the other hand, when the standard is not met, man's existence can be described as sub-rational and, in this respect, characterized by suffering, violence, and destruction. These realities must be reduced and society must go through the process of secularization if this is to become reality. For instance, the pre-industrialized notion of hell must be understood in materialistic terms in order for it to make sense in modern scientific society. If hell is described as a reality which exists in history and is being created by man as well as by nature, hell can be rationally understood as the product of a society "whose rationality is still irrational".[15]

Irrationality must be dealt with and eliminated in order for modern society to be able to master nature and turn it into history.[16] Marcuse is convinced that man's joy and happiness are the result of his capacity to transform nature. He even refers to the transcendence of nature, but the idea of transcendence here is the equivalent of control over nature.

---

[15] Marcuse, *One-Dimensional Man*, 234-237.

[16] Ben Agger, *The Discourse of Domination: From the Frankfurt School to Postmodernism* (Evanston, IL: Northwestern University Press, 1992), 127.

When nature is made subject, civilization can be said to have flourished and secularization is thus at work. Liberation and pacification of man's existence in the world follow but only if nature is kept under strict control, which means the liberation of nature from brutality, insufficiency, and blindness through reason. To be sure, everything which escapes the power of reason is a sign of the lack of civilization, which brings with it the possibility of conflict, destruction, and illusion. This indicates that secularization must happen, at the end of the day, through the constant application of reason within the modern scientific society, which involves the acute awareness that technology must be mastered to the same degree that nature must be kept under control. When secularization becomes a fact, Marcuse points out that reason transforms itself into post-technological rationality, which becomes what he calls "the art of life" because a rationality that civilizes human existence by purging it from mystification is a life-changing form of art. This is why, in Marcuse, the function of reason coincides with the function of art.[17]

When it comes to art, Marcuse shows that art has the capacity to revalidate metaphysics. Such revalidation though does not imply a return to sub-rational beliefs pertaining to man's natural – not yet civilized and demystified – life, but rather a rethinking of metaphysics from the perspective of science and technology. Thus, secularization can make use of the concept of metaphysics for as long as what informs it and provides it with content is the material reality as understood through the transformation of society by means of science and technology. The immediate result of such transformation is liberation and a pacified existence for the human being, which both sum up the essence of Marcuse's idea of secularization as desacralization and destruction of sub-rational values through the proper use of reason.[18]

---

[17] Charles Reitz, *Art, Alienation, and the Humanities: A Critical Engagement with Herbert Marcuse* (Albany, NY: State University of New York Press, 2000), 154.

[18] Marcuse, *One-Dimensional Man*, 237-243.

3

Dismissing the Otherwordliness of God: Karl Rahner

Secularization and Demythologization

Karl Rahner's extremely complex notion of secularization can be deciphered by noticing its fundamental connection with the idea of demythologization.[1] While demythologization points – in a rather distinct way – to the traditional doctrine of Christ, secularization should be followed in Rahner's Christology as a process which explains not only how Christ should be understood today, but also how the world can be pictured within the secularized mind of today's human being. The fact that secularization is juxtaposed with demythologization reveals not only Rahner's conviction that Christology should no longer focus on the traditional conviction that Jesus Christ needs to be conceived in divine and human terms – both ontologically true and real – but also his desire to discuss the issue of Christology from the perspective of this world. The traditional "otherworldliness" of Christ is therefore dismissed because the orientation towards the reality of this world is not only the immediate result of demythologization in Christology but also the preoccupation of secularization as an inevitable and irreversible process.

It is important to highlight here that, in Rahner, secularization is not to be seen exclusively through the lens of demythologization; such a connection – although extremely important – is only one facet of the problem. In Rahner, secularization is described as the consequence of the will of Christianity itself. This is indicative of Christianity's capacity to bear secularization within its very doctrines and then, most likely, within its history. As a religion, Christianity is able, according to Rahner, not only to capture but also to initiate the process of secularization which eventually leads to demythologization. This ability of Christianity also provides its theology with the power to convey ideas which helps human beings see reality in a specific way. In this respect, Rahner points out that the world becomes a new reality for the human being.

---

[1] For details of demythologization in Rahner, see Walter Kasper, *Jesus the Christ* (Mahwah, NJ: Paulist Press, 1976), 48-50.

Thus, the world is not only a given; something which the human being finds as existent and wherein the human being itself realizes the factuality of its existence. Through secularization, the world itself turns into a "material" which is not only at man's disposal but also within his reach to be transformed in a radical way. To be sure, the transformation of the world as a result of secularization can be achieved through technology; in this sense, secularization not only assists the human being in discovering the reality of the world as a possibility of manifesting his innate capacity to create, but it also reveals the world's material constitution. The world presents itself to the human being as a material reality; the world is seen in terms of matter, which indicates the fact that it can be transformed, molded, and rendered useful to humanity in a way that is brought about through the mediation of technology.[2]

Consequently, in Rahner, secularization should be understood as a process in which the human being discovers the world in a specific way, namely as a material reality that can be altered in order to serve man's needs as a result of his creativity. In this respect, secularization unveils the world to humanity as matter, which can be turned into virtually anything through the agency of technology.[3]

Secularization affects everything, and the entire *corpus* of Christian dogma is radically altered as a result of the process of secularization. In this respect, Rahner makes reference to the doctrine of Christ since the very connection between secularization, demythologization, and technology was made within a specifically Christological context. Christology is important because it is perhaps the first traditional doctrine which can reveal the practical results of the application of secularization to Christian doctrine. This is why Rahner makes it clear that Christology – as a fundamental dogma of Christianity – should no longer be understood in what he calls a "mythological way".[4] Although Rahner does not offer many details about what this "mythological way" entails, one can see that secularization tends to force theology out of its traditionalism into a modernism that can be known and experienced "with certainty". Evidently, the traditional doctrine of Christ which stipulates that he is the actual incarnation of a divine person whose existence is believed as ontologically real lies beyond man's capacity to know and experience it with certainty. This is why, in Rahner, the idea of certainty as applied to

---

[2] Details about Rahner's view of technology can be found in Richard Lennan, *The Ecclesiology of Karl Rahner* (Oxford: Oxford University Press, 2002), 117-118.

[3] Karl Rahner, *Theological Investigations*, vol. V (Baltimore, MD: Helicon Press, 1966), 190.

[4] See also Steven G. Ogden, *The Presence of God in the World: A Contribution to Postmodern Christology based on the Theologies of Paul Tillich and Karl Rahner* (Bern: Peter Lang, 2007), 189.

dogma is crucial because it proves not only his acceptance of secularization but also his understanding of secularization as a tendency to see the world as material reality which can be known and experienced with certainty.

Whatever man lives, experiences, and knows must go through the filter of certainty despite the doctrine's nonmaterial constitution. Ideas, though, are part of the materiality of the human being, so they must be known the same way matter can be known. Ideas or doctrines must be experienced the same way matter can be experienced. This conviction is again the result of Rahner's idea of secularization seen as demythologization because since demythologization pushes the divinity of Christ into his humanity, secularization pictures the human spirit as part of his materiality.[5] In other words, Rahner's secularization as demythologization postulates the unity between spirit and matter. While this is not a reference to homogeneity, Rahner explains that the human being should be seen as the "existent" in which matter manifests its fundamental tendency to "to discover itself in spirit". This discovery, however, should be made through self-transcendence, which points to the fact that the human being has reached the point in history when it can see itself as fundamentally and totally part of the world.

To put things into perspective, Rahner's complex explanation indicates that secularization is the process which allows man to understand his existence as part of the world; his existence, though, is essentially material and, in this respect, there is a clear connection between the matter of the world and the matter of man. Any reference, however, to the spirit should be accepted within the same material perspective on the world, in the sense that man's spirit is inextricably united with his bodily matter, so the two entities are in fact one single reality. This unified perspective on reality – regardless of whether it refers to the world or to the human being, since the two are essentially one single reality – confirms that the marrow of secularization is demythologization since the image of Christ speaks about the reality of man in the world.[6]

Incarnation and Creation

The connection between Christ and the reality of man in the world is highlighted by what Rahner calls "the evolutionary view of the world". This is the context for a proper understanding of Christ and this is also the context for a correct understanding of man in the world as a reality

---

[5] See also Paul G. Crowley, *Rahner beyond Rahner: A Great Theologian Encounters the Pacific Rim* (Lanham, MD: Rowman & Littlefield, 2005), 27.

[6] Karl Rahner, *Foundations of Christian Faith: An Introduction to the Idea of Christianity* (New York, NY: Crossroad, 1978/2005), 180-181.

which blends spirit and matter.[7] The fact that Christ is not a distinct being from human beings in general is proved by Rahner's conviction that the phrase "hypostatic union" should be applied to man as a human being, not to Christ as a divine-human being. The evolutionary view of the world confirms that secularization as demythologization works both in the realm of the Christian doctrine of Christ and in the field of the Christian doctrine of man. Thus, Christology and anthropology show together – in a rather clear way – that secularization as demythologization refocus theology from the traditionally dualist perspective on the world that accepts a twofold reality (worldly and otherworldly or material and spiritual, or even human and divine) to a contemporary, scientific, and technologized understanding of reality as the unique blend of spirit and matter. This does not mean that the spirit has an existence of its own but that the spirit should be conceived as part of matter.

Consequently, Rahner speaks about the God-Man, but the God-Man is not Christ, and certainly it is not only Christ. The God-man is not a reality which distinguishes Jesus from the rest of humanity; he is a reality which shows that Jesus was a mere man, like the rest of humanity. Thus, the God-man is a phrase which speaks of every human being in the sense that it must be found in every human being as an indication of his capacity to think about God within – as well as despite of – his material constitution. Man is able to think about what Rahner calls "the absolute mystery" and, in doing so, man equates the absolute mystery with God. Nevertheless, God as absolute mystery is nothing but man himself and his capacity to transcend himself; man's ability to think of himself in spiritual and material terms is what the idea of hypostatic union entails in reality.

This understanding of the uniqueness of the blend between matter and spirit as reference to one single reality has a powerful impact on the doctrine of incarnation.[8] Thus, incarnation no longer refers to Jesus Christ based on the traditional belief that God's *logos* became incarnate in the person of Jesus in the sense that two ontologically distinct beings met within the same human person; on the contrary, incarnation is the "divinization of the world", as Rahner puts it. Incarnation is not a movement from a metaphysical God whose ontology and spiritual reality are beyond doubt towards the physical man who lives in the material world. Quite the opposite, incarnation is a movement from man, who – because of the process of secularization as demythologization – is able to

---

[7] For details, see David Torevell, *Liturgy and the Beauty of the Unknown: Another Place* (Aldershot: Ashgate, 2007), 149-150.

[8] See George Vass, *A Pattern of Doctrines, 1: God and Christ*, vol. III: *Understanding Karl Rahner* (London: Continuum, 1996), 111-112.

understand that reality is one, essentially material, but which can be described in spiritual terms. Thus, man's capacity to think of the world spiritually can be described as incarnation; when man speaks of matter using the terminology of the spirit, matter can be said to have been divinized. Incarnation does not proclaim the special character of Jesus' traditional image as divine and human, but rather man's ability to see himself in spiritual, divine terms.[9]

In Rahner, the essence of secularization as demythologization not only leads to the affirmation of the hypostatic union as a feature of humanity in general and the confirmation of incarnation as divinization of the world; it also points to the fact that Christian theology cannot be discussed without reference to the "evolutionary view of the world" which is fundamentally scientific and technological.[10] From this perspective, his idea of secularization focuses the theological discourse on the world of man, because it is here where man feels "competent" and "at home". This is why, according to Rahner's idea of secularization, theology should no longer be occupied with seeing God beyond this world, but rather with investigating God within this world. The focus of theology should not be heaven any longer, but the world.

In other words, Rahner's concept of secularization is based on his belief that there must be a reconciliation between Christianity and modern thought, which is actually an attempt to explain Christian doctrines from the perspective of, as well as based on, the reality of contemporary science and technology. Christianity – and especially the doctrine of Christ – must not be concerned with pointing to a reality which is said to exist beyond the material universe; in contemporary times, Christianity should delve into the study of matter, the human being, and its existence within the world. Rahner underlines that people today feel alienated because of metaphysics and religious statements; thus, any metaphysical discourse and religious claims made in the traditional sense must be avoided. In turn, what must be underlined as relevant for today's scientific minds is the discourse about the unity of reality. Matter and spirit are one, this world and the other world are one, earth is one with heaven – in a word, everything which can be said to exist belongs to the same, unique reality that is essentially material. This is why, in Rahner's theology, the traditional expression "the *logos* became flesh" should be read as "the spirit became matter", so the most important task of Christology is not to proclaim the traditional coexistence of divinity and humanity in Jesus Christ but to underscore

---

[9] Rahner, *Foundations of Christian Faith*, 181.

[10] For details about the divinization of the world in Rahner, see Veli-Matti Kärkkäinen, *An Introduction to the Theology of Religions: Biblical, Historical, and Contemporary Perspectives* (Downers Grove, IL: InterVarsity Press, 2003), 193.

that divinity is in fact humanity.[11] When this happens, the divinity of the traditional Jesus Christ becomes an affirmation of his humanity and the promises of traditional theology concerning the otherworldly reality of heaven are nothing but confirmations of the worldly reality of the material universe.

Such scientific belief modifies not only the doctrine of incarnation but also that of creation since, in Rahner, the traditional Christian belief in the creative work of God does not point to the fact that all things were created by what humanity has always called God but rather to the conviction that all things have one single cause. The affirmation of the existence of one single cause as the foundation for the existence of all things points to "a *single* world". This is to say that what has been traditionally designated by the concepts of matter and spirit has more aspects in common than differences. In Rahner's terms, matter and spirit are actually one; the notions of matter and spirit make reference to one single reality, to one single world, which is essentially material. The same pattern of thought is to be applied to Christology, in an attempt to prove that the materiality of Jesus' being is the only factual and real aspect of his existence, while his spirituality is nothing but a characteristic of his material constitution. This is why Rahner stresses the paramount importance of matter as "an inescapable given". Matter allows man to perceive himself as part of the world and the world as the context for his existence; matter is the reality which determines man's feeling of alienation in the world but also helps man understand his purpose within nature.

In other words, matter causes and heals man's estrangement because of its capacity to "make possible the objective other"; therefore, man is able to see himself as part of the world but also as different from the world because of matter and – at the same time – man has the capacity to make sense of his material existence in the world due to the power of matter to objectify reality. Rahner makes it clear that man exists in time, space, and history, but such understanding of the human being is possible only because of matter. Once the human being realizes this aspect, then he is able to communicate with other human beings in time, space, and history since they are all able to understand their existence within the same coordinates.[12]

---

[11] See also Aidan O'Boyle, *Towards a Contemporary Wisdom Christology: Some Catholic Christologies in German, English, and French, 1965–1995* (Roma: Editrice Pontificia Università Gregoriana, 2001), 241.

[12] Rahner, *Foundations of Christian Faith*, 181-183.

Man's Self-Transcendence and God's Self-Communication

When matter becomes so important for Rahner, it is clear that something else must change. Matter not only designates this world; matter is this world and Rahner's entire theology is an attempt to revert attention from traditional theology – whose focus is the other world, the transcendent, metaphysical and ontologically real world of God – to a modernistic approach of the world, thoroughly based on the idea of secularization, which leaves behind any reference to transcendence in order to include it within the reality of the material world.

Thus, in Rahner, the notion of transcendence is detached from traditional theology as a reference to the metaphysical world of God and is attached to man's reality in the world. This is why Rahner speaks about "active self-transcendence" as indicative of man's capacity to relate to himself.[13] Man is matter and spirit, and the relationship between matter and spirit – Rahner explains – is essentially not static because it happens in history. Whatever occurs within the reality of history, which is fundamentally tied to nature and matter, time and space, as well as man's awareness of himself and of the world, is therefore designated as active, so man's self-consciousness is included here. When man is aware and conscious of himself, Rahner writes that the human being becomes present to itself. Man's presence to himself comes with an awareness of his previous existence in the world based on his relationship with himself and the world. When the human being is able to relate itself to the world and its own being, so that he realizes his presence in the world and within his own interiority, then one can speak of "active self-transcendence". Man is therefore able to go beyond his own self into realizing his place in the world as a being which is conscious and totally aware of himself. Spirit and matter cannot be detached from one another, so the materiality of man is informed of its own transcendence – which is in fact a self-transcendence – by man's spirituality.

In Rahner, self-transcendence is accompanied by the idea of becoming; in other words, man reaches out beyond his own self towards a progress of his own being in a spiritual way. Man, who is essentially matter, is able to step outside his own self spiritually, so man is radically open to his own identity to the extent that he is able to reach what Rahner calls "the ultimate point of identity". This ultimate point of identity is called "God", so in Rahner the idea of God is actually a notion which is used to define man's becoming his own identity through his self-transcendence. In other words, man goes beyond his naturalness and materiality into the reality of the spirit, which is in fact his own

---

[13] See also Gregory C. Higgins, *The Tapestry of Christian Theology: Modern Minds on the Biblical Narrative* (Mahwah, NJ: Paulist Press, 2003), 102.

consciousness.[14] In doing so, man becomes aware of the infinite possibilities which lie ahead of him and help him accomplish the fullness of his own being. Thus, man takes a huge leap into his own consciousness, into his own ontological interiority, so man transcends himself in an active way from the limitations of his biological materiality to the absoluteness of his conscious spirituality. When man's active self-transcendence reaches the radical self-awareness of man's absolute spirituality, one can say that the idea of God has been incarnated within the human being.[15]

Rahner's secularization cements the human being within materiality, naturalness, and consciousness, so – based on his conviction that matter and spirit are united into the one single reality of the world – it means that God must be sought within the same reality. There is no other choice for man: if he really wants to find God, then God must be searched for within this world. Rahner explains that self-transcendence assists man in performing a thorough investigation of the mystery of reality, which in Rahner is described as grounding everything. God, on the other hand, is "the inexpressible infinity of mystery", so when man is able to realize the ineffability of the mystery of existence – of the universe and of himself – then God has been found.[16] This is to say that man must look for God within the world and within his own being. The macrocosmos and the microcosmos are both aspects which speak of the same uniqueness of reality and God is to be found in both. Or, to be more precise, God is to be found in the one single reality of the universe which reflects itself in the materiality of nature and of the human being.

Man is aware of the materiality of the world and of his own being in a spiritual way; he is infinitely open to this reality and the fullness of its realization prompts him to understanding his openness to it, to its mystery, and ineffability – in other words, his openness to the absoluteness of the mystery which lies within the existence of the universe itself, namely the idea of God.

God, therefore, becomes known to man through self-communication and, as God can be found in nature and in man's own being, it means that God's self-communication is actually man's awareness of himself and

---

[14] For details about consciousness in Rahner, see Werner G. Jeanrond, "Rahner's Theological Method and a Theology of Love", 103-120, in Pádraic Conway and Fáinche Ryan (eds.), *Karl Rahner: Theologian for the Twenty-First Century*, vol. III: *Studies in Theology, Society, and Culture* (Bern: Peter Lang, 2010): 118.

[15] Rahner, *Foundations of Christian Faith*, 183-188.

[16] Gaspar Martinez, *Confronting the Mystery of God: Political, Liberation, and Public Theologies* (London: Continuum, 2001), 1.

of the universe.¹⁷ This is why, in Rahner, the person of Jesus Christ becomes a particularization of the human being's relationship with God, which is his self-awareness of himself and the world, as well as his capacity to step beyond his materiality into a conscious relationship with himself and the world. Jesus exemplifies the reality of both incarnation and creation, in the sense that he is representative of man's capacity to be aware and conscious of his infinite openness towards his own spirituality. If God is to be found through his self-communication, which is man's awareness of his own consciousness, then Jesus is the particularization of man's capacity to discover God within himself and within the material reality of the universe as the ineffability of the mystery which characterizes the depth of existence. In Rahner, this is the most evident result of secularization – the fact that God can only be found within the materiality of existence, in man's interiority and the universe's exteriority, through the self-transcendence of the human being which perceives its spirituality as God's self-communication.¹⁸

---

[17] For details of God's self-communication in Rahner, see William V. Dych, *Karl Rahner* (London: Continuum, 2000), 154.

[18] Rahner, *Foundations of Christian Faith*, 189-198.

4

Stripping Nature of Sacred Meanings: Mircea Eliade

Desacralization and Rationalization

In Mircea Eliade the issue of secularization is often discussed in conjunction with the reality of nature. He speaks in fact about the secularization of nature because in his thought nature is the reality which contains sacred meanings. The sacralized perspective of nature is man-made, but in modernity nature is no longer seen through the lens of the sacred, so its religious meanings are gradually abandoned. Secularization is, therefore, a process within a process, in the sense that secularization is the process of stripping nature of its sacred meanings, which happens as part of the process of the desacralization of the world.[1]

In Eliade, the desacralization of the world is in fact a huge transformation of the world, which is also associated with the desacralization of the cosmos seen as the creation of God. Eliade points out that the transformation of the world through the desacralization of the cosmos and the secularization of nature was triggered by industrialized societies and the actions exerted by the scientific discoveries of physics and chemistry. The process of secularization and desacralization seems to move on and one cannot tell for a fact whether or not it will be possible in the future to regain the sacred dimension of the world.

What is important for Eliade to establish is the fact that, despite the serious secularization and desacralization, modern man still retains a significant number of habits, as well as a behavior which shows reminiscent traces of what used to be sacred in times past. The most industrialized societies still keep within themselves manifestations which remind their members of the sacred beliefs from the past. Thus, it is clear that, in Eliade, the past is associated with pre-modern beliefs which are in turn marked by religiosity and sacredness. By contrast, modern beliefs are devoid of religiosity, so the dimension of the sacred

---

[1] See also Walter J. Ong, SJ, *The Presence of the Word: Some Prolegomena for Cultural and Religious History* (New Haven, CT: Yale University Press, 1967/Binghamton, NY: Global Publications, 2000), 161-162.

is on the verge of extinction. It has not been totally dismissed from man's life though, so his current behavior still shows that pre-secularized, pre-desacralized, and pre-industrialized convictions remain part of today's scientific society.

One of the reasons why the sacred survives in modern society despite secularization appears to be connected with man's living in a home. According to Eliade, traditional societies – namely those in which the sacred exists unaltered by secularization – place a huge emphasis on the sanctification of the home or the house because it is the image of the world.[2] Since the world is perceived as God's creation in traditional societies, it is evident that the home is seen in similar terms. Thus, the sacralization, or rather the sacredness, of the house is based on the sacredness of the world, which is believed to be God's creation. Now, the world may be seen as non-sacred, even profane, in modern societies as a result of secularization, but the fact that man lives in his own house – which is quite difficult to desacralize since it is man's own creation – could explain why traces of the sacred are still noticeable within today's post-industrialized and scientific societies. This could indicate that, in Eliade, secularization is not a natural process, but rather an attempt to counter the natural tendency of the human being to sacralize its existence. Whether or not the cosmos and the house are sacred is not important; what is crucial though has to do with the fact that, in traditional society, it is natural for man to consider the cosmos and his house sacred. This is why what happens in industrialized and scientific societies in the form of secularization seems to be the modern man's attempt to secularize and desacralize his existence by unnaturally going against what the human being has always considered sacred.[3]

Secularization is not only a process of desacralization, but also an enterprise which is characterized by rationalization.[4] Eliade makes it clear that it was rationalization which led to secularization with the end-result that the whole cosmos is emptied of its religious content. Nevertheless, one cannot speak of the definitive secularization of the world because the religious feeling, so traditional for the human being, continues to manifest itself within the experience of many modern individuals. When it comes to modernity, however, Eliade shows that despite the sacred nature of the house which still maintains some sacredness in the experience of the modern man, secularization was made

---

[2] See also Darlene M. Juschka, *Feminism in the Study of Religion: A Reader* (London: Continuum, 2001), 580.

[3] Mircea Eliade, *The Sacred and the Profane: The Nature of Religion*, trans. Willard R. Trask (New York, NY: Harcourt, 1987), 50-51.

[4] For details about rationalization and its effects on religion in Eliade, see Inger J. Birkeland, *Making Place, Making Self. Travel, Subjectivity, and Sexual Difference* (Aldershot: Ashgate, 2005), 128.

possible through the rationalization of some specific events in man's life which were devoid of their ritual character. For instance, if secularization proved to be successful in modernity, that was the result of the fact that ritual was no longer seen as part of man's life and especially of events such as birth, marriage, and death. Thus, according to Eliade, the secularization of the world began with the rationalization of individual existence and the first aspects to be emptied of their religious, sacred, and ritual character were birth, marriage, and death. In other words, for the modern areligious man, birth, marriage, and death mean nothing but the actual fact of one's birth, marriage, and death. Despite the rationalization and secularization of these critical aspects of human experience, Eliade points out that a totally areligious experience in a pure state is extremely rare even in societies which have reached an unprecedented level of industrialization, technology, and scientific achievements. This is a fact today, but it could change in the future. This is why Eliade admits that a totally areligious experience is possible in the more or less distant future – which also indicates that secularization can indeed reach a peak when religion, sacredness, and ritual are totally excluded from human life – but for now secularization is evidently mixed with traditional reminiscences of religious, sacred, and ritual elements that still find a way to show up in the lives of most contemporary individuals.

There is, however, a "profane world" which is acknowledged by Eliade as a reality within today's society and is characterized by what he calls "a radical secularization of death, marriage, and birth". The abolished religious behaviors of the past, though, continue to exist despite modern rationalization, secularization, and desacralization. To be sure, however, the essence of secularization in modern, post-industrialized, and scientific societies is based on the transformation of the pre-industrialized ideal of humanity as anchored in a superhuman sphere into a reality which is essentially human.[5] In other words, Eliade explains that secularization is nothing but the rational attempt of the modern man to see his achievements as part of this world, the world which he can see and rationalize, not as endeavors which place himself outside the naturalness of the world. If religion is an attitude towards the world, so is secularization. Eliade indicates that the religious man wants to be different from what he is in his natural state; this is why he attempts to complete and perfect his life in accordance with an ideal image of himself which was revealed to him through myths. Thus, the secular man wants to do exactly the opposite: complete and perfect his

---

[5] See also Douglas Allen, *Myth and Religion in Mircea Eliade* (London: Routledge, 2002), 67-68.

life in accordance with how he understands the world based on reason. This is why secularization as desacralization and rationalization is also explained by Eliade as the conscious rejection of traditional religious myths.[6]

The Acknowledgment of the Sacred

While secularization is in general an attempt to purge the profane of any sacred influence, in Eliade the effectiveness of secularization seems to include the very important aspect of the recognition of the sacred, both as history and as a key human component. Secularization cannot be achieved unless the sacred dimension of humanity is fully acknowledged. This is why, for Eliade, the knowledge of the spiritual side of man, the sacred side of his naturalness, is paramount for a better understanding of the human being in general. To be sure, secularization can never reach its goal until the human being is known in all its aspects, traditional and modern, pre-industrialized and industrialized, pre-scientific and scientific, and – in the end – sacred and profane.[7] There is an aspect of the sacred which has long been surpassed – that of primitive religion and ancient religious culture – but in order for secularization to achieve its purpose, these historical manifestations of the sacred must be known competently. Eliade's main reason for the knowledge of man's religious past has to do with his conviction that contemporary humanity exists in its actual "form" due, to a large degree, to man's religious past, the knowledge of which is essential for contemporary awareness about the human being in general. We are what we are, Eliade writes, because of our religious past and because of the religious convictions of our ancestors, so – as they are part of our history – it is normal that we should want to be aware of their beliefs, customs, and traditions.

Thus, in Eliade, the effectiveness of secularization depends on the knowledge of the religious man, who is characterized by some distinctive features: first, the religious man assumes a specific mode of being in the world, which is based on the deep conviction that the sacred – as absolute reality – transcends this world and has its own real existence beyond the naturalness and materiality of this world; second, the sacred manifests itself in this world and, in doing so, it sanctifies it and makes it real; and third, the religious man believes in the sanctity and sacredness of human life, which becomes more actualized as it clings to its religious dimension. Thus, the foundation of religious thought resides

---

[6] Eliade, *The Sacred and the Profane*, 158-159, 186-187.
[7] See Bryan S. Rennie, *Reconstructing Eliade: Making Sense of Religion* (Albany, NY: State University of New York Press, 1996), 31-32.

4. Stripping Nature of Sacred Meanings: Mircea Eliade 47

in man's conviction that the more he founds his existence on the sacred dimension of his life as based on his faith in the metaphysical reality of a transcendent world, the richer his life becomes spiritually.[8] Religious man believes in God or in gods, in the world as God's creation, in some civilizing heroes who perfected God's creation, and in the history of God's actions in the world which were all preserved as myths.

Now, it has to be underlined that the conviction that the history of the acts of God in the world should be understood as myths is essentially modern, so it is a product of secularization, but what Eliade points out here is that man has a fundamental need to re-actualize his sacred history. In other words, the religious man wants to imitate divine behavior and, in doing so, to stay close to gods, because for him this means staying within what is truly real and meaningful. This is to say that religion provides humanity with meaningfulness and gives the human person the feeling of "reality" within the indifference of nature's materiality. The process of secularization needs to take this into account if it is to be efficient because in diminishing the influence of religion, secularization also replaces man's traditional belief in the meaningfulness of the sacred with something totally different, which is no longer to be found beyond this world but in this world.[9]

From this perspective, secularization tries to replace the religious man with the areligious man, who has three main features: first, he rejects transcendence in the sense that he does not believe in the ontological reality of a transcendent world; second, he embraces the relativity of reality, which means that he is more than willing to live with the idea that more interpretations can be given to the same reality, and third, he sometimes doubts the meaning of his existence.[10] While acknowledging the possibility that areligious people existed in ancient, archaic religious cultures, Eliade shows that it was only in modern times – especially in Western heavily industrialized societies – that the areligious man manifested his presence in a plenary way. This entails a sheer conviction that history is all that matters; the world as it exists in space and time is the only source for the areligious man's reality. The areligious man is the agent of secularization because his set of personal convictions does not include what Eliade terms "the call to transcendence". The areligious man is therefore interested only in the *saeculum*,

---

[8] See John A. Saliba, "Homo Religiosus" in *Mircea Eliade: An Anthropological Evaluation* (Leiden: Brill, 1976), 98.
[9] Eliade, *The Sacred and the Profane*, 202-203.
[10] On Eliade's areligious man, see further L. Eugene Thomas, "The Way of the Religious Renouncer: Power through Nothingness", 51-64, in L. Eugene Thomas & Susan A. Eisenhandler (eds.), *Aging and the Religious Dimension* (Westport, CT: Auburn House/Greenwood Publishing, 1994): 59.

in the existence, affairs, and development of this world, so if there is any meaning whatsoever to be found for human existence, it must be looked for within the materiality of the natural world. The areligious man sees himself as a subject and agent of history; this is why transcendence is totally meaningless for him.[11]

As a result of secularization, the areligious man is not willing to accept models for his humanity; the only thing which works for him is the actuality of the human condition as it manifests itself throughout history. Specific historical moments can shed some light on the human condition and, in doing so, they highlight distinct characteristics of humanity: this is all that the secularized mind of the areligious man can accept as rational and meaningful. This is why the areligious man cannot accept that his existence depends on something or somebody else. The idea of God, the sacred, and the transcendent tells him nothing. The areligious man creates himself, so one of the most important religious aspects which are modified by secularization is the notion of the world – as well as of the human being – as creation. Secularization promotes a man without belief in religion, a man whose ability to create himself depends on how much he manages to desacralize the world and himself. For the areligious man, the sacred is a serious hindrance for him; the sacred prevents the secularized man from reaching the full potential of his personal freedom. The areligious man wants to be himself but in order for him to achieve this goal he must emerge as a demystified human being, so his total freedom depends on his capacity to kill the gods.

In order, however, for these ideals to be accomplished, the areligious man must be aware of his religious past; this is why, in Eliade, the knowledge of the sacred history of humanity is essential for the realization of the process of secularization in an effective way. The areligious man originates in the religious man, which also means that secularization originates in religion. In Eliade, religion itself seems to contain the seeds of secularization, which become activated in history when humanity reaches a certain level of industrial, technological, and scientific progress based on a history of rationalization that began long before the modern breakthrough in the practical field of science.[12]

Consciousness and Unconsciousness

Science seems to be the catalyst of secularization, but when accepted as part of one's existence secularization does not prove totally capable of

---

[11] Marty Glass, *Yuga. An Anatomy of Our Fate: A Companion to Spiritual Practice* (Hillsdale, NY: Sophia Perennis, 2001), 232.
[12] Eliade, *The Sacred and the Profane*, 203-204.

detaching religion from the interiority of the human being. This is why, according to Eliade, nonreligious or areligious people may believe in science and the materiality of the universe, but the essence of what has been considered religious through the entire history of humanity still remains within them and forces them to adopt pseudo-religions or degraded mythologies. The secularized man is the product of the religious man, which explains the mythological and religious traces still left within man's consciousness or even unconsciousness.[13] Eliade is convinced that a purely religious human being is an abstract concept, so it does not practically exist in the reality of today's society since rationality and irrational, unconscious experiences define the totality of a human being regardless of whether one's mind frame is secularized or not. Since the actual content as well as the structures of human unconsciousness bear evident resemblances to mythological images and figures, it is obvious why secularized people continue to manifest themselves in a way which can be considered – if not religious – at least pseudo-religious and partially mystified.

At this point, Eliade makes it clear that this does not mean that religions are the product of human unconsciousness; on the contrary, religion and mythologies are the product of man's reason and experience since they become unveiled as myths, which means that a certain event took place and that event, or a central figure thereof, exerted a powerful influence on a certain community to the point that various narratives about that event gradually turned into a myth. Eliade's stress on the origin of myth is extremely important because it seems that reason plays a crucial role not only in the formation of myth but also in the appearance of secularization. Thus, the desire to create as well as to detach from myth – namely sacralization and secularization – are both the result of human reason. At the same time, the pseudo-religious manifestations of today's people within the general context of secularization have nothing to do with active reasoning because, while people want to rid themselves of religion, they still unconsciously retain religious and mythological elements in the deepest structures of their spirituality.[14]

In other words, secularization – although scientific and conscious, rational and expressly willful – is also characterized by a certain degree of unconsciousness precisely because the areligious man's behavior is

---

[13] For details about how the areligious man is the product of the religious man in Eliade, see Simon Stander, "The Commodity", 71-90, in Paul Zarembka (ed.), *Why Capitalism Survives Crises. The Shock Absorbers* (Bingley: JAI Press/Emerald, 2009): 84-85.

[14] See also Daniel Chapelle, *Nietzsche and Psychoanalysis* (Albany, NY: State University of New York Press, 1993), 223.

not totally devoid of religious influences. The human being in all its manifestations is essentially existential, which means that religious and areligious people go through existential crises which deeply impact their lives. This is important because, in Eliade, the existential crisis literally confounds itself with the sacred, which means that the sacred is actually present – more or less unconsciously – within the life of the areligious man. Consequently, reason and a secularized way of thinking are not the answer for the areligious man in search of meaning; the mere fact of one's desire to find meaning for one's life is proof of the existence of a religious dimension within one's life. Consequently, the solution to the existential crisis is profoundly religious, transcendent, and otherworldly, because this is the way which must be pursued if the areligious man wants to overcome his personal situations and, in doing so, to open himself to the realm of the spirit.[15]

The process of secularization goes hand in hand with the permanent activity of human unconsciousness. The former cannot do without the latter, so in Eliade secularization is at least partly religious. Despite his capacity to rationalize his existence in the materiality of the world, the areligious man of today's secularized society is still confronted with unrest and existential issues which need solutions.[16] Secularized or not, areligious or religious, the human being must face a wide variety of symbols on a regular basis and, given man's innermost need for meaningfulness, he will have to deal with them one way or another. In traditional religious societies, man confronted symbols with religion which provided him with a religious, transcendental, and metaphysical explanation of his material existence within the world, seen as God's creation. In modern areligious communities, man is still confronted with symbols, but he is unwilling to use religion to decipher them in a metaphysical, transcendent, and otherworldly way; consequently, there is no meaning attached to an areligious, secularized, and rationalized solution to the modern man's existential crisis.

A solution, however, must be found for the restoration of psychical balance, but the solution does not come from the conscious use of reason; on the contrary, it comes from the sphere of man's unconsciousness even if the individual shares a deep commitment to secularization, desacralization, and demystification. This is why, for Eliade, man's unconsciousness fulfills – despite secularization and within today's secularized society – the traditional role of religion, which is to offer integrity to human existence. Thus, the trumpeting of secularization in today's society as a dismissal of religion, mythology, and sacred-

---

[15] Eliade, *The Sacred and the Profane*, 210-211.
[16] See also James L. Cox, *A Guide to the Phenomenology of Religion: Key Figures, Formative Influences, and Subsequent Debates* (London: Continuum, 2006), 186-187.

ness is nothing but an equally important recognition of the continuous presence of it within the deepest recesses of man's unconsciousness. Secularization therefore must admit that while the modern, scientific mind of the secularized man may have lost the capacity to live religion in a conscious way, he still unconsciously lives it in a fashion that continues to shape his experience in the world. The modern, secularized man of today's scientific and rationalized society is definitely unable to understand and assume religion consciously; his unconscious though works deep within his being.

In other words, the traditional search for God does not end with or because of secularization. Man continues – in a clearly unconscious way – to search for God, but while the traditional religious may have looked for God in a transcendent world, the secularized man looks for God, namely for meaning, value, and integrity, in this world. This is why, in Eliade's thought, secularization should be described as religion since it is, in a way, a second "fall".[17] The first fall caused man to lose religiosity in his torn consciousness, so he began to search for meaning outside this world; with the second fall – which is secularization – man's innate religiosity sinks even deeper, in the abyss of his own unconsciousness, so his search for meaning remains rationally confined to this world while performed in a desacralized and demystified way.[18]

---

[17] Jonathan Z. Smith, *Map Is Not Territory: Studies in the History of Religions* (Chicago, IL: University of Chicago Press, 1993), 93.
[18] Eliade, *The Sacred and the Profane*, 212-213.

5

Lessening the Importance of God: Edward Schillebeeckx

The Lessening of God

Edward Schillebeeckx discusses the issue of secularization within his analysis of how we should correlate our image of man – and also of the world – with our image of God. In other words, between how we perceive the world and how we see what we know as the idea of God there must be a correlation.[1] As a matter of fact, this correlation seems to be some sort of equalization since our image of the world and of man as living in the world is not only placed at the same level with how we understand God; it is more than that, it is how we explain what we mean by God. This implies that the traditional understanding of God as having an existence different from man is dismissed from the start. If in traditional theology God and man were two distinct existences – namely two different and separate substances – in Schillebeeckx, God and man look like one single, unified, and unique existence in the material world of nature. The God of traditional theology loses his former importance; what becomes crucially vital for people today is our image of man, of who we are in the world. This is why the first – as well as the fundamental – aspect of Schillebeeckx's idea of secularization is the waning of God, which is explained through three main concepts: the world, man, and relationship.

In order to understand what Schillebeeckx means by secularization, one should accept the fact that the word "God" no longer produces the impact which it managed to induce in the past. For today's men and women, the word "God" does not signal any kind of palpable presence; for today's people, God is rather silent, so his impact in the world is considerably lessened. When God is silent – and the most evident aspect of today's society is that God is indeed silent according

---

[1] Aloysius Rego, OCD, *Suffering and Salvation. The Salvific Meaning of Suffering in the Later Theology of Edward Schillebeeckx* (Louvain and Grand Rapids, MI: Peeters and Eerdmans, 2006), 49.

5. Lessening the Importance of God: Edward Schillebeeckx

to Schillebeeckx – one can say secularization has already taken its toll on today's society. Schillebeeckx admits that the idea of secularization is a dualistic concept, in the sense that it has a non-religious connotation but also a meaning which can be tied to the actual manifestation of religion in the world. In its primary meaning, secularization has nothing to do with God; it focuses exclusively on the world. The word itself comes from the Latin *saeculum*, which speaks of the world. Secularization is understanding the world.[2]

In today's society, though, the concept of "world" cannot be detached from the idea of "God"; one has to deal with both God and the world in order to understand what the world really means. Secularization investigates what the world is and how it exists, but in order to do that there has to be a redefinition of the world with reference to the idea of God. In this respect, Schillebeeckx mentions that the traditional understanding of God involves the fact that God reigns over the world as his creation, so the world is understood through the reality of a God who ontologically transcends it.

Such an understanding of the world is clearly dismissed by Schillebeeckx, who criticizes traditional theology for having imposed the notion of "salvation" on man's perception of the world. Everything which happened in history was seen as God's act of salvation; God acted in the world in order to rescue the world and the human being. God therefore was beyond the world trying to get involved in the world in order to save the world.[3]

Science and technology, however, changed all this, and nowadays the world no longer needs God's salvation; in fact, today's world needs neither salvation, nor God. This explains Schillebeeckx's move in defining secularization from the world to the reality of man. When the world is no longer seen as God's creation or object of salvation, the world becomes pure nature, and the material existence of nature includes the existence of humanity, men and women. Consequently, it is not God who can be described as the world's creator; on the contrary, man is presented as the one who creates, shapes, and reshapes the world through science and technology.[4] It is no longer God who can be seen in the world; it is now man who can be connected with the material reality of the world's natural and physical existence. God is no longer the creator of the world and neither is he the one who reveals

---

[2] Erick Borgman, *Edward Schillebeeckx: A Theologians in His History*, trans. John Bowden (London: Continuum), 334.

[3] Edward Schillebeeckx, *World and Church*, trans. N.D. Smith (London and Sydney: Sheed and Ward, 1971), 78-79.

[4] See also Philip Kennedy, OP, *Schillebeeckx* (Collegeville, MN: The Liturgical Press, 1993), 76.

himself in the world; man creates and recreates the world through what Schillebeeckx calls "the supremacy of technology", so it is man who now reveals himself in and to the world.[5]

Secularization implies the degradation of God's image in today's society and the strengthening of man's image within the same context through the control of nature. There is a shift from cosmocentrism – which also implies theism – to anthropocentrism, in the sense that nature is no longer the subject of man's control, but the object of man's control through science and technology. In other words, the world no longer bears the image of God, but the image of man. As Schillebeeckx puts it, the world lost its capacity of being *theophanous*; the world does not show us God any more. What the world shows us today is the image of man, so the world turned into a *hominized* reality. Secularization is thus seeing the world through the lens of man, not of God, but the reality of man's existence is fundamentally diverse and multifaceted. Man exists as a community of individuals, which indicates that the most fundamental existence; that of relationships between each human subject. From the standpoint of secularization, an adequate definition of it has to include a dramatic change in what Schillebeeckx terms "man's relationship with the world". Thus, man should no longer see the world exclusively as nature; man does not relate only to the exteriority of nature. Man is fundamentally connected with other human beings as they all exist in the world of nature as the only objective reality. God is ousted as creator and savior of the world, while man is enthroned as the "demiurge" of the world and the crafter of his own existence in the reality of material nature.[6]

The Move Away from the Church

The second aspect of secularization in Schillebeeckx is what he himself calls "the movement away from the church". If the first element of secularization is the redefinition of the world, which presupposes a drastic reconsideration of the idea of God, moving away from the church is the next logical step. Through secularization today's society rids itself of the traditional understanding of God – but not necessarily of the concept of God itself – so the world is no longer seen from God's perspective but from man's point of view. Such reshaping of theology leads quite naturally to Schillebeeckx's movement away from the church, because as society does not share a common preoccupation

---

[5] For an excellent discussion about man's capacity to create, see Marguerite Abdul-Masih, *Edward Schillebeeckx and Hans Frei. A Conversation on Method and Christology* (Waterloo, ON: Wilfried Laurier University Press, 2001), 70.

[6] Schillebeeckx, *World and Church*, 79-80.

for God, it is logical that the church should be somewhat left aside in an attempt to promote some kind of ecumenism which leaves nobody outside the sphere of religion.[7] Any movement away from the church, though, implies coming closer to the active reality of society, so secularization means learning and appropriating the current issues of today's society in an attempt to address them and, when necessary, solve them. Schillebeeckx's idea of secularization is based on his conviction that the human being must reshape its own experience in the world. By moving away from the church and delving into the current problems of today's society, man learns a new experience, an experience of the world as material reality which presents itself as the only objective reality of man's existence. In other words, man should no longer understand the world theologically, but rather sociologically. Even the idea of God should be seen anthropologically and sociologically; secularization as the process of focusing the human being on the current issues of the world has no room left for a divine, transcendental understanding of God. Secularization teaches man to understand himself from the perspective of his own experience, and such a perspective also changes the very definition of experience.[8] Experience thus becomes the standard for how man comprehends the surrounding reality; experience is man's new epistemology. Man learns how to understand, investigate, and accept the world through his own experience in the material context of physical nature. At the end of the day, man learns how to embrace his own reality through experience. Schillebeeckx is convinced that experience leads to knowledge, so the only realities we can know for a fact are those which can be experienced.

To be sure, man understands the world through his experience in the world, and this is exactly the way he should also understand the idea of God. God must be known from and based on man's experience in the world simply because one cannot experience a God who exists beyond the world, namely beyond the possibility of man's direct experience. Consequently, through secularization, man not only learns how to understand the world and his own experience; man also learns how to use his experience in order to redefine the religious realities of his life, of which the most important is the idea of God.

---

[7] On Schillebeeckx's inclusivist perspective, see Susan F. Parsons, "Watch and Pray. A Reflection on the Meaning of *Ut*", 81-92, in Francesca A. Murphy and Christopher Asprey (eds.), *Ecumenism Today: Universal Church in the 21st Century* (Aldershot: Ashgate, 2008): 87.
[8] For the relationship between secularization and experience, see Kathleen A. McManus, OP, *Unbroken Communion: The Place and Meaning of Suffering in the Theology of Edward Schillebeeckx* (Lanham, MD: Rowman & Littlefield, 2003), 24.

Schillebeeckx's redefinition of experience is crucial here mainly because he rejects the traditional understanding of experience which is shaped by theology; in our secular society, experience shapes theology. If in traditional theology, human experience was molded by man's concept of God as an objective being that exists beyond creation, now human experience dictates the very content of the doctrine of God, so it is not man who conforms to God's requirements but the other way around: God conforms to man's requirements.[9]

If knowledge is possible only based on man's experience, it means that man can only learn about the world in which he lives through his own perceptions. Man must be aware of the world, of how the world can be known through experience, and also of his own perception about himself. Man must enter an active and sensible relationship with himself if he or she really wants to know the world in a meaningful way; once such knowledge is attained, then a redefinition of the idea of God becomes possible.[10] As a result, man understands that the essence of secularization is seeing God in a brand new way, which has nothing to do with his traditional out-of-the-world transcendental existence. God cannot exist outside this world because, if so, he would be beyond the reach of man's capacity to know him. This is why, Schillebeeckx underlines, God must be conceived in terms of this world; God must somehow exist in this world if man wants to know him. When it comes to God's presence, however, Schillebeeckx writes that "God can only be present in the manner of absence", which means that only reference to God as being present in the world points to man's awareness that God is in fact absent from the world.[11] In other words, when the secular man expresses his conviction that God is present in this world, he actually states his belief in God's total absence from the world. God is therefore a concept which enriches man's spirituality because man's experience does not allow for an idea of God which professes his objective presence in man as God's creature. Schillebeeckx underlines that this is not the cancellation of religion; it is only embracing religion in a secular way. God is not removed from man's experience; on the contrary, Schillebeeckx, argues, God is present in the secularized man's religion, but in a totally different way. God is seen as a concept whose presence is in fact his sheer absence from the world, so the secularized man must accept this new under-

---

[9] Schillebeeckx, *World and Church*, 80-81.

[10] See also Robert J. Schreiter, CPPS, "Edward Schillebeeckx", 152-161, in David F. Ford (ed.), *The Modern Theologians: An Introduction to Christian Theology in the Twentieth Century* (Oxford: Blackwell, 2004): 156.

[11] This is also true in Jesus' case, so Schillebeeckx's idea of God's absence has practical implications for Christology. For detail see Matthew W. Levering, *Sacrifice and Community: Jewish Offering and Christian Eucharist* (Oxford: Blackwell, 2005), 20.

standing of God in an atheistic way. At the same time though it is not only God who must be seen in atheistic terms; the human being itself must be understood through the lens of atheism as a being which is no longer driven by the perception of a God that is present in the world.

The shift from theism to atheism in defining God and humanity is Schillebeeckx's way to explain that secularization is in fact a process of desacralization which presents God, religion, and the human being in social terms. God, religion, and the human being are part of this world, and it is only through the direct experience of the world that the human being is able to know both God and religion. Today's secularization leads to an atheistic view of God and humanity, which does not cancel religion or theology but redefines God and the human being from a sociological perspective as inherent realities of the material world.[12]

Critical Thinking about God

The third aspect of Schillebeeckx's understanding of secularization is the need to think critically about God.[13] For Schillebeeckx, this is urgent, because modern secularized people have to experience what he calls "authentic Christianity" in a brand new way, but this cannot be done unless criticism is applied to all traditional values of Christianity, the image of God included. Experiencing God in accordance with traditional theology equals having a less authentic Christian experience for Schillebeeckx, so whatever was considered Christian in the past needs to be critically reevaluated and most likely discarded. Alternatively, the content of doctrines can be dramatically redefined, but this also implies giving up what Schillebeeckx dubs the "old forms" of Christianity. Schillebeeckx's problems with traditional Christianity seem to be related to his understanding of history. In other words, he appears to have an unrealistically optimistic perspective on the progress of history, which for him coincides with the progress of science, so whatever belongs to a past period in history, when scientific progress was not as strong as it is today, seems to be outdated. In fact, the past does not belong to the present for the simple reason that the past is not temporally connected with the present. For Schillebeeckx, the past seems to be detached from the present, so the things of the past, the

---

[12] Schillebeeckx, *World and Church*, 82-84.

[13] This presupposes the use of historical criticism, especially with reference to Christology. See Janet M. O'Meara, "Salvation. Living Communion with God", 98-116, in Mary C. Hilkert & Robert J. Schreiter (eds.), *The Praxis of the Reign of God: An Introduction to the Theology of Edward Schillebeeckx* (2nd edn, Bronx, NY: Fordham University Press, 2002): 98.

doctrines of the past, and even the science of the past must be left behind because the past is not literally connected with our contemporary times. Since this link is non-existent for Schillebeeckx, the past cannot have any meaningful significance for the present. Consequently, the modern man of today's world needs to find meaning for his life in our contemporary times; there is no authenticity of life in the past, when science and technology were underdeveloped while man's understanding of God shared the same pitiful fate. The past may have been relevant to people who actually lived in the past, but it cannot be relevant to people living today. What can be relevant for the people living today is a new and contemporary perspective on God, which can only be reached following a thorough criticism of the "old", traditional understanding of God which was common in the past. Christianity must go through a process of *aggiornamento*, and so must the church even if bringing doctrines up to date means understanding God and humanity in atheistic terms and moving away from the church.[14] For Schillebeeckx, moving away from the church is a sociological truth, which he interprets through the lens of theology in the sense that the actual situation in which today's people exclude the church from their lives is a theological manifesto against traditional Christianity. Thus, today's people who move away from the church must find a new understanding of God and, as they are already detached from the church, what they should do is criticize traditional theology in order to find a new understanding of God. This new understanding of God must be characterized by a critical attitude if today's people really want their secularized society to make sense.[15]

A new and critical understanding of God implies not only thinking of God in atheistic terms and moving away from the church, but also – as Schillebeeckx points out – the possibility of abandoning religion altogether. It follows that atheism and agnosticism take clear shape as vital characteristics of secularization as an attempt to find meaning for a society whose lay consciousness needs a reasonable explanation for fundamental human concepts such as God. This is why, Schillebeeckx underlines, Christians must not only embrace secularization, but also promote it. It is evident that Schillebeeckx takes secularization for granted in the sense that it is a sociological datum. Instead of fighting it based on traditional theology, Schillebeeckx reverses the whole argument and supports the idea that far from being countered, secularization should be promoted by Christians, although this implies thinking

---

[14] In this respect, Schillebeeckx's thought resembles liberation theology. See Patricia McAuliffe, *Fundamental Ethics: A Liberationist Approach* (Washington, DC: Georgetown University Press, 1993), 194.

[15] Schillebeeckx, *World and Church*, 84-85.

of God in critical, atheistic, and agnostic terms and excluding the church from one's life. The meaning of life is no longer to be found in the traditional doctrine of God or even in the traditional teaching of the church; indeed, for Schillebeeckx, the meaning of life today can no longer be found in the church. If one really wants to have a meaningful life, then he or she must step outside the church, go into the world, and find an authentic life in moving away from God and the church. Giving up God, disbelief in God, criticism of God, belief in God's non-existence can all be forms of a genuine, meaningful, and authentic life, in Schillebeeckx's secularized perspective on what life is and how life should be led today. This is why, for Schillebeeckx, secularization implies the total desacralization of contemporary society.[16] No God, no church, no sacred, no anything which belongs to the past is relevant any longer. Today's secularized man should change his perspective, so while leaving God and the church aside or even behind, he should focus on believing in his fellow men. The man of our contemporary secularized society should no longer believe in God but in man; he should no longer trust the church but science and technology. Spiritual counseling should be rejected as outdated; psychology, sociology, and medicine are the new realities worthy of man's trust.[17]

In the final analysis, in Schillebeeckx, secularization is man's attempt to find relevance and authenticity for his life in today's society, and if this means giving up God, the church, and whatever is considered traditional for Christianity in general, then this is the best solution. Whatever serves the purpose of finding meaning for one's life is good and needs to be embraced; our experience is what brings meaning into our lives, and if this presupposes a life without God or a life based on the conviction that God does not exist, then this is the step to be taken. Ultimately, for Schillebeeckx, secularization is man's desperate search for theological and existential meaning in a world where God is no longer welcome.[18]

---

[16] For the impact of desacralization on the church, see Teresa Whalen, *The Authentic Doctrine of the Eucharist* (Kansas City, MO: Sheed & Ward, 1993), 135-136.

[17] For Schillebeeckx's confidence in science, see also Francis Schüssler Fiorenza, "Systematic Theology: Task and Methods", 1-88, in Francis Schüssler Fiorenza and John P. Gavin (eds.), *Systematic Theology: Roman Catholic Perspectives*, vol. I (Minneapolis, MN: Augsburg Fortress, 1991): 57-58.

[18] Schillebeeckx, *World and Church*, 86-88.

6

Keeping God at a Distance: John Hick

The Christological Confusion

In John Hick's religious philosophy, the idea of secularization seems to coincide with the process that leads to what he calls "the established secular world view", which is based on the conviction that a historical individual cannot see himself in terms of God. In other words, secularization is the type of religious or theological thinking which keeps God away from any identification with the human being. To be more precise, it is the human being that needs to be kept at a secure distance from God if claims to divinity made by one single individual are to be avoided. This is clearly a hint at the Christian doctrine of Christ, so secularization in Hick has to do with keeping Christ in Jesus' "shoes", while God is left on his own beyond the realm of Jesus' humanity and, evidently, of humanity in general.

Hick's program of secularization can be squeezed into three distinct stages which range from the attempt to recognize the current state of Christology that – if one listens exclusively to Hick – is dominated by sheer confusion, to the dismissal of classical or traditional Christology as mythological and also to the promotion of a global – essentially inclusive – religion that is able to speak of Jesus in non-offensive ways when compared with other religious leaders.[1]

For Hick, the first step is crucial because it aims at tainting traditional Christology with the opacity of confusion so that no clear exposition of Jesus could be said to have been proclaimed within Christianity. Recognizing the Christological confusion reflects, therefore, Hick's intention to portray Christianity as a religion which is not sure of its image of Jesus. If Hick is right, then Christianity speaks of a Jesus who can be presented in so many ways which are not only fundamentally divergent, but also point to the lack of unity within Christianity's religious understanding of its own doctrines. Hick's argument is based on

---

[1] For further details, see Harold A. Netland, *Dissonant Voices: Religious Pluralism and the Question of Truth* (Vancouver, BC: Regent College Publishing, 1991), 243.

his conviction that a serious theological analysis of Christology should start from how the situation looks today and, as far as he is concerned, the words which best describe the current state of Christianity regarding its understanding of Jesus are "confusion" and "uncertainty". Every contemporary attempt to speak of Jesus is literally under the assault of confusion and uncertainty to the point that the image of the historical person who lived in Palestine in the first century can no longer convey a clear conviction about who Jesus was.[2]

What Hick seems to imply here is that there is a sharp distinction between the historical reality of the person named Jesus and the subsequent beliefs about him as professed through the entire history of the Christian church. It is one thing to believe in the historicity of Jesus and a totally different issue to see Jesus as he was. This "distance" between who Jesus was and who Jesus is said to be provides Hick with the chance to claim that traditional Christianity is no longer capable of coming up with a unique image of Jesus that reflects the actual reality of his historical existence.[3]

To be sure, the historical existence of the person known as Jesus of Nazareth is a fact that must be acknowledged. On the other hand, though, how this Jesus was seen under the name of Christ through the whole of church history is in itself a reality which, despite its importance for the church, has little in common with the truth of Jesus' actual existence. Hick is not willing to accept that the wide variety of descriptions of Jesus can be brought under the same Christology; for him, the sheer diversity of Christological images of Jesus is the proof of the current state of confusion which afflicts today's Christology. The subsequent religious uncertainty only adds to what seems to be an unfortunate state of affairs for Hick, because it allows Christianity to parade in the "boots" of religious superiority over other world religions. This is why, for Hick, secularization also appears to contain his desire to bring Christianity to the same level as all other world religions, so Christianity's claim that Jesus is the only savior must be downgraded to a religious conviction that promotes Jesus as a mere religious leader among many.[4]

---

[2] See also Stephen T. Davis, *Encountering Jesus: A Debate on Christology* (Louisville, KY: Westminster John Knox Press, 1988), 171.

[3] John Hick, *The Metaphor of God Incarnate* (London: SCM Press, 1993), 40, and John Hick, "Jesus and the World Religions", 167-185, in John Hick (ed.), *The Myth of God Incarnate* (London: SCM Press, 1993): 167.

[4] Terrence Merrigan, "The Historical Jesus in the Pluralist Theology of Religions", 61-82, in Terrence Merrigan & Jacques Haers (eds.), *The Myriad Christ: Plurality and the Quest for Unity in Contemporary Theology* (Leuven: Peeters, 2000): 76.

In order to achieve this goal, Hick has no option but to insist that the various images of Christ that speak of the historical life of Jesus of Nazareth are conflicting, confusing, and ambiguous. For instance, Hick's idea of secularization cannot accept that harmony can in fact exist between images of Christ – in order to portray Jesus in all his complexity – put together seemingly opposite features, such as sternness and tenderness, wrath and grace, love and justice, transcendence and immanence, pacifism and punishment, majesty and humility. The list can go on and on, but Hick is still firm in his conviction that such complexity in describing the image of Christ is the result of what he believes to be the confusion of the church, which plagues today's Christianity with uncertainty and megalomania – especially based on the church's belief in Jesus' exclusive capacity to act as the sole savior of the entire humankind.

This is why, for Hick, the complexity of religious images about Christ are in fact the effort of the church, in various stages of its development, to project its understanding of Jesus in a specific image of Christ in order to serve its purposes and especially the ideals of its members. The greatest problem of this ecclesiastical effort seems to be – for Hick – that all these images of Christ managed to build a supernatural understanding of the man Jesus; in other words, Jesus of Nazareth, the historical person who lived in Palestine, was proclaimed as being no less than God himself.[5] In Hick's system, secularization should sever Jesus of Nazareth from the church's claims that he was in fact God incarnate. Supernaturalism and transcendence are concepts which should no longer be attached to Jesus; for Hick, secularization implies the preservation of Jesus' humanity within the confines of history and nature. Anything that goes beyond history and factuality should be understood in terms of mythology, and secularization is the very process that acknowledges the validity of mythology for all religions, including Christianity.[6]

Mythology and the Image of Christ

Hick seems convinced that mythology is a necessary component of religion without which religious truths cannot be expressed and conveyed in a meaningful manner. Mythology needs to be considered the core of religion, otherwise some religious teachings may appear odd to people of today, for whom secularization is a fact of contemporary history. When it comes to Christianity, Hick seems to suggest that

---

[5] Paul D. Molnar, Incarnation and Resurrection: Toward a Contemporary Understanding (Grand Rapids, MI: Eerdmans, 2007), 248.
[6] Hick, "Jesus and the World Religions", 167-168.

while other religions are not reluctant to embrace their mythical content, Christianity is anything but ready to accept that mythology can easily be read into its doctrines; in fact, mythology is the very way its core doctrines should be explained in order for the image of Christ to be relevant for today's secularized consciousness.[7]

According to Hick, Christianity should give up its imperialistic attitude towards other religions and the first step in doing so is accepting its truths and doctrines in a mythological way. This also keeps Christianity away from any claim of superiority; in today's world, Hick contends, superiority is not a word which should be used in religious dialogue. There is no place for such a concept in today's pluralistic society, so Christianity – or any other religion for that matter – should not consider itself, and is not, superior to other religions. In Hick, the refusal of mythology as part of any religion – although he obviously targets traditional Christianity here – equals religious imperialism and a lame sense of superiority. In order to avoid both, Christianity needs to embrace mythology, especially with reference to Christology.

In other words, Christianity has to understand that its various images of Christ are the result of mythological thinking, so what needs to be done is for Christian theology to get back to the historicity of Jesus' life as the founder of the Christian religion in order to rediscover its equal status as compared with other religions. Accepting that only the proclamation of a historical Jesus is valid these days goes hand in hand with the mythological perspective on the image of Christ, which is no longer relevant for the world. Jesus may be of interest for the world in as much as he is considered the founder of Christianity; Christ, however, seen as savior, presents no interest for the world unless embraced as a mythological figure whose claims may work within Christianity but certainly not outside its dogmatic and ecclesiastical systems. Thus, Christ as savior – or, to be more precise, Christ as mythological savior – is no better than other religious figures that promise salvation; in other words, salvation as proclaimed by Christianity needs to be understood within the general context of all salvific promises which already exist in other religions.[8]

As a result of seeing Christ in mythological terms, Christianity is just one way to salvation among many in the world; for Hick, this is an essential part of what can be seen as the secularization of today's idea of

---

[7] See also Daniel W. Hardy, *God's Ways with the World: Thinking and Practising Christian Faith* (London: Continuum, 2005), 289.

[8] For more information about Hick's idea of salvation in world religions, see Todd Miles, *A God of Many Understandings? The Gospel and Theology of Religions* (Nashville, TN: B&H Publishing Group, 2010), 146.

religion with special reference to Christianity. What Hick proposes here is the dissolution of Western theology into a religious movement which promotes a mythological understanding of its founder, very much in line with what other religions have to say about their key figures. The Christian Christ must not be allowed to be the only character that speaks about salvation to the world in a meaningful way; each religion has this right, according to Hick, so Christianity must align its doctrines to the tenets of other religions by accepting that its understanding of Christ is mythological thinking about the historical life and person of Jesus of Nazareth.[9]

Hick seems willing to accept that what he considers to be the mythological understanding of Jesus produced – over many centuries – an image of Christ which gave Christian theology the chance to claim superiority over other religions; the life of Jesus must have been profoundly religious for such mythological responses to be triggered in the minds of so many people throughout history. Nevertheless, it is the duty of today's secularized society to translate the impact of Christ in mythological terms so that no religion is offended and Jesus occupies a fully human role in the development of Christianity as religion. Embracing mythology as the key to deciphering Christian theology means that concepts like transcendence and supernatural existence cannot be used in connection with Jesus any longer. From a purely religious point of view, which is evidently promoted by Hick, Jesus was a man and remained a man until the moment of his death; in fact, his death spoke of his humanity, so he continued to be seen as a mere man even beyond his own death.[10] What happened to the image of Christ, which pictured Jesus as God himself, is a totally different matter, but secularization implies either giving up the image of Christ entirely or reading it mythologically, which is what Hick actually proposes.

A total renunciation of the image of Christ would be detrimental to the Christian church, so Hick knows that in order for the church to function as a historical manifestation of the Christian religion, Christ must remain a landmark for it. It does not really matter whether the image of Christ is accepted in divine terms as long as it remains confined to the ecclesiastical purposes of the church. When taken outside the church, Christ must be accepted and promoted as a myth, otherwise he either makes no sense for today's secularized consciousness or he produces disquiet amongst other religions. For as long as the church recognizes the mythological character of Christ, it is free to talk about

---

[9] Hick, "Jesus and the World Religions", 182.

[10] For Hick's understanding of Jesus, see also Nicholas I. Mbogu, *Christology and Religious Pluralism: A Review of John Hick's Theocentric Model of Christology and the Emergence of African Inculturation Christologies* (Berlin: LIT Verlag, 2006), 79.

Jesus in any possible way as, for instance, the Son of God, or maybe God the Son, the Logos of God, God's incarnate Logos, or the God-man.[11] These phrases, though, which all describe the way Jesus has been perceived as Christ through centuries of church history, must remain the basis for ecclesiastical language. In other words, they must remain confined to the church and its ministry for itself. Once they go beyond the church into the world and especially into active dialogue with other religions, these Christological expressions must be professed as fundamentally mythological in nature if Christianity is to be part of the great family of world religions. Christian theology must not only embrace Christ as a myth; it must also go beyond this mythology in order to promote a religion which is able to produce a global impact in the world, alongside other religions.[12]

Global Religion and Freedom

Following the recognition of today's so-called Christological confusion and the willingness to read the impact of Jesus in mythological terms, the next logical step for Hick's process of secularization is to promote a global religion.[13] If Jesus was a mere man and the reality of divinity cannot be attached to his historical person at all, then it means that his influence over centuries of church history was not the result of God's work in the world but the outcome of popular beliefs which saw Jesus as the divine Christ. What one needs to do these days is to admit that such belief is no longer relevant, so Jesus should not be seen as the divine Christ but rather as the mythical Christ. When this happens, Christ is no longer a figure that is claimed to be the only savior of humanity; he thus becomes a mere man, who – alongside many other more or less illustrious but certainly influential personalities – can be considered a founder of a world religion, in this case what has gone down in history as Christianity.

Embracing Christ as myth should lead, Hick believes, to what he calls "a global religious vision" which first and foremost is concerned with the promotion of the fundamental unity of humanity. This unity of mankind unfolds in history "before God", as Hick puts it, as if his image of God were somewhat transcendent and superior to humanity. Hick does not elaborate on this, but his way of expressing himself

---

[11] See also Chiara Bottici, *A Philosophy of Political Truth* (Cambridge: Cambridge University Press, 2007), 61.

[12] Hick, "Jesus and the World Religions", 183.

[13] For a critical position about Hick's quest for a global religion, see Donald G. Bloesch, *A Theology of Word and Spirit: Authority and Method in Theology* (Downers Grove, IL: InterVarsity Press, 1992), 131.

seems to certify such understanding of divinity as transcendent to humanity. He speaks of "God's way" and "God's equal love for all men", then about man's capacity to "see God", which all point to some sort of belief in something which hovers over humanity – or at least over the materiality in which all human beings live as natural entities – and can be described as God.[14]

What seems to be going on here is Hick's attempt to promote the equality of all religions and especially of all religious claims to salvation; this is why God is presented as positioned "above" humanity. All religions have the same importance; all their claims concerning man's salvation share an equal amount of relevance for contemporary humanity. Nobody and nothing is more important than anybody or anything else.

What is peculiar in Hick's case has to do with his attempt to build an image of a global religion which is under the influence of one single reality known as God. Global religion means that all religions can be ultimately described as "religion", in the sense that religion *per se* – but also its historical manifestations regardless of their number – promotes the very same idea of God. It does not really matter how God is perceived and what each religion means by the term "God" as long as the mythical character of the concept is fully acknowledged in order not to cause disquiet among other religions.

Hence the idea of God in Hick seems to be a mythical concept whose transcendence and superiority over religion and humanity in general is not ontological but rather linguistic. All religions must accept the fact that the word "God" should be the reality which is meant to drive each religion; no individual perception of "God", though, should be presented in terms of exclusivity or superiority over other such perceptions. The equalization of all religions' perception of God in Hick is probably the core aspect of his idea of a global religion.[15]

Global religion means a pluralistic understanding of religion because man is able to understand the revelation of God or the self-disclosure of the divine due to his freedom.[16] Hick seems to be convinced that the degree of freedom humanity enjoys in contemporary society is bigger than in the past, so man is now free to search for God in a way that was practically unavailable before. This freedom encompasses the awareness that each religion has the same importance and God needs to

---

[14] For details about Hick's presentation of God and how it moved from personalism to an impersonal definition of God, see David Cheetham, *John Hick: A Critical Introduction and Reflection* (Aldershot: Ashgate, 2003), 134-135.

[15] Hick, "Jesus and the World Religions", 180.

[16] More information about Hick's understanding of freedom can be found in Lindsey Hall, *Swinburne's Hell and Hick's Universalism: Are We Free to Reject God?* (Aldershot: Ashgate, 2003), 170.

be looked for in what Hick calls the "state of 'natural religion'." In other words, natural religion seems to be the only way religion in general can exist. The forms and manifestations of religion are unimportant as long as each religion can be described as natural. Man has to search for God in the world, in the reality and materiality of nature, so that each religion and its preoccupation with God is given an equal chance as to validity and doctrinal claims. The reality of God can be explained by each religion in its own, specific way and each explanation of God is equally valid. This is because God is a concept, not a being; God is a linguistic reality with a mythical content which is available to all religions.

Hick offers an example by attempting to present the reality of God from a Christian perspective. Thus, Christians have the right to believe that God is the ultimate reality which created everything so that all "human animals" – as Hick dubs people – are considered children of God.[17] This God offers his salvation to all human beings, and the reality of divine salvation is presented through expressions such as "eternal Logos", "cosmic Christ", "God the Son" and some other phrases that designate the same concept.

Hick is very keen to underline that all religions speak of the same salvific realities in their own terms, so Christians are justified in their claims that they are saved by the Logos. They can even say that they are saved by Christ; what they cannot claim, however, is that they are saved by Jesus. The historical person of Jesus of Nazareth can be said to have encountered the Logos, but claiming that Jesus is the only person whose life coincides with the reality of the Logos is exclusivistic, negativistic, and profoundly unfair to all other religions. As far as Hick is concerned, the Logos describes God's salvation in all religions, irrespective of the way they actually describe the reality of salvation. In Hick, though, salvation is liberation, which means that salvation represents man's awareness that all religions share the same importance within the larger context of the world. This is an indication of the fact that all religions make up one single global religion which expresses man's belief that whatever is described as "ultimate reality" has the capacity to influence human consciousness.[18]

---

[17] See also R. Douglas Geivett, *Evil and the Evidence for God: The Challenge of John Hick's Theodicy* (Philadelphia, PA: Temple University Press, 1993), 206-207.
[18] Hick, "Jesus and the World Religions", 180-181.

7

Growing Responsible towards the World: Paul van Buren

Spiritualization and the Totality of Reality

In the 1960s, Paul van Buren spoke of secularism – and implicitly of the process which leads to it, namely secularization – in close connection with what he called the "secular meaning of the Gospel", a clear reading of the metaphysics of traditional theology in less metaphysical terms; in fact, such reading was concerned only with the worldly aspects of theology.[1] The things that can be seen acquired a greater importance compared with those unseen, so the traditional preoccupation for the metaphysics or the transcendence – both ontological in nature – of God became subject to the new wave of materialistic concerns, which affected theology and consequently turned it into some sort of social philosophy.

The life of God – so prominent in traditional theology – was slightly but surely removed from the general interest of theological studies; in this respect the life of man became much more significant in light of modern secularizing tendencies. To be sure, the life of God as the core of traditional theology faded away and the life of man as the essence of radical theology emerged as a salient disposition of the modern mind. Within this specific intellectual context, secularism as well as the way to it – described as secularization – began to promote a paramount concern for the issues pertaining to man's existence in the world as it develops throughout history.

Van Buren speaks of the "beyond" as the totality of reality; the complexity of whatever can be described as existing regardless of whether the human being is or is not able to see or perceive it by its own senses. The "beyond" in van Buren appears to be approached in a dualistic way, in the sense that it has two sides to it. The materiality of the world – in fact the material constitution of the physical universe of

---

[1] See also David A. Pailin, *God and the Process of Reality: Foundations of a Credible Theism* (London: Taylor and Francis, 1989), 44.

nature – is merely one side of the beyond and secularization shares a deep preoccupation for it. By contrast, any attempt to investigate the other side of the beyond – which most likely has to do with what cannot be seen or perceived by human senses – is traditional theology and plays no role in secularization. Speaking of secularization, it displays an evident bias towards nature, the world, and matter in general; this is why the life of the human being as it exists in nature, the world, and matter in general is undoubtedly the target of secularization which attempts to ascribe a consistently growing awareness of the intellectual preoccupations of today's people. In van Buren, the beyond must be investigated with responsibility, so the idea of responsibility is attached both to unseen and seen realities.[2] Balance in responsibility needs to be completed by balance in the investigation, assessment, and understanding of the "beyond". Any exaggeration in man's research of the beyond is anything but desired in contemporary theological, philosophical, and religious endeavors; consequently, two distinct attitudes result from the faulty – specifically unbalanced – understanding of the beyond as the encompassing reality of what can and cannot be seen. Thus, the lack of balance in scrutinizing reality inevitably leads either to spiritualization or to secularization.[3]

This distinction, however, seems to be a later development in van Buren – oftentimes associated with his 1980s productions – who sees spiritualization and secularization as opposing perspectives on the world. From the perspective of the idea of responsibility – or rather the lack thereof – spiritualization is connected with God, while secularization has to do with the world.[4] To be exact, spiritualization is a lack of responsibility to God and secularization is lack of responsibility to the world.

What van Buren wants to say by referring to the two opposing *Weltanschauungen* has to do with the fact that an overemphasis of either God or the world is not in line with how man should perceive reality in contemporary society. According to van Buren, spiritualization is wrong because it differentiates too sharply between the matter and spirit or between the seen and the unseen. Spiritualization tends to make reference to the biblical distinction between flesh and spirit,

---

[2] For details about the idea of responsibility in radical theology, see David Tracy, *Blessed Rage for Order: The New Pluralism in Theology* (Chicago, IL: University of Chicago Press, 1975), 72.
[3] Paul van Buren, *The Secular Meaning of the Gospel based on an Analysis of Its Language* (New York, NY: Macmillan, 1966), xiii, xiv.
[4] Peter Ochs, "Judaism and Christian Theology", 607-625, in David F. Ford (ed.), *The Modern Theologians: An Introduction to the Christian Theology in the Twentieth Century* (2nd edn, Oxford: Blackwell, 2004): 610.

which for van Buren is superfluous. Flesh and spirit, matter and spirit, the seen and the unseen are merely concepts which speak of reality; since reality though is so complex that some aspects of it can be seen while others remain hidden to man's senses, spiritualization is dismissed as insufficient and consequently faulty.

Likewise, secularization is dismissed as placing too heavy an emphasis on the realities that can be seen, to the detriment of those that remain unseen. When secularization is accepted as being normative without a critical appraisal of it, when culture is considered identical with what van Buren calls "the Way" – a rather confusing reference to man's existence in the world, which can be apprehended with or without reference to God – and when the "faith" of secular culture translates as one's own trust, then secularization must be given up.[5]

Although van Buren is critical of secularization in these terms, his thought is certainly not less secular, because walking "the Way" is based on his unshaken conviction that reality must be accepted on one's individual terms, without any external constraints. In other words, one is free to understand reality however one wants: as seen and unseen put together, as seen devoid of any references to the unseen, or even as matter with or without enlightenment from God.

Secularization is bad when it promotes values which become normative to everybody; secularization is good, however, if it allows individuals to select their own values through which they would then be able to see reality in their own, specific, and personal ways. If secularization forces man to repeat what has been said over and over again, namely accept previous patterns of thought, then it is a bad thing. On the other hand, if secularization offers man liberation from cemented antecedent ways of seeing reality, then secularization should be embraced, promoted, and recommended as a profitable method in assisting the human being to understand the world. What is important for van Buren is neither the fact that the previous patterns of thought were bad in themselves nor that the new ways of thinking were good by contrast; van Buren is concerned to promote freedom, man's individual capacity to decide for him- or herself how to see, understand, and accept the surrounding reality. Regardless of whether one adopts old or new understandings of the world, what must be present in their awareness is freedom and criticism. Nothing should be accepted uncritically because this denotes not only lack of freedom but also irresponsibility. These go hand in hand with an equally frightening lack of concern for what van Buren calls "our worldly involvement".

---

[5] For an assessment of van Buren's theology and his interpretation of "the Way", see Gregory Baum, *The Twentieth Century: A Theological Overview* (London: Continuum, 1999), 83-84.

In other words, the human being must be preoccupied with the affairs of the world, which must be dealt with in freedom, with responsibility, and also with an attitude of positive criticism. The idea of God may or may not be of help in this enterprise, but the fundamental concern for the world can and should never be detached from man's frame of mind, which at the end of the day is nothing but a strong affirmation of secularization as the marrow of man's attempts to understand the world for himself.[6]

The Death of Jesus and the Value of Life

God does have a paramount importance in van Buren's thought, but merely as a concept. It should be noted that, while he uses a rather biblical kind of language with significant references to the Bible itself, van Buren does not understand God in the traditional, metaphysical, and ontologically transcendent way of classical theology. This is why his thought can indeed be considered a manifestation of contemporary secularization; van Buren's interest in God is purely historical and emerges from his preoccupation with Jesus of Nazareth. It goes without saying that, in van Buren's thinking, Jesus was undoubtedly a historical character who managed to capture the imagination of many illustrious writers, among them the apostle Paul himself.

Van Buren's interest in the Bible and the writings of the apostle Paul reveal his high appreciation of the Jewish people, but this is also the result of his historical awareness. Jewish wisdom is according to van Buren a special type of human reasoning; it is thus worthy of the consideration of today's society because it promotes ideas which can be useful for a better understanding of humanity in general. In order, however, to understand Jesus properly, one has to consider the actual and historical event of his death, the meaning of which is capable of bringing together Jews and Gentiles – in a word, the whole of humanity – as they all walk the same Way, the same path of experience in the world.[7]

Van Buren highlights one key aspect from the writings of the apostle Paul, namely that death is man's last enemy. This piece of Jewish wisdom can speak powerfully to humanity in contemporary times because

---

[6] Paul van Buren, *Discerning the Way: A Theology of Jewish-Christian Reality* (New York, NY: Seabury Press, 1980), 1-2, 57-59.

[7] For a critical perspective on van Buren's view of the death of Jesus, see Edward H. Flannery, "The Cross in Jewish-Christian Relations", 235-248, in Alan L. Berger, Harry J. Cargas & Susan E. Nowak (eds.), *The Continuing Agony: From the Carmelite Convent to the Crosses at Auschwitz* (Lanham, MD: University Press of America, 2004): 242-243.

it informs humanity of the connection that exists between Jesus and God. Since van Buren does not believe in the metaphysical existence of God, the liaison between Jesus and God should not be deciphered strictly in theological terms, but rather in historical and perhaps philosophical realities. From the standpoint of history, the certainty of death goes beyond any doubt; van Buren, however, mentions the resurrection of Jesus which is also presented – alongside his death – as a historical reality. While Jesus' death may have been read as a historical reality, it certainly does not mean that it was a historical event. As a historical reality, Jesus' death does not happen as an event but rather it bears historical and real meaning for the historical reality of humanity as it exists in the world. According to van Buren, the apostle Paul left humanity a most important lesson, namely that death should not only be taken seriously as it is part of this world, but also that death should not be seen as man's last enemy.[8] This is where van Buren's thought can be seen as the result of contemporary secularization, and this has to do with his conviction that the prospect of death is meaningful for man's existence. In other words, if adequately understood from the perspective of man's existential expectations, death can be seen as a good human reality.

This means that – as van Buren puts it – death can be faced; it no longer has to scare people as the end of life. Death can be seen as a good thing if it comes after a "good life". If so, the definition of man's demise can be described as a "good death".[9]

Jesus' death, though, was not a good death; it was untimely, brutal, and mutilating – Jesus died young, he suffered horrendously, and was entombed after being whipped as a criminal. There was nothing fair in Jesus' death, unless perhaps the fact that it showed humanity something crucial, namely that the Gentiles were saved by it.[10] This is another indication that van Buren's thought is the result of contemporary secularization. In this respect, one can say that the death of Jesus is representative for humanity. In his death each human being can find a bit of existential significance. Each individual can find healing in the fact that Jesus suffered a gruesome death for his fellow human beings.

At this point, van Buren's rather obscure idea of secularization takes shape when he points out – quite emphatically – that the healing brought about by Jesus' death should not be understood as a metaphysical theory, but as a historical sequence. By stripping Jesus' death of its

---

[8] See also Tom Frame, *Losing My Religion: Unbelief in Australia* (Sydney: University of New South Wales Press, 2009), 158.

[9] Van Buren, *Discerning the Way*, 194-195.

[10] See also Eugene B. Borowitz, *Exploring Jewish Ethics: Papers on Covenant Responsibility* (Detroit, MI: Wayne State University Press, 1990), 479-480.

metaphysical significance, van Buren obliterates the traditional perspective on sin and especially of salvation from sin: a clear token of religious and theological secularization. What remains is the historical aspect of Jesus' death, which underlines two distinct aspects: first, that the death of Jesus happened in real history and second, that Easter – which deals with Jesus' resurrection – cannot be accepted in historical terms.[11]

In other words, Easter did not happen in history; it is an "event" which needs more than just history for a correction interpretation. Even if it cannot be accepted as a historical event, Easter still has to be dealt with as part of history. In other words, as the death of Jesus happened in history, the resurrection of Jesus also happened in history – not in a ontologically real way, but rather as wisdom. Jesus never rose again to life – this is quite clear in van Buren although he does not say it so plainly – but what happened in the aftermath of Jesus' demise in history can be seen as an equally significant part of the history of humanity. Thus, after Jesus died, the apostles said that he had come back to life. Although not a real, historical event, Jesus' coming back to life or his resurrection had profound historical implications especially because it was seen as some sort of elevation of the importance of man's humiliation. In other words, as part of today's secularization, van Buren's thought sees Jesus' death as a means to promote the existential meaningfulness of humiliation; Jesus' death told humanity that the debased, the humble, and the poor needed special attention and the realization of this necessity enriched Christianity with a perspective on humanity which promotes the ontological worth of each human being. Jesus' death not only shows that the reality of death can be coped with; it also demonstrates that the impending character of death has a profitable existential significance for each human being. Faced with death, humanity is forced to value life: individual and community existence as well as hope for the future. Van Buren's secularized thought does not allow for metaphysical interpretations of Jesus' death; on the contrary, his death is historical and is capable of conferring existential significance to the historical lives of all human beings. Despite being seen as the end of life, death – and especially Jesus' death – is a means to see the entirety of human existence through the lens of hope.[12]

---

[11] James F. Ross, *Portraying Analogy* (Cambridge: Cambridge University Press, 1981), 176.

[12] Van Buren, *Discerning the Way*, 195-196.

Hope and the Notion of Messiah

In van Buren, hope is the characteristic of "the Way", man's progress towards the goal of humanity, which is a society of righteousness and peace. Van Buren is open to pluralism in all its aspects – mainly religious, philosophical, social, and political – but he underlines that while the Way is one and unique, the ways in which humanity walks it can be quite varied. Human beings are by nature incapable of pursuing one single kind of walk as they go through life. Life itself is unique, but the ways in which individuals lead it differ greatly. Van Buren is convinced that the legitimacy of one's walk is beyond question; any walk for that matter is valid as individuals go through the daily reality of the Way.

Van Buren's secularization derives from his pluralistic convictions, especially when he singles out Marxism as a legitimate, valid, and worthy way for one's life.[13] It needs to be said here that van Buren's pluralistic understanding of man's experience in the world – mostly as connected with Marxism – is much too optimistic. Not having lived in any Eastern European, South American, or even Asian Communist societies, he has no firsthand experience of the practical side of Marxism as developed by Communism, so his readiness to accept Marxism as valid may be philosophically correct or logical, but it is socially and practically imbued with too much hope. He clearly shows that the Way of Christianity is different from the way of Marxism but, in the end, both search for a goal and in both people find meaning and purpose.

Another sign of secularization in van Buren's thought has to do with his willingness not to "prejudge history"; in other words, history may prove everybody wrong when it comes to nurturing hopes in various ways of thinking and living. What some consider valid and worthy today may prove false and unworthy in the future; and the opposite is also true. On the more practical side, Marxism and Christianity may prove to be wrong in the future – the theoretical possibility of this happening is allowed for in van Buren – but what matters today is that humanity should find hope in the different ways it pursues, as individual human beings search for meaning, righteousness, and peace in their lives. For as long as responsibility is not excluded from one's walk in the Way, van Buren is more than ready to see that particular kind of walk in legitimate terms.

In van Buren, secularization arises from his conviction that hope necessarily points to God, while God is to be seen in everybody's attempt to secure hope for his or her individual lives. Based on his plu-

---

[13] For more information about how Marxism influenced van Buren's theology, see Friedrich-Wilhelm Marquardt, *Auf einem Weg ins Lehrhaus. Leben und Denken mit Israel* (Frankfurt am Main: Otto Lembeck, 2009), 171-172.

ralistic ideas, van Buren seeks to cancel the traditional religious distinction between Jews and Gentiles; at a deeper level, it seems that he wants to annihilate the differences between Judaism and Christianity, and, by extension, between all world religions. While conceptual differences cannot be erased completely, the nature of hope that is common to all religions is here to stay. For instance, van Buren writes that Jews are God's elect people and Gentiles are God's elect church; in other words, the conceptual difference between the two religious phrases is more than evident.[14] The similarities, though, are much more obvious and what really counts in this respect are the aspects which unite the two – and not only the two – religions. The fact that both – and all – religions believe in God, that humanity defines itself through the mediation of the idea of God is far more significant than the huge variety of conceptual religious terms that promote divisiveness. All religions and the human being in general share the hope that "God is with us", van Buren says, and this is what really supports the pursuit of hope as men and women walk the Way.[15]

It seems that van Buren's secularization is an attempt to prove that all human beings share the same election by God as well as the same hope for their lives. In other words, all religions nurture the same hope so their quest for meaning is equally valid. By extension and going beyond the borders of religion itself, the quest of all human beings for existential meaning is equally legitimate, regardless of whether one actually believes in God or not. Van Buren says: Metaphysics is definitely not the proper way to understand God; what counts in one's pursuit of meaning is the reality of hope. When it comes to hope, though, its practicality can be seen in the person of Jesus of Nazareth.[16] There is hope to be found for each man's life if Jesus is embraced as an example of what a human being should be and how it should act in life. Hope should only be pursued; hope is not only a human desire, it is a practical reality of life and this can be seen in Jesus.

What van Buren wants to do by pointing to Jesus is not to emphasize his Jewishness but rather to point out that the Jewish understanding of redemption can be appropriated by all those who want it,

---

[14] For details of van Buren's idea of election as connected with religious pluralism, see Richard Harries, *After the Devil: Christianity and Judaism in the Shadow of the Holocaust* (Oxford: Oxford University Press, 2003), 110.

[15] Van Buren, *Discerning the Way*, 197.

[16] For a critical perspective on van Buren's idea of hope as related to his reinterpretation of the resurrection of Jesus as the courage to die for what one believes, see Carl E. Braaten, "The Crux of Christianity's Case: The Resurrection of Jesus", 23-34, in Michael Shahan (ed.), *A Report from the Front Lines: Conversations on Public Theology. A Festschrift in Honor of Robert Benne* (Grand Rapids, MI: Eerdmans, 2009): 26.

mainly because it promotes the redemption of the entire creation, of the whole world. Van Buren points out that the Jewish word which speaks about the hope that can be nurtured for the entire world is Messiah.[17] What matters is that the word Messiah, although Jewish in nature, speaks of a reality which concerns the entire world, not only the Jewish nation. Messiah is a concept that underlines the fact that the hope of humanity for the improvement of the world in the direction of righteousness and peace is a practical reality. Messiah does not promote the relevance of Judaism; on the contrary, it speaks about the relevance of man's quest for meaning and hope. In van Buren, Messiah seems to be the equivalent of hope itself; it is a notion which allows humanity to exist in a meaningful way as well as in total openness to the future. As far as van Buren's thought is concerned, its secularizing essence is evident in the emphasis he places on the final character of hope. It does not matter if people believe in God or not; it does not matter if human beings pursue different religions. What really matters is that all humanity shares the same "final hope", which concentrates man's whole attention on the Way, namely on the reality and actuality of human experience in the world. When all human beings hope for the best of the world, for the realization of righteousness and peace in the world, hope has been achieved in a way and the image of Messiah has proved its legitimacy, relevance, and veracity. This is thus van Buren's idea of secularization: the unification of all religions under the idea of hope, made practical to humanity in the person of Jesus of Nazareth. Van Buren invites all human beings to accept that the life of Jesus of Nazareth is able to show the world that hope and meaningfulness can be practically achieved for each individual human experience in the world.[18]

---

[17] See also Harvey Cox, *Common Prayers: Family, Faith, and a Christian's Journey through the Jewish Year* (New York, NY: Houghton Mifflin, 2001), 144.

[18] Van Buren, *Discerning the Way*, 198-199.

8

Reducing Religion to a Human Phenomenon: William Hamilton

Radical Theology and Language

In William Hamilton secularization is described in terms of radicalism. Secularization affects everything in contemporary society and, as the process evolves, it is clear that its most important characteristic has to do with the fact that it produces radical changes in all the aspects of today's world. With reference to religion, secularization is a process which acts against religion, not necessarily to destroy it, but certainly to diminish its capacity to influence the world in a significant way. When religion is rendered unimportant and when its traditional power has been dealt with in a way which places religion under the authority of the secular state, then secularization can be said to have achieved its main purpose.[1] For Hamilton, secularization seeks to turn religion into a phenomenon which no longer produces, maintains, and defends privileges for those associated with it. Hence secularization aims at reducing the importance of religion to the point that religion is recognized as a mere human phenomenon, whose impact and significance in the world cannot be said to be above other human phenomena irrespective of the specificity of the domain in which they manifest themselves.

Religion, however, cannot simply be reduced to a mere phenomenon by just preaching the importance of having it placed under the subjection of the secular. Action in this respect is paramount and it should be carried out in a wide variety of fields, such as technology, mass media, and science. All the aspects of today's society must work together in a secular way, so that the role and the importance of religion are reduced to such a degree that religion should no longer be considered prevalent in contemporary society.

---

[1] See also Philip L. Vickeri, "The End of *Missio Dei* – Secularization, Religions, and the Theology of Mission", 27-44, in Volker Küster (ed.), *Mission Revisited: Between Mission History and Intercultural Theology* (Münster: LIT Verlag, 2010): 28.

Consequently, for Hamilton, secularization means autonomy, especially autonomy from religion in its traditional forms, but at the same time it refers to a determined movement away from God, understood as the traditional being who is said to be man's problem solver. This is not to say that secularization attempts to destroy the idea of God; on the contrary, God as a notion may well continue to exist and man should feel free to think about having a relationship with God. Secularization, though, points to the fact that man's relationship with God should no longer be presented by means of concepts such as dependence and need. To be sure, secularization promotes a theology in which man does not see himself as being dependent on or as being in need of God. As for God, he should no longer be believed or trusted as the one who needs to fulfill man's needs or solve his problems.[2] Man is autonomous – and so is God for that matter – and his autonomy from God, which can sometimes be seen even as a total independence from him, is the most important aspect of secularization.

The theology of man's declared independence from God is, for Hamilton, not only secularized but also essentially radical. This is why, in his thought, radical theology is the first feature of secularization and it does not attempt to extract religion from man's life. On the contrary, radical theology recognizes the importance of religion in man's existence, but not also in the secular constitution of today's society. The fundamental notion of religion, which is God, may remain critical for religious thought, but it must be redefined from the perspective of man's language. God is a word and, in its capacity of being a word, God cannot just be given any significance. The word "God" has a history and secularization should never take it for granted that the historical meaning of the word "God" can be changed in order to convey whatever meaning one desires. In other words, secularization should never attempt to redefine the most fundamental meaning of the word "God". Nevertheless, the word "God" must be understood in light of contemporary society, based on secularized and secularizing convictions, as a result of how technology and science are seen these days, and certainly as a mere word which has a limited ability to convey the wide range of meanings inherent in the idea of God.[3]

The recognition that language is limited in transmitting the complexity of the notion of God lies at the very foundation of radical the-

---

[2] Details about the Bonhoefferian origin of Hamilton's idea of God as a problem-solver, see Douglas Sloan, *Faith and Knowledge: Mainline Protestantism and American Higher Education* (Louisville, KY: Westminster John Knox Press, 1994), 129.

[3] William Hamilton, *The Quest for the Post-Historical Jesus* (New York, NY: Continuum, 1994), 12. See also William Hamilton, "Dietrich Bonhoeffer", 113-116, in Thomas J.J. Altizer & William Hamilton, *Radical Theology and the Death of God* (Indianapolis, IN: Bobbs-Merrill, 1966): 114.

ology as a vehicle of secularization.[4] Given the complexity of the word God, radical theology should promote the awareness that one single religion is no longer capable of explaining God all by itself. This means that, through the mediation of radical theology, secularization disseminates the idea that the content of the word God should be extended over the confessional, theological, and even religious boundaries of Christianity. As such, Christianity should be considered just one religion amongst the ocean of world religions; the God of Christianity is merely one expression of the reality which the word God is able to hold and express in today's secularized society. Defending one single religion – Christianity for instance – is categorically not the task of secularization. The promotion and the defense of all religions as equally valid is, though, one of the most important tasks of the process of secularization, given that no religion in particular rises above the others or above the significance of secular thought. This is an indication that while secularization keeps religion under the gird of the secular power, it also promotes religion in general as a human phenomenon which could exert a beneficial influence in the world. As a result of such a conviction, secularization is not interested in the veracity or truthfulness of religion; on the contrary, secularization manifests an open interest in the usefulness of religion within today's religionless environment. Radical theology is a means to promote religion despite, as well as with the help of, secularization.

Extremes, however, must be dismissed. For Hamilton, secularization is able to make good use of religion provided that it moves between atheism and the "new" polytheism; in other words, religion must be kept away from radical convictions about God's existence or nonexistence. Radical theology does not mean radical beliefs in God or in the fact of whether or not he exists; radical theology means belief in the concept of God as expressed by means of language to the benefit of contemporary secularized society. As far as Hamilton is concerned, traditional atheism and traditional belief must be avoided at all costs because they are both based on how certain people understand an experience with God. Believers who profess faith in a living God are convinced that they do have an experience with God, while atheists express the conviction that experience with God is essentially absent.

As an essential feature of secularization, radical theology must find a way to move between atheism and classical faith, so it must found its

---

[4] For the importance of language in the death of God theology, and also in Hamilton, see John C. Cooper, *The "Spiritual Presence" in the Theology of Paul Tillich: Tillich's Use of St. Paul* (Macon, GA: Mercer University Press, 1997), 124-125.

principles on what Hamilton calls the "experience of an absence".[5] Radical theology believes in the fact that God is absent from the world, that God – the traditional God of faith, the God against whom atheists are always ready to declare their unbelief – is nothing but dead. In Hamilton's words, the radical theology of secularization seeks to investigate "the hole where God use to be"; this is why he should no longer be perceived as a presence. In radical theology, God is utterly absent because he is dead.[6]

The Death of God and Monotheism

In Hamilton, the death of God has nothing to do with ontology; this is simply because faith in a living God, a God who exists as a transcendent and supernatural being has absolutely no point of contact with an intellectual conviction that accepts God as a word, a notion which speaks about what and how God has been perceived through history. As far as Hamilton is concerned, God is only part of the realm of language and this is precisely why the secularization's idea of God – which sees God as dead – belongs to the same world of language. In other words, the death of God is a metaphor, which cannot and should not be detached from other equally important metaphors that speak about God. The death of God by no means points to the actual demise of the ontological God of traditional Christianity; if its veracity were beyond doubt, the actual death of God – of the supernatural and transcendent God of traditional faith – would be out of the question. For the radical theology of secularization, though, there is no such thing as the ontology of God; the only reference to God which makes sense is the metaphor of God, the literary character of God as a concept.[7] Consequently, radical theology is able to provide secularization with an image of God which is essentially characterized by absence. God is dead – and one must remember that God is a word belonging to the realm of literary metaphors – because he is absent. God is dead because he is silent; God is dead because he has disappeared. Hamilton therefore speaks about "the eclipse of God", about the fact that the traditional God has been "covered" by another image, which pictures him in the clarity of his absence, silence, and disappearance.

For radical theology, however, the death of God is nevertheless speech about God for – as Hamilton himself points out – eclipses do

---

[5] See also Donald E. Gowan, *Theology in Exodus: Biblical Theology in the Form of a Commentary* (Louisville, KY: Westminster John Knox Press, 1994), 21.

[6] Hamilton, *A Quest for the Post-Historical Jesus*, 12-13.

[7] For how God works as a metaphor in death of God theology, see Zachary Braiterman *(God) after Auschwitz: Tradition and Change in Post-Holocaust Jewish Thought* (Princeton, NJ: Princeton University Press, 1998), 94.

not last forever, silence is followed by discourse, and absence "becomes" presence. Within the realm of literary devices, the metaphor of God's death does not reveal the actual death of the traditional God. On the contrary, when faith in the traditional God and his transcendentally supernatural ontology is displaced by a secularized pattern of thought, one can no longer speak of faith. What remains appears to be discourse, and discourses are constituted by literary devices; the death of God itself is such literary device which presents God in terms of absence, silence, and disappearance.[8] This absent, silent, and vanished God offers the secularized mind another image of God. From a literary – specifically metaphorical point of view – the fact that God is said to be dead, absent, silent, and obscured does not diminish its literary content as God. The word God remains the word God, whether or not one attaches to him various characteristics such as presence or absence, talk or silence, revelation or disappearance. This explains Hamilton's conviction that radical theology and its secularizing tendencies do not promote the continuous impossibility of any language about God. Quite the reverse, language about God is possible indeed despite belief in God's lack of ontology, his silence, absence, and disappearance. The world of language is full of possibilities, Hamilton stresses rather emphatically, and so seems to be the realm of radical theology and secularization. In other words, anything can happen within it: resurrections, for instance, are possible, so despite God's death, reasonable discourse about the notion of God can be pursued with a significant degree of success. The fact that the secularized mind of today's people perceives God as dead does not mean that one cannot or should not talk about God. So radical theology is in constant search for a meaningful explanation of the metaphors which speak about God, especially the metaphor that presents God as dead.[9]

The death of God or, more precisely, the discourse about God's death makes sense to the secularized thought of contemporary people due to three main recent historical developments which Hamilton discusses briefly, and they all have to do with traditional – specifically monotheistic – religion as exemplified by Christianity, Judaism, and Islam. Evidently, the three religions are founded on belief in the supernatural, transcendent, and ontological character of God, so the God of these three religions is beyond the actual realm of language. What Hamilton attempts to argue here is that in all these three religions, God should be restricted to the world of language and metaphors because

---

[8] See also Richard Grigg, *Gods after God: An Introduction to Contemporary Radical Theologies* (Albany, NY: State University of New York Press, 2006), 8.
[9] Hamilton, *A Quest for the Post-Historical Jesus*, 13.

three historical events, or rather clusters of events, proved that the traditional view of God is no longer relevant on an empirical basis. Thus, Hamilton points to the rise of science, the experience of radical evil, and belief in the natural goodness of man.

First, the rise of science informs contemporary society that human beings are no longer controlled by nature. On the contrary, human beings have learned to harness nature through industrialization, technological development, and scientific progress. While Christianity, Judaism, and Islam appeared in "an agricultural climate", as Hamilton puts it, our post-agricultural society, which is heavily industrialized, technologized, and scientifically informed, cannot accept the control of nature any longer. Pre-industrialized and pre-scientific thought may have coped with an ontological view of God very well but secularized thinking is not willing to accept that kind of God. The ontological God of Judaism, Christianity, and Islam is dead – from the standpoint of the radical theology of secularization – so the only God which is available to contemporary lay consciousness is a literary God which, by comparison with the ontological God of traditional theology, is dead.[10]

Second, the experience of the radical evil as manifested in concentration camps is – Hamilton believes – totally incapable of explaining the presence of God in a world where evil manifested itself on such a huge scale. This is why the traditional image of God as present should be reconsidered and, given the experience of radical evil, a discourse about a dead God, a God who can be perceived as absent, would make more sense. Hamilton admits that such a reconsideration of God from traditional ontology to secularized language can produce either sorrow or relief. Whatever the end-result, though, Hamilton is convinced that today's secularized minds of most Westerners will eventually have to deal with the very definition of God. The best course is evidently to see God as dead.[11] The dead God, though, can be accepted as "living" provided that he is kept within the realm of language, so the dead God of radical, secularized theology is very much "alive" if seen through the lens of metaphor and language.

---

[10] See also Christian Wiese, "'God's Adventure with the World' and 'Sanctity of Life': Theological Speculations and Ethical Reflections in Jonas's Philosophy after Auschwitz", 419-460, in Hava Tirosh-Samuelson & Christian Wiese (eds.), *The Legacy of Hans Jonas: Judaism and the Phenomenon of Life* (Leiden: Brill, 2008): 443-444.

[11] The idea of God's death is supposed to make God-talk accessible to everybody, not only to theologians or religiously devout people. See Judith M. Buddenbaum & Debra L. Mason (eds.), *Readings on Religion as News* (Oxford: Blackwell, 2000), 265-266. For a critical perspective on death of God theology, see Paul S. Fiddes, "The Quest for a Place which Is 'Not-a-Place': The Hiddenness of God and the Presence of God", 35-60, in Oliver Davies & Denys Turner (eds.), *Silence and the Word: Negative Theology and Incarnation* (Cambridge: Cambridge University Press, 2002): 44.

Third, belief in the natural goodness of man will have to replace the traditional belief in the natural evil of man. Hamilton seems convinced that monotheistic religions turn good people in evildoers. In other words, people are born good in this world but once they adhere to either Christianity, Judaism, or Islam, they suddenly become evil. This is a poor understanding of religion, but Hamilton also discloses his conviction that monotheistic religions inculcate in the minds of many people the very offensive belief that one can believe in as well as possess "the one truth". This runs against the equality and validity of all religions – so desperately preached by radical theology and secularization adherents – so the definition of God as dead at least places monotheistic religions on the same level with any other religion in the world. Evidently, Hamilton is not bothered by the traditional claim that "the one truth" can be discovered; what worries him is the fact that one particular religion claims that its teachings are the only ones which offer access to "the one truth". Hence, the need for each traditional religion to revisit its doctrines from a perspective which is based on language, not on ontology. Christianity could offer a good example in this respect by rethinking its understanding of Jesus.[12]

The Post-Historical Jesus

Jesus is important for any theology, and Hamilton cannot avoid the issue of Christology either. What he makes clear from the start is that his Christology has definitely nothing in common with the traditional understanding of Jesus in classical Christianity. This truth is revealed not by Hamilton's evident dismissal of traditional Christology, but by his reference to the fact that Jesus should be understood as post-historical. He underlines, though, that post-historical does not mean post-modernist; to be sure, Hamilton does not like postmodernism, for his lack of purpose and theology – as based on language – should serve some purpose. What he likes is modernism, which reportedly saved him from "suburban boredom" in his teenage years. Modernism had not only a purpose but also a passion for understanding theology in a certain way. This passion cannot be found in post-modernism, which – according to Hamilton – seems to lack every single bit of interest in the aspects of theology in general, traditional or not. Post-modernism displays no interest in purpose as much as they have no interest in meaning, which are both compulsory ingredients in any theological enterprise.

In declaring his lack of interest in post-modernism, Hamilton categorically places himself and his thought within the spectrum of

---

[12] Hamilton, *A Quest for the Post-Historical Jesus*, 13-15.

modernism and, in doing so, he also reveals his interest in Jesus. While not at all traditional, Hamilton's desire to delve into the depths of research into Jesus is based on what he calls "a consensus" about Jesus.[13] He emphatically shows that this "Christological consensus" is merely "a consensus", so while it does not necessarily represent a wide range of ideas accepted by a huge majority, it does nonetheless express his position in terms of what he means by Christology and especially how Jesus can be known. Although his explanation of what he means by the post-historical Jesus lacks detail, Hamilton does put down what he considers obligatory for a correct understanding of Christology in post-modernity despite the prevalence of post-modernity. As a matter of fact, Hamilton attempts to rekindle a spark of modernism in the midst of a post-modern world. The device he uses in this respect is Albert Schweitzer's book *A Quest of the Historical Jesus*, published in 1906, a work which put an end to the liberal search for a historical Jesus. Theological liberalism was indeed of manifestation of modernism – and Schweitzer's book is no less modern – but what he shows in his work is the fact that historical access to the historical person of Jesus of Nazareth is impossible.[14] To close the circle, Hamilton tries to do the same, namely to show that there is no historical means whereby the person of Jesus could somehow be accessed in the sense of being known as a historical person. Thus, like Schweitzer at the beginning of the twentieth century, Hamilton strives to prove – in his case at the end of the same century – that modernism is right in admitting that the historical Jesus cannot be known in a historical fashion.[15]

If Jesus cannot be accessed historically, then theology should not bother to look for a historical Jesus. What can be done instead is to search for a post-historical Jesus, which does not mean that Jesus was not a historical person. It simply means that while admitting that Jesus was a historical person, theology should also accept that fact that the historical person of Jesus is beyond the reach of contemporary historiography, experience, or anything else.[16] This is why Hamilton lists three aspects which are compulsory for a correct apprehension of the post-historical Jesus: first, the fact that Jesus cannot be reached *via* history. To put it in his words, "Jesus is inaccessible by historical means".

---

[13] See also Alan G. Padgett, *Science and the Study of God: A Mutuality Model for Theology and Science* (Grand Rapids, MI: Eerdmans, 2003), 57-58.

[14] See also Tim Murphy, *Nietzsche, Metaphor, Religion* (Albany, NY: State University of New York Press, 2001), 111-112.

[15] Hamilton, *A Quest for the Post-Historical Jesus*, 14-16.

[16] See also Alan G. Padgett, "Advice for Religious Historians: On the Myth of a Purely Historical Jesus", 287-307, in Stephen T. Davis, Daniel Kendall & Gerald O'Collins (eds.), *The Resurrection: An Interdisciplinary Symposium on the Resurrection of Jesus* (Oxford: Oxford University Press, 1998): 297.

The only piece of information contemporary society knows about Jesus is the fact that "he has come". Such an understanding of Jesus suggests that the reality of faith has nothing to do with the actual historical existence of Jesus. While it is important to know that Jesus did exist as a human being, the historical life of Jesus seems to bear little significance for faith. Faith is able to believe in Jesus with or without the awareness of the details of his historical existence. Second, the things which the contemporary world could find about Jesus are not important for people living two thousand years after his life and death. Third, a mixture of the first two aspects can also be accepted or, as Hamilton puts it, "an elegant blend" can also be of help. What is evident as a result of Hamilton's three-point list is a particular understanding of the Gospels. Accepting Jesus as post-historical does not only mean that Jesus cannot be known in a historical way; it also means that the Gospels cannot and should not be accepted as historical accounts of Jesus' life. This is why Hamilton stresses that the Gospels were not intended to be investigated as history or as contemporary society understands the idea of history. Certainly, for Hamilton, the Gospels are not history. Whatever is written there about Jesus has nothing to do with what happened in actual history or in the particular history of Jesus. The Christological consensus on which Hamilton founds his entire view of Jesus hangs on the conviction that the Gospels are not works of history, but of fiction.[17] For Hamilton, such an understanding presents to the contemporary world a new range of possibilities, especially with reference to the fact that extra-canonical sources become equally valid in being researched as fundamental sources for a better understanding of Jesus.

Thus, Hamilton's idea of secularization proposes the reinvention of Christology as post-historical, in the sense that the totality of information that is accessible today about Jesus is not necessarily historical but rather fiction and is based on all the sources that speak about Jesus, canonical and extra-canonical. This is the image of the secularized Christ in Hamilton: a fictional portrayal of a historical figure who cannot be known by historical methods, but only through literary, fictional, and imaginative devices. That is why the death of God is a metaphor which includes the post-historical view of Jesus as fiction (not history) and radical theology as experience of God's absence (not experience of his presence).[18]

---

[17] See also Alexander J.M. Wedderburn, *Jesus and the Historians* (Tübingen: Mohr-Siebeck, 2010), 26.

[18] Hamilton, *A Quest for the Post-Historical Jesus*, 17-21.

9

Being Aware of Temporality and Finitude: Gabriel Vahanian

Secularity and Secularism

In the thought of Gabriel Vahanian one must distinguish between secularization, secularity, and secularism. In doing so, the first step is to understand the crucial distinction between secularity and secularism, which afterwards leads to the very definition of secularization itself. Thus, for Vahanian, secularity and secularism must be placed in sheer opposition since they reflect two distinct, as well as contrary, positions concerning religion in general and Christianity as a religion in particular.[1] Secularity refers to the realm of man's existence; it is the world of nature wherein man not only exists but he also works. In Vahanian's terms, secularity points to "the sphere of man's action". He then points out that the delineation of man's realm in terms of what man does underlines the fact that one of its most important characteristics resides in its temporality. The world of man is a space defined by time, and this places it in contrast with the traditional understanding of divinity and God, which are characterized by eternity. In other words, the realm of man exists in contrast with the realm of God and the first aspect which highlights this reality is temporality.

There is, however, another issue which strengthens the fundamental distinction between man's world and God's realm; in addition to temporality, there is also finitude. The world as man knows and experiences it has two basic features: temporality and finitude, which both contrast with the eternity and infinitude of God's realm as understood in traditional terms. Consequently, secularity is concerned with the sphere of man's existence in the world – more precisely, with the temporality and finitude of man's existence in the material world of nature – which indicates that while man can be considered a being that exists as "God's image" (especially given his creativity) he is nonetheless not

---

[1] See also Keith W. Clements, *The Theology of Ronald Gregor Smith* (Leiden: Brill, 1986), 81.

a divine being himself. It is clear that, in Vahanian, secularity focuses on man's being and his existence in the world of nature and matter, but this is done under the auspices of man's power to create. Man's creativity, however, has nothing to do with God or with any other characteristic which could point to man's connection with divinity. Secularity, as Vahanian understands it, is meant to show that man's realm is totally separated from what traditional theology promotes as God's realm; in other words, man exists in the material reality of nature without any connection with God or with a world which is said to exist beyond nature itself. Secularity can indeed make reference to traditional concepts, but in doing so, secularity redefines them from the perspective of man's existence in the world and especially from the standpoint of man's finitude, temporality, and materiality as he exists in the world. This is why, in Vahanian, secularity reveals its preoccupation with man's existence in the world and how man perceives himself as a being which exists in the world.

Since man's most important characteristic is creativity, secularity also points to man's "cultural manifestations" in the world with or without reference to whether he sees himself as a creature of God or not.[2] Vahanian points out that man's "cultural manifestations" include not only art and culture in general, but also theological and ecclesiastical issues (with all their liturgical and credal complexity), so the concept of secularity includes religious and non-religious expressions of man's existence in the world.[3]

The fact that secularization embraces both religious and non-religious forms of human manifestation discloses not only Vahanian's willingness to confine the realm of religion to the world of culture, but also his desire to treat religion in cultural terms. This is why, in his thought, there is only one fundamental reality which includes religious and non-religious forms of man's manifestation, and this is the world itself. The world, in which man lives and works, is the material nature that constitutes the very reality of human culture; human culture, on the other hand, makes reference to art and religion in all their intricate forms.[4] Secularity thus points to the unique reality of this world as man's realm of existence and action which includes religious and non-religious expressions of human culture. Therefore, from Vahanian's

---

[2] For details about man's creativity and its role in Vahanian, see Robert O. Johann, SJ, "Modern Atheism", 348-369, in Ralph M. McInemy (ed.), *New Themes in Christian Philosophy* (Notre Dame, IN: University of Notre Dame Press, 1968): 360-361.

[3] Gabriel Vahanian, *The Death of God. The Culture of Our Post-Christian Era* (New York, NY: George Braziller, 1967), 66.

[4] On Vahanian's theology of culture, see further Clayton Crockett, *A Theology of the Sublime* (London: Routledge, 2001), 21.

perspective, the sacred and the secular point to one single reality, the reality of the world. The world, where temporality and finitude define man's material existence in nature, is the only reality that can be said to exist in objective terms. So in Vahanian, everything is sacred and, at the same time, everything is profane.

The Bible itself, he believes, propagates this understanding of human reality since – according to its teachings – there is "only one valid distinction: the holy and the not yet holy". In other words, there is only one reference point according to which one should judge reality. Whether that is referred to as "holy" or not does not really matter. The world as it is constitutes the only standpoint for man's reality. Some people judge the world from the perspective of the "holy", which can be described in terms of divinity, God, infinitude, and eternity, while others would rather cling to the things which can be seen, to humanity, finitude, and temporality.[5]

Either way, however, there is only one reality which includes both divinity and humanity, namely culture, and culture is an essentially human construct that includes man's religious and non-religious convictions, manifestations, and expressions. To be sure, in Vahanian, culture is the real focus of secularity, which distinguishes between the sacred and the profane only in theoretical terms; in practice though secularity embraces both religious and non-religious forms of expression as essentially human cultural manifestations. By contrast, secularism is the attitude which attempts to force religion into the category of non-religious culture.

For Vahanian, secularism is to be compared with religion, because neither is willing to accept the validity of the other. While religion preaches that the ultimate validity of man's life is to be found in God and, in doing so, excludes the reality of nature from any claims of ultimate truth, secularism does the same – in reverse – and glorifies man's naturalness to the detriment of his religious attitudes. So for Vahanian, secularism is "an inverted or concealed religious attitude", which replaces the tyranny of religious supernaturalism with the despotism of non-religious naturalism. In other words, neither religion which promotes the sacred to the detriment of the profane, nor secularism, which defends the profane against the secular, is a proper understanding of the complexity of man's existence in the world. The only correct way to a proper understanding is secularity, which in Vahanian is theoretically able to reconcile religion with secularism, the sacred with the profane, and the theological understanding of the world with a non-theological perspective on it. In the end, therefore, the whole

---

[5] See also Rosemarie Freundorfer, *Dein Reich Komme. Das Zentrum in Rosemary Radford Ruethers Theologie* (Münster: LIT Verlag, 2004), 176.

process which leads to the establishment of secularity as the only proper way to see man's life and actions in the material world of nature, based on his awareness of finitude, temporality, and cultural complexity, can be described as secularization.[6]

Christology and Anthropology

Secularization manifests itself in many aspects of religion, and especially of Christianity as a religion, but one of the most evident is dogma. Christian doctrines are the first to go through the process of secularization, with the evident result that they change from containing references to supernatural realities to tenets that point to merely human values. When it comes to the secularization of dogma, Vahanian notices that Christology is among the first to take the hit of the secularizing wave of contemporary thought. Vahanian is able to trace the Christological alterations which characterize the secularization of Christian doctrine from the biblical "new man in Christ" to what he calls the "secular Adamic man", and eventually to the "Christic man".

In distinguishing between the new man in Christ, the secular Adamic man, and the Christic man, Vahanian discloses the three stages of secularization, which first and foremost affect Christology. Thus, in order for Christian doctrine to be secularized, one needs to focus on Christology, so secularization must affect the Christ-event if it is to be effective. By the Christ-event, Vahanian understands "God's redemptive act through the person and the work of Jesus Christ".

In describing the Christ-event in terms of redemption, which in turn is linked with the reality of God and then manifested in the person and work of Jesus Christ, Vahanian of course traces the characteristics of Christian traditionalism. For instance, in traditional Christianity, the Christ-event is seen from a double perspective: first, the reality of God's supernatural world, and second, the reality of man's natural realm. The Christ-event places supernaturalism and naturalism together in one single reality, which is meant not to unify God's supernatural world with man's natural world, but to point out that the two meet for the sake of the human being. Furthermore, the supernatural Christ reveals himself in the natural world of man in order to redeem him, so the blend of supernaturalism and naturalism is what constitutes the essence of traditionalism in Christian theology.[7] This initial juxtaposi-

---

[6] Vahanian, *The Death of God*, 67.
[7] For a different reading of Vahanian, who is said to have contrasted the sacred with the profane, see Charles W. Winquist, "Theology, Symbolism, and Language in the Thought of Langdon Gilkey", 259-273, in Jeff B. Pool & Kyle A. Pasewark (eds.),

tion of transcendence and immanence with reference to what can be called reality began to undergo the effects of secularization, which was evident in the modifications of Christology from traditional supernaturalism to a rather wide range of modern and contemporary naturalist understandings of Christ.

Thus, traditionalism is associated with the new man in Christ, which underlines the awareness of man that he can be redeemed by a divine, transcendent, and supernatural Christ who reveals himself to him in the reality of material nature. This is an indication that, in traditional Christianity, Christology is more important than anthropology, in the sense that God's redemptive act in Christ is what defines the reality of man in the world. The supernatural Christ works the redemption of man so that man is then able to lead a new life "in Christ"; so Christology informs anthropology. When the process of secularization began to corrode traditional Christianity, a dramatic shift happened so Christology was no longer seen as the foundation of anthropology but the other way around. Secularization does not start from Christology in order to define anthropology, but it establishes anthropology as the basis of Christology.[8] In other words, the supernatural Christ who redeems man is no longer the figure which counts in the religious equation; on the contrary, man is the one that deciphers the complexity of Christ. Christ is no longer considered a person who incorporates divinity and humanity in one single being; as a result of secularization, Christ is accepted as a mere notion, which is able to inform the natural reality of man's existence in spiritual terms.[9]

In Vahanian, the alteration of the Christ-event through secularization not only shifted the interest from the traditional supernaturalism of God to the modern and contemporary naturalism of man. Secularization was much more powerful than that, so it actually deprived man's natural reality of any supernatural connotations. If in traditional theology, man was able to look above at God's supernatural reality as a result of God's redemptive work in Christ, in secularized thought man only looks around, at the natural reality of the material world. The new man in Christ, so characteristic of traditional theology, was aware of a dual reality: his life on earth and his future life beyond it, with God. The new man in Christ, though, disappears when secularization sweeps Christian theology away and a new kind of man emerges from

The Theology of Langdon B. Gilkey: Systematic and Critical Studies (Macon, GA: Mercer University Press, 1999): 262.

[8] For the effects of secularization as presented by Vahanian, see also Richard A. Muller, *The Study of Theology: From Biblical Interpretation to Contemporary Formulation* (Grand Rapids, MI: Zondervan, 1991), 28.

[9] Vahanian, *The Death of God*, 16-18.

the powerful interest in the affairs of the world: the secular Adamic man.

It is interesting to notice that, for Vahanian, both the new man in Christ of traditional theology and the secular Adamic man of secularized religious thought are visualized in terms of "myth".[10] In other words, they are both mythical images of humanity which display strong convictions about how ultimate reality should be depicted. If for the new man in Christ, ultimate reality is the supernatural being of God, for the secular Adamic man, ultimate reality consists of the natural constitution of the material world in which he himself lives. Vahanian places both images within the category of myth because neither accepts the validity of the other; the images appear to be mutually exclusive. In this respect, the secularization of Christian theology moved from Christological traditionalism to anthropological secularism or, in other words, from one extreme to another.

Vahanian also shows that secularization produced a dramatic transfer of values. If traditional Christianity was characterized by hope and faith, secularized society focuses on progress and the natural goodness of man, but neither – in Vahanian's view – seems to speak the truth about humanity.[11] The existence of man in the world cannot be solely considered in terms of hope and faith or exclusively as moving between progress and the natural goodness of man. All these values, however, appear as features of humanity in general, so the process of secularization should not stop with the excursion from the new man in Christ to the secular Adamic man. They both need to be kept together in what can be called the Christic man. Hope and faith must not be replaced by progress and belief in the natural goodness of man; the former must be completed by the latter, so that a more comprehensive view of man is proposed to contemporary people, an image of humanity which includes the traditional values of faith and hope as well as the secularized values of progress and the natural goodness of man.

One needs to realize, though, that the Christic man is a major departure from traditionalism because the role of Christ in man's redemption is actually usurped by the Christic man who – as a result of secularization – seeks to present himself in Christological terms. The traditionally supernatural attributes of Christ are, in a way, transferred upon the Christic man who, despite his sheer unbelief in traditional

---

[10] See also Charles H. Lippy, *Pluralism Comes of Age: American Religious Culture in the Twentieth Century* (Armonk, NY: M.E. Sharpe, 2002), 141.

[11] See also Charles N. Bent, SJ, *The Death of God Movement: A Study of Gabriel Vahanian, Paul van Buren, William Hamilton, and Thomas J.J. Altizer* (Mahwah, NJ: Paulist Press, 1967), 9.

supernaturalism, thinks of himself in terms which allow him to live up to the secularized values of progress and natural human goodness. In fact, the Christic man finds hope and faith in the fact that he is able to perceive himself as the promotor of progress and natural goodness. According to Vahanian, the Christic man represents the secularizing tendency to universalize the qualities of the traditional Christ by extending them to the actuality of man's existence in the world.[12]

Faith and the Dead God

As secularization modifies the entire corpus of Christian doctrine, and especially its Christology from a supernatural Christ who redeems humanity to a natural man who thinks about himself in Christ-like (almost "supernatural" in the sense of "extraordinarily natural") terms, humanity is left to search for meaning in this world – simply because there is no other world beyond this one. If there is no other world beyond this world, then there is no God beyond this world, so if one really wants to speak of God in our contemporary, highly secularized society, then one must look for this God in this world. Traditionally, however, God is believed to exist beyond this world and – as there is no world beyond this one – the very concept of God (in its traditionally Christian denotation) becomes superfluous. In other words, there is no God outside this world, which means that there is no God in this world either.

Man – most notably contemporary man – is free to think of himself in Christ-like terms but this does not make him divine in any sense of the word whatsoever. Consequently, secularized society and the scientifically informed mind of contemporary people are left without God. This is why, for Vahanian, God is dead, in the sense that today's world is not willing to believe in a supernatural God, as traditional Christianity does, so any discourse about God is in fact a discourse about God's death.[13]

According to Vahanian, however, the open recognition of God's death is nevertheless an equally open confession of faith; contemporary people express their faith in the death of God. In other words, they believe that God is dead; he may have served specific purposes in past times but this is no longer the case. This indicates though that the reality of faith continues to inform contemporary society; in the past, it

[12] Vahanian, *The Death of God*, 18-20.
[13] For details of how Vahanian understands the death of God and how his theology differentiates itself from other "Death of God" approaches, like those of William Hamilton, Paul van Buren, Thomas J. J. Altizer, and Harvey Cox, see Richard Lints, *Progressive and Conservative Religious Ideologies: The Tumultuous Decade of the 1960s* (Farnham: Ashgate, 2010), 164, note 3.

was faith in a supernatural God, while in the present it is faith in a natural, conceptual God or even faith in a dead God. One way or another, man seems totally incapable of ridding himself of God; irrespective of whether God is considered alive or dead, man cannot do without him or it. The traditional faith in a living God informed and transformed the lives of many generations of Christians; in fact, such faith was a reality which shaped and reshaped culture in a radical way. The same radicalism, however, can be felt in today's modern and contemporary faith in a dead God for the mind of today's secularized man is still in search for meaning regardless of whether God is dead or alive. It is quite obvious that either way faith is the vehicle which carries meaning and relevance in man's life; his very existence in the world cannot be detached from the reality of faith. Faith brings with it the reality of God and – dead or alive – God is there to give meaning to man's experience.[14] What is interesting for Vahanian is the fact that despite Christianity's belief in a supernatural God – in other words, despite faith in the otherworldliness of God – Christianity managed to have a great impact in this world, which indicates that the seeds of secularization lie within Christianity itself.[15]

Another key feature of secularization is its capacity to describe contemporary times as a "post-Christian" era.[16] Consequently, Christianity – or at least its traditional forms, manifestations, and beliefs in a supernatural God – is behind today's society. Nevertheless, the very times wherein contemporary people live are described in connection with Christianity. Post-Christianity is the result of secularization but, although Christianity itself is left behind in all respects, the redefinition of contemporary life cannot be done without reference to Christianity itself. This is because, despite secularization and its evident achievements, neither the idea of God nor that of Christianity can be extracted from man's existence in the world. God is here to stay and the fact that he is believed to be dead or alive is no longer of any importance. God still informs and transforms the experience of today's man, very much as the idea of Christianity continues to exert a remarkable influence on contemporary society despite the fact that the actuality of traditional Christianity and its living God have long been dismissed as irrelevant. People – ancient, or modern, or contemporary – cannot think of

---

[14] See also Steven H. Propp, *And with All Your Mind: A Novel about Evangelical Theology* (Bloomington, IN: iUniverse, 2010), 119.
[15] Vahanian, *The Death of God*, 47-48.
[16] See also Robert Asa, "Classic *Star Trek* and the Death of God: A Case Study of '*Who Mourns for Adonais?*'," 33-60, in Jennifer E. Porter & Darcee L. McLaren (eds.), *Star Trek and Sacred Ground: Explorations of Star Trek, Religion, and American Culture* (Albany, NY: State University of New York Press, 1999): 40.

themselves without defining themselves by pointing to God; this is why Vahanian writes that "people try God ... as others try the newest medicine".

The evident results of secularization, though, cannot be dismissed as easily. For instance, God may have been kept in man's consciousness to the present day but for many people God is dead. At the same time, Christianity may well continue to influence today's society, but it does so from the position of a religion whose influence belongs to the past. This is why today's society is post-Christian, but in being post-Christian the contemporary world continues to relate itself to what people living today think about God and the Christian religion.[17]

Vahanian identifies three aspects which confirm the fact that today's society is essentially post-Christian: first, Christianity is synonymous with religiosity; second, Christianity has lost its capacity to inspire culture, and third, Christianity is no longer a hegemonic religion. In other words, secularization managed to displace Christianity from its leading religious position to a lower state, which literally inserts Christianity among other world religions. So, for Vahanian, the most evident result of secularization is religious pluralism; the fact that Christianity is now perceived as a mere religion among other religions. As a result of secularization, Christianity is no longer the only religion or the best religion. Vahanian's sense of history allows him to conclude that, as any other religion in the world, Christianity is to be accepted as a religion whose God is dead, very much like the Gods of other religions. Believing otherwise – that Christianity can be either the only or the best religion in the world – is offensive, and today's society seems unwilling to build its values on aggressive or even obnoxious beliefs. Writing back in the 1960, Vahanian's perspective on secularized Christianity seems unrealistically optimistic because he could not have envisaged the resurgence of traditional Christianity in various parts of the world as developed in the late 1990s. His views on secularization though, do highlight, as well as explain the decrease of the influence which was traditionally exerted by Christianity in various geographic locations where Christianity is no longer the dominant religion.[18]

---

[17] See Sally R. Munt, "Queer Spiritual Spaces", 1-34, in Kath Browne, Sally R. Munt & Andrew K.T. Yip (eds.), *Queer Spiritual Spaces: Sexuality and Sacred Places* (Farnham: Ashgate, 2010): 9.

[18] Vahanian, *The Death of God*, 49-59.

10

Accepting God as Dead: Thomas J.J. Altizer

De-Christianization and Re-Christianization

In Thomas J.J. Altizer, secularization cannot be discussed apart from the essential notion of the death of God, which explains how Christianity should be understood in contemporary society. Altizer admits that secularization is a modern phenomenon, which consists at the same time of a program of de-Christianization and an attempt to offer a re-Christianization to a world that is in constant need of symbolism despite its current preoccupation with its material constitution. For Altizer the fact that secularization is simultaneously de-Christianization and re-Christianization can be explained through the traditional phrase *coincidentia oppositorum*, which allows for the features of two distinct entities to be used interchangeably.[1] This is why, Altizer hopes, secularization is not the end of Christianity but rather the chance of a new beginning for Christianity as a world religion.

Secularization works with the idea of the death of God if the whole process of diminishing the role, power, and importance of religion within contemporary society is discussed from the perspective of the secular world. The secular world in fact is the reality which not only started but also supports the program of secularization, so religion must lose its influence in matters pertaining to a society that is no longer willing to accept its tenets. Thus, from the angle of the secular world, the waning of religion can only be achieved if the concept of God – so fundamental for traditional Christian thought – is attached to the notion and reality of death. With God dead, Christianity loses its grip of society and its institutions, which gives society itself the opportunity to extend its influence over the realm which was previously dominated by Christianity.

---

[1] For a better understanding of Altizer's use of the *coincidentia oppositorum*, see David Jasper, *The Sacred Desert: Religion, Art, and Culture* (Oxford: Wiley-Blackwell, 2004), 147.

When Christianity loses its importance in society to the benefit of the non-religious state, one can evidently speak of secularization as de-Christianization. On the other hand, though, secularization is also re-Christianization, and this has to do with the awareness that the Christian world, namely the totality of those who still believe that God is not dead, not only rejects the idea of the death of God but also promotes the notion of the crucifixion – a reference to belief in Jesus' death and resurrection in traditional theology – as the heart of its understanding of the world.[2] Thus, secularization is ultimately a particular perspective on Jesus; in fact, one's acceptance of secularization is based on the conviction of Jesus' connection with the idea of God. In traditional Christianity, Jesus is God, so his crucifixion points not only to his death but also to his resurrection. In modern thought – obviously under the pressure of secularization – God is Jesus, which means that Jesus is not God but rather that the idea of God can be seen in the person of Jesus. When this realization is achieved, namely that Jesus is no longer seen as God but rather as a man in whom the idea of God can be said to have achieved a plenary manifestation, secularization is no longer a process of de-Christianization but an attempt at re-Christianization.

Thus, in Altizer, secularization is the de-Christianization of modern society by showing that God is dead for contemporary non-religious people, but also the re-Christianization of the same social realm by the promotion of the awareness that the idea of God can be said to exist in the life of Jesus.[3]

It is important to notice, however, that Altizer's fundamental polarization of secularization as de-Christianization and re-Christianization is possible only after secularization is accepted in terms of a non-religious attempt to put an end to the powerful impact of traditional religion. Thus, secularization is a radical process with accelerating tendencies which attempts to reduce the importance of religion and, in doing so, to decrease the power of religion in its traditional form. Such an endeavor can only be successful in a world of technology and mass media, which are powerful vehicles for promoting secularization.[4] Thus, secularization is primarily a negative phenomenon which aims at the reduction of religion's influence in contemporary society and second-

---

[2] Lisa McCullough, "Historical Introduction", xv-xxviii, in Lisa McCullough & Brian Schroeder (eds.), *Thinking through the Death of God: A Critical Companion to Thomas J.J. Altizer* (Albany, NY: The State University of New York Press, 2004): xxii-xxiv.

[3] Thomas J.J. Altizer, *The Contemporary Jesus* (Albany, NY: State University of New York Press, 1997), xxiv; Thomas J.J. Altizer, *The Gospel of Christian Atheism* (Louisville, KY: Westminster Press, 1966), 44.

[4] See also Ted R. Spivey, *Flannery O'Connor: The Woman, the Thinker, the Visionary* (Macon, GA: Mercer University Press, 1997), 24.

arily a positive promotion of religion as philosophy of life through the image of Jesus that incorporates – and also practically displays – the idea of God.

When it comes to the idea of God, Altizer shows that secularization – and, of course, the secularization of the idea of God itself – is achievable exclusively with reference to the notion of apocalypse. Secularization as de-Christianization and re-Christianization must take into account the notion of apocalypse because this is what explains how Jesus functions as the marrow of religion regardless of whether one sees him from the standpoint of traditional Christianity or that of modern secularization. To the secularized eye, however, Jesus is a figure that explains both Christian theology and the contemporary secularized understanding of it. In traditional Christianity, Altizer points out, Jesus pointed to a God beyond him, while in contemporary society, God is to be found in the reality of the man Jesus. Likewise, in traditional Christianity, Jesus was expected to come into the reality of history in order for the world to be united with God; in secularized thought, Jesus is expected to represent the idea of God in every human being living in the world. Either way, apocalypse is what explains Jesus to man: in terms of God for traditional theology and in terms of showing God in man within our secularized society. Consequently, secularization is the process which accepts what Altizer calls "the apocalypse of God", in the sense that God's absolute transcendence and immutability from traditional theology is turned – through "an apocalyptic reversal" as Altizer puts it – into "absolute actuality".[5] God is no longer beyond us; on the contrary, God is "all in all". The God of traditional theology and religion is dead, so he cannot be conceived as a personal, metaphysical, and transcendent being any longer. When this happens, secularization has already occurred through the apocalypse of God, which comes up with a new definition of God. The metaphysical God is dead; the new God – the one that is immanent in each human being as a concept that is relevant to man's most profound feelings and his actual existence in the world – seems to have begun to exert his influence over today's technological world as a result of secularization.[6]

---

[5] For a critical perspective on Altizer's understanding of the necessity that transcendence should be abandoned in contemporary religious thought as reportedly informed by Eliade, see Bryan S. Rennie, *Reconstructing Eliade: Making Sense of Religion* (Albany, NY: The State University of New York Press, 1996), 30.

[6] See also Thomas J.J. Altizer & William Hamilton, *Radical Theology and the Death of God* (Indianapolis, IN: Bobs-Merrill, 1966), 114; Altizer, *The Contemporary Jesus*, xxv-xxvi.

Criticism against Christianity

Altizer sees his theology as radical; as for himself, he is a radical theologian who condemns religion for promoting a false dualism between flesh and spirit. A particularity of his system resides in the fact that his criticism of religion – and he clearly emphasizes this aspect of his thought – must not be considered a condemnation of all religions. In fact, his criticism is directed against Christianity because, as he explains, the non-Christian religions cannot and do not fall within the same category. In other words, world religions in general – without the notorious exception of Christianity – cannot be accused of tearing the spirit apart from the reality of the flesh to the degree promoted by Christianity. Consequently, although secularization aims at diminishing the capacity of religion to exercise control over contemporary society, in Altizer this specific program is launched especially against Christianity and its tenets which distinguish – in a rather sharp way – between the reality of the spirit and that of the flesh, or the body.[7] The two, flesh and spirit – but also body or even matter and spirit – must coexist in a way which extends its validity beyond any possibility of tearing the two asunder; for Altizer, such realization can only be achieved in radical theology or in what he calls a "religionless Christianity".

Despite the oddity of such a juxtaposition where the reality of Christianity is placed together with the idea of non-religiosity, Altizer is convinced that Christianity must be embraced these days not as a religion, but rather as a staunch belief in the reality of the "Word". If described as a religion, Christianity should also be labeled as repressive – a reality which produces, fosters, and harbors opposition to the "Word".[8] Thus, in traditional Christianity, the Word becomes flesh but in a way that does not put the body of Jesus together with the reality of divinity.

While claiming such a unity between the divinity of the Word and the humanity of Jesus, Altizer seems to be convinced that traditional Christianity still keeps divinity away from humanity because the two realities do not blend in the person of Jesus; on the contrary, they coexist within the same person which means that they are fundamentally kept apart from one another. What needs to be done, Altizer proposes, is to reverse the classical meaning of the incarnation in the sense that

---

[7] See Hans Schwarz, *Theology in a Global Context: The Last Two Hundred Years* (Grand Rapids, MI: Eerdmans, 2005), 322.

[8] For an informative discussion about the importance of the Word in Altizer and his opposition to Mark C. Taylor, see J. Stephen Fountain, "Postmodernism, A/Theology, and the Possibility of Language as Universal Eucharist", 131-158, in Stanley E. Porter (ed.), *The Nature of Religious Language: A Colloquium* (Sheffield: Sheffield Academic Press, 1996): 142.

divinity and humanity should no longer be accepted as separate and distinctive realities within the person of Jesus. Radical theology or religionless Christianity is able to accept such a reversal of the incarnation in which divinity and humanity, spirit and matter, are blended together in one single, mixed, and complex reality. Spirit and matter must be intermingled in order to reflect the actual reality of how humanity exists in history, otherwise Christianity promotes dualism in a way which is far from the truth of everyday life. This is why, in Altizer, it is only Christianity which should be criticized as a religion for separating matter from the spirit, which does not do justice to the complexity of the human being as it exists in the natural world.[9]

Such an understanding of secularization as criticism against Christianity as a religion which reportedly keeps the spirit away from matter is not supposed to stop here. In order for the complete reunification of the spirit with matter to occur, Christianity must first and foremost abandon its belief in the objectivity of supernaturalism. This is because when matter and spirit constitute the only true reality that exists in whatever man considers to be reality, then the idea of the spirit as detached from matter or as having an ontologically real existence on its own without matter is excluded from the start. It follows that the God of traditional Christianity is seen as an illogical doctrine which has no contemporary relevance for a society that is totally unable to grasp the meaning of spirituality – or the idea of God for that matter – without making constant reference to matter, the body or simply the notion of sensible substance. When the God of traditional Christianity who is able to live in a spiritual way without the necessity of matter is out of the picture, any other concept that is defined with reference to God's spiritual being is criticized – and excluded – as well. For instance, radical Christianity should rid itself of the concepts of sin and guilt because neither has meaning without the objective existence of a supernatural, totally spiritual God.[10] This is why, in Altizer, secularization must target Christianity because only this particular religion is said to have "reduced human existence to sin and guilt".

Altizer's secularization, though, aims to destroy the traditional alterity of God; God cannot exist as a subject outside the personal reality of the human being. If this happens, then it means that God's existence, alterity, and superiority over the human race is at least postulated theoretically, which leads to a "broken" image of humanity that is constantly oppressed by God. Altizer appears to hate any concept which places

---

[9] Altizer, *The Gospel of Christian Atheism*, 44-45.
[10] Thomas A. Idinopulos, *Betrayal of Spirit: Jew-hatred, the Holocaust, and Christianity* (Aurora: CO, The Davies Group, 2007), 182-183.

humanity in submission to a God which is characterized by sheer alterity. This is why his discourse about God must go through a process of intense secularization first; God must be de-Christianized as a wholly other being as compared to the human being in order for it to be re-Christianized as a concept which keeps together the spirit and matter in one single being, namely the human being. Secularization must reject the alterity of God because such a God is totally abstract, without life, isolated from humanity because of its transcendence, and also estranged from the personal character of the human being.[11] Such a God – and this is only the God of Christianity understood in its traditional form as belief in a supernatural deity – must die. Altizer's secularization is an attempt to kill God together with anything else which separates the spirit from the natural reality of matter. From this perspective, in Altizer, secularization is an attempt to put together divinity and humanity in a unique reality which can be said to reflect the actuality of man's existence in the world. In this case, what dictates in Altizer's program of secularization is not the spirit which is supposed to be forever united with matter, but matter itself, which seeks to be explained in a spiritual way. For Altizer, though, the only way in which matter can be explained spiritually, or in a way which makes sense to contemporary people, is through promoting the specific death of the Christian God.[12]

The Death of the Christian God

Since for Altizer the death of God actually means the death of the Christian God, it is crucial to see how the death itself really happens. In order for the death of God to occur effectively so that Christianity is no longer religious but non-religious, what one has to do is deprive incarnation and crucifixion of their "once-and-for-all" historical character. In other words, neither incarnation nor crucifixion should be embraced as events which happened in history – although they did happen to the person of Jesus of Nazareth – so radical theology takes them and assimilates them into images of the progression of human redemption.[13] This means that incarnation and crucifixion can be understood as metaphors of man's attempt to acquire redemption; consequently, redemption loses its metaphysical character since sin and guilt

---

[11] See also Simon D. Podmore, *Kierkegaard and the Self before God: Anatomy of the Abyss* (Bloomington, IN: Indiana University Press, 2011), 81.

[12] Altizer, *The Gospel of Christian Atheism*, 45.

[13] For details about how Altizer sees the necessity to understand crucifixion and resurrection in an apocalyptic way, see Orrin F. Summerell, "Introduction: When God Is Not Deity", 1-13, in Orrin F. Summerell (ed.), *The Otherness of God* (Charlottesville, VA: The University Press of Virginia, 1998): 8.

are no longer objective realities judged by a supernatural God. In Altizer, sin and guilt simply do not exist, so the traditional understanding of redemption as salvation from sin and guilt no longer applies in radical theology. Redemption thus becomes an analogy for man's progress towards self-understanding, while sin and guilt turn into images or metaphors of how this progress develops through history.

This also implies that Jesus was born into the world, lived, and died on a cross, but after all these events happened, nothing else followed. Jesus was indeed considered God, but since Altizer does not believe in Jesus' actual resurrection, the Jesus who was believed to be God never rose again, so he died for ever. Even more importantly, the idea that Jesus was God died with him, and this is how the death of God – and particularly the death of the Christian God – can actually happen.

In other words, for Altizer, God died in Christ; he died with the person of Jesus of Nazareth and since Jesus never returned to life, the image of God which was associated with him remained amongst the dead as well. In order for the death of God to occur for real, one must negate religion and turn Christianity into a metaphorical reality which enables humanity to understand its spiritual progress within this world and without anything or anybody else that does not pertain to this world. At the same time, the death of God cannot be achieved unless man takes a decisive step towards breaking the bondage with the transcendent God; such an image of deity serves no practical purpose in Altizer's theology.[14] God must be dead in order to make sense for today's man, so secularization must preach a dead God, a God who dies in Christ and never comes back to life. Altizer's secularization which is built on the death of God denies the historical character of Jesus' incarnation and crucifixion as real events but, at the same time, it promotes the death of God as a "final and irrevocable event". According to Altizer, if the death of God is such an important event which happened in Christ, then God has been dead for quite some time. Consequently, secularization is not only the full recognition of the death of God in Christ, but also the process which popularizes the death of God through history in order for the "self-negation" of God to become a significant part of man's experience in the world. Certainly, the death of God is meant to confer meaning to human experience, and this is the core of secularization in Altizer's radical understanding of theology.[15]

---

[14] See John D. Caputo, "Spectral Hermeneutics: On the Weakness of God in the Theology of the Event", 47-88, in John D. Caputo & Gianni Vattimo, *After the Death of God*, ed. Jeffrey W. Robbins (New York, NY: Columbia University Press, 2007): 68.

[15] Altizer, *The Gospel of Christian Atheism*, 102-108.

Altizer makes a clear distinction between traditional Christianity, which is religious and traditional, and contemporary Christianity, which is religionless and radical. By extension, the contemporary Christian is a person who not only believes in the death of God, but also manages to detach him- or herself from any form of religion, transcendence, and guilt as a result of sin. In other words, the end product of secularization is the contemporary Christian who liberates himself from what Altizer calls "the most alien, the most distant, and the most oppressive deity in history" – evidently the supernatural God of traditional religious Christianity. Secularization, however, thrives in promoting the opposite image of God; a dead God who makes sense for today's people only if conceived as a natural concept that speaks of the "descent of the Word" into the complexity of man's existence and experience in the material world.

According to Altizer, man does not need a God that cannot be seen because of his transcendence and detachment from the word; on the contrary, he needs to see the world as it is, he must see the complexity of matter, the complexity of his being, and then he should be able to make sense of what happens to him, his person, and his existence in the world. God must be moved from outside the world into the world, but when he reaches the world he ends up dead in Christ.

In other words, the spirit – which is traditionally associated with God – must be brought into the reality of the material world; spirit and matter must become one in the body of the human being. Secularization can do this provided that the death of God is actualized in man's experience, so whatever man means by divinity – except for its traditional perspective as objectively supernatural – can make perfect sense to man's contemporary understanding of the world if brought down to the level of "the profane".[16]

In Altizer, secularization brings the sacred together with the profane to the point that the sacred loses itself in the profane. God dies in Christ, divinity melts into humanity, and transcendence becomes diluted in immanence; in a word, the spirit become matter in order to make man's experience meaningful in the material world of nature. Thus, in Altizer, secularization is the celebration of the death of God and the liberation provided to contemporary people from any representations of transcendence as attached to divinity. Secularization emerges as triumphant in the world when man escapes the bondage of the "alien power" of the transcendent God of traditional and religious Christianity. Today's people must understand that transcendence, and especially the

---

[16] For the influence of Mircea Eliade on Altizer's understanding of the profane, see Douglas Allen, *Structure and Creativity in Religion: Hermeneutics in Mircea Eliade's Phenomenology and New Directions* (The Hague: Mouton, 1978), 126.

image of God as a transcendent personal being, can only be described in terms of emptiness and darkness.

When this realization is fully embraced in today's society, Altizer expresses his conviction that the proclamation of the "good news" of the death of God has been manifested as a result of secularization and as the embodiment of radical Christianity. Secularization does not promote the traditional image of God, but only his death; in this respect, secularization also welcomes the paramount importance of man's experience, which reigns supreme, of the dead God and "the triumphant realization" of his "self-negation".[17] In Altizer secularization is finally complete when the image of God is no longer attached to a transcendent image of divinity, but to the immanent, historical, and material reality of humanity.[18]

---

[17] Discussion of the self-negation of God in Altizer can be found in Paul S. Fiddes, *The Creative Suffering of God* (Oxford: Oxford University Press, 1988), 243-244.

[18] Altizer, *The Gospel of Christian Atheism*, 109-112, 130-131.

11

Turning to Humanity: Hans Küng

The World, Religion, and Theology

In Küng, the idea of secularization begins with the notion of the "turn to humanity".[1] It is quite obvious that by using the notion of the "turn of humanity", Küng attempts to place his theological thinking outside the fences of traditional Christianity, which is characterized by a constant "turn to divinity". The attention of today's theology, therefore, should no longer be God and the idea of divinity but rather man and the concept of humanity. As far as Küng is concerned, it seems that pursuing traditional theology and its orientation to God or the very preoccupation with divinity lie within the sphere of deception. In other words, man deceives himself if today he is still in pursuit of God and divinity, when in fact he should be investing his powers of reason in the active research of the realm of humanity. Even theology, which used to be forced into investigating God and divinity, should nowadays be sprinkled with the freshness of whatever Küng means by the "turn to humanity". What used to be the ancient theology of divinity which is permeated with the notion of God should turn into today's man-oriented theology of humanity.[2]

In order, however, for traditional theology and its preoccupation with God and divinity to develop into a contemporary search for man and humanity, one needs three distinct aspects which must be dramatically reconsidered from the perspective of the "turn to humanity" –

---

[1] For an interesting presentation of how the "turn to humanity" can be understood, see Linda Woodhead and Paul Heelas, *Religion in Modern Times: An Interpretative Theology* (Oxford: Blackwell, 2000), 406-410.

[2] See also Christian Smith, "Secularizing American Higher Education: The Case of Early American Sociology", 97-159, in Christian Smith (ed.), *The Secular Revolution: Power, Interests, and Conflict in the Secularization of American Public Life* (Berkeley and Los Angeles, CA: University of California Press, 2003): 145.

and Küng lists them in a clear sequence: first, the modern world itself; second, religion; and third, theology.[3]

With reference to the first aspect mentioned by Küng, man should no longer deceive himself when it comes to the reality of the contemporary world, which is characterized through the idea of "modernity". The contemporary world, our world, is a modern world, and modernity is defined by science, technology, and culture. There is a high degree of confidence in all these three aspects of modernity in Küng, so man should no longer deceive himself that the world has not evolved in these three respects. Theology should be changed from divinity to humanity because the modern world has reached a stage of development in all these directions; science has attained an unprecedented level of understanding, technology has propelled the human being far beyond what was conceivable only a century ago, and culture has provided the human being with a perspective on itself that is no longer informed by the objectivity of God and divinity.[4] The subject of the human being is not God – not any longer, if we are to believe Küng; what really counts these days is the objectivity of man's material existence in the world; what lies beyond – which is most likely non-existence in terms of material objectivity – is no longer the concern of modern man. The man of today's society is a person whose interests are powerfully connected with what he can see, hear, and feel with his senses. The modern man lives in the world, so he is concerned with the world; anything that pertains to the world is of interest to him, even theology – which in former times was occupied with what lay beyond the world – should turn into an attempt to delve into the mysteries of the world. Such a goal can be achieved if the modern man pays heed to science, technology, and culture – all accepted and widely used only if permeated by this "turn to humanity", so even God should be seen through the lens of humanity.

According to Küng, contemporary science, technology, and culture raise the question of what being a man should be, and the answer to what being a man is should also inform the question of what being Christian is. Looking at God through the lens of humanity should not make finding an answer to what being Christian is more difficult; on the contrary, it should make it easier to grasp, because today's world seems to have found an answer to what being man entails, based on the progress of science, technology, and culture. People of today should be

---

[3] Hans Küng, *On Being a Christian* (trans. Edward Quinn; New York, NY: Pocket Books, 1976), 26.
[4] Egbert Schuurman, *Faith and Hope in Technology*, trans. John Vriend (Toronto, ON: Clements, 2003), 87-88.

preoccupied with the world, not with God; in other words, they should be *secularized*, namely all their interests should revolve around the reality of the *saeculum*, the world as it exists in its material reality of the natural world.

When it comes to the second aspect, Küng points to religion. In Küng, religion is not static; on the contrary, it appears to be a dynamic reality which develops throughout history and the development of modern religion has not been hindered by the unprecedented evolution of science, technology, and culture. On the contrary, religion has learned how to adapt to the new challenges of the modern world, in the sense that religion itself became preoccupied with the world; religion itself is now secularized and, once it accepted that its new focus was no longer God but humanity, it reached the conclusion that God is dead.[5] The modern man of today's secularized society is no longer able to believe in accordance with what belief used to be in the past; in other words, the secularized mind of today's people is incapable of putting its faith in God. God is dead but the need to believe remains intact; this is why Küng points to the fact that the death of God and man's modern incapacity to believe in God reveals what Küng calls "the new need" to believe. Man may no longer believe in God as an objective reality outside the world, but he most definitely is able to believe in something else; he can believe in a God who is fashioned according to modern science, technology, and culture. In other words, man should be able to believe in a secularized God which is thoroughly informed by the faculties and features of the modern human being.

The third aspect on Küng's list is theology, which despite all the crises of the human spirit that had direct repercussions on its content, has not reached the end of its wisdom and – as Küng himself puts it – has never become bankrupt. Küng is convinced that the theology of the last two centuries – a more than evident reference to the rationalism of post-Enlightenment philosophy and especially religious philosophy – which is the result of the tremendous work of entire generations of theologians provided today's secularized society with a better understanding of the world and the human being. Theology is better prepared than it has even been before, so Küng is confident that it should be able to answer the question of what it means to be Christian in today's secularized world of modern science, technology, and culture.[6]

---

[5] Stephen V. Monsma, Clifford Christians, Eugene R. Dykema & Arie Leegwater, *Responsible Technology*, ed. Stephen V. Monsma (Grand Rapids, MI: Eerdmans, 1986), 49-50.

[6] Küng, *On Being a Christian*, 26.

Emancipation, Equalization, and Autonomy

Küng's idea of secularization is founded on his overly optimistic perspective on the contemporary world as well as on what he believes to be the abilities of the modern man through the support of science, technology, and culture. A secular world consists of a society which is formed by people who want to live in a human world. He starts from the idea that, in our modern society, man wants to be and live like man, which means that he does not want to be a super-man (most likely a hint at traditional believers who profess their salvation as deeply rooted in the divinity of Christ) or perhaps less than a man (again, possibly a reference to religions that project God beyond the material nature of the human being). Today's world should consider itself secular because the advances that the human race has made in recent history are outstanding: for instance, man has recently managed not only to leap into the universe which lies beyond our little planet but also to delve into the depths of our innermost psychological constitution. In other words, secularism presupposes a staunch belief in the power of the human being and its ability to conquer not only the macrocosm, but also the microcosm.

At the same time, though, secularization is also the undeterred conviction that man is able to harness both matter and the spirit, nature as we see it outside ourselves and nature as we feel it within ourselves. Küng points out that secularization is a complex word, which points not only to the transfer of church property into usage by the lay state – and this is the primary meaning of secularization – but also to nearly all the important aspects of human life, such as science, economics, politics, jurisprudence, culture, education, medicine, social work, and the internal affairs of the state. In other words, secularization is the process which promotes the interests of the human being – or rather the immediate social interests of the human being – in a way which diminishes or even cancels the influence of the church, theology, and religion.

For Küng, minimizing the role of the church, theology, and religion in today's modern society is not only the key feature of secularization but also the responsibility of the modern man, who has become a secular being. Indeed, contemporary secularization should be defined through the word "emancipation",[7] which Küng compares with the release of the child from the authority of his parents or with the act of setting slaves free from the ruling power of their masters. In addition to "emancipation", secularization also means "equalization", especially with reference to social justice. All human beings are equal, Küng

---

[7] Gaspar Martinez, *Confronting the Mystery of God: Political, Liberation, and Public Theologies* (London: Continuum, 2001), 72.

appears to believe, and this means that all human beings should be released from any relationship of dependence; for instance, secularization means promoting self-determination or autonomy to the detriment of heteronomy.[8] Individual human beings should be given the chance to govern themselves; nothing and nobody should exert power over individuals, and creating the necessary conditions for such society rests with the process of secularization. Thus, secularization is emancipation and equalization, which are realized through the self-determination of all national, confessional, and cultural minorities, which include peasants, workers, women, and Jews – to list only a few categories picked up by Küng himself. At the end of the day, the contemporary secular man should free himself from any "blind" and "illegitimate" authority, regardless of whether this has to do with the limitations of nature, society, or even other individuals. Being secular means being free; nothing and nobody else – except for one's individual self – has the right to exert authority over any human being whatsoever.[9]

There is another aspect which needs to be highlighted in Küng's understanding of secularization. Thus, secularization is a process during which man learns to place himself in the center of the world, so he no longer needs God or even belief in God.[10] In the past, everything was in society and his own perception of himself was connected with the Christian faith. As such, Christian faith – Küng contends – influenced man's experience, knowledge, and ideas, so the human being was under the oppressing authority of the church. Today's world has managed to shake off such religious and theological tyranny – Küng seems to imply – so all the domains of human life have begun to be perceived less and less from the perspective of God's world. Man has learned to see and look at himself not from God's perspective, but from his own, and this is what secularization ultimately entails. Man's decisions should not depend on belief in the existence of God's world; on the contrary, they must be shaped by the reality of this world.[11] Küng is convinced that in today's secularized world, the influence of the church and theology, the prevalence of religion, and the meaning of doctrines and rituals have lost almost all their influence; for Küng the control of the church is a reminiscence of the Middle Ages and anything pertaining

---

[8] See also Brian Griffiths, "The Business Corporation as a Moral Community," 205-218, in Parth J. Shah (ed.), *Morality of Markets* (New Delhi: The Academic Foundation and the Centre for Civil Society): 214.

[9] Küng, *On Being a Christian*, 27.

[10] For details about the modern man's dismissal of belief in God, see George, R. Hunsberger, *Lesslie Newbigin's Theology of Cultural Plurality: Bearing the Witness of the Spirit* (Grand Rapids, MI: Eerdmans, 1998), 63.

[11] Sayyed Hossein Nasr, *The Need for a Sacred Science* (Albany, NY: The State University of New York Press, 1993), 45.

to the influence of religion in general or theology in particular is a medieval flaw which must be eradicated on a large scale.

Küng realizes that his optimism concerning the actual progress of science, technology, and culture may be called into question and the spiritual turn, which also led to a specific awareness, of the last fifty years or so may or may not be shared by everybody. What really counts when it comes to the reality of secularization is the state of theology on the one hand, and the attitude of the church, on the other. His main concern is not society – although his understanding of secularization draws heavily on today's social realities – but the church and its theology and how the institution which calls itself the church is able to respond to the challenges of today's secular society. It seems, though, that Küng attempts to level the boundaries of the traditional church in order to scatter the members of the church throughout today's secular society. If today's society is unable to attach any meaning whatsoever to the reality of God – at least not in the traditional sense of the word – then the church must find a way to speak about God in the secularized terms of our modern world, which once again dismisses God's classical ontology, objectivity, and personhood.[12]

Openness, Social Awareness, and Freedom

In order for secularization to get a good grasp of Christian theology, the Christian church itself must become secular. Such transformation cannot be achieved unless the church opens itself to the secular world.[13] The idea of openness is not static in Küng; on the contrary, it is progressive movement through which the church teaches itself to see the world in a brand new way. Thus, the world should never appear to the church as evil, or sinful, or even pagan. The church must embrace the world; it must take an affirmative or positive stand as far as the world is concerned. In a word, the church must shape the world by assuming its most fundamental values. It is as if the church should level its traditional boundaries which formerly delineated it from the values of the world; now, according to Küng, the church should somewhat fluidize its boundaries. The church must pour itself out into the world, while the world pours itself out in the church through an exchange of values which do not go from the church to the world but rather the other way around: the values of the world force themselves into the church, which must accept them as its own.

---

[12] Küng, *On Being a Christian*, 27-28.
[13] See also Wacław Hryniewicz, *The Challenge of Our Hope: Christian Faith in Dialogue* (Washington, DC: The Council for Research in Values and Philosophy, 2007), 125.

What Küng proposes in fact is that the church should be more socially aware and pay constant heed to the immediate social, economic, and even political needs of the world.[14] Thus, the church must work with the world to solve the world's urgent problems. While one may rightly ask oneself about the problems of the church and whether the church is taken care of by the world, Küng suggests – quite insistently – that it is the church that should adapt itself to the world and, at the same time, open itself to and become more aware of the problems of the world. The church which lives in today's secular world must open so much to the world that not only its boundaries become fluid and its values become united with the world's way of thinking, but also its most essential spiritual drive must be reset in such a way that the church develops a constant curiosity about the world. It is clear that it is not the world which should be curious about the church as in traditional theology; it is the church which must find a way to develop its curiosity about the world in order to solve its most pressing problems. This means that the church must leave behind its "untimely" traditional orthodoxy because, unless it does so, the church will never be able to be scientifically honest towards its doctrines and the Bible.

Today's Christians – Küng proposes – must find a new freedom and a new openness for themselves in doctrines, morality, and ecclesiastical life, but all these must conform to the secular values of the world. What the church must do is eventually to become some sort of social organization which, according to Küng, must be actively involved in developing the social dimension of all human beings, protect human rights and religious freedom, fight against economic, social, and racial injustice, promote international understanding and world peace, oppose the proliferation and dissemination of weaponry, attempt to extinguish illiteracy, hunger, alcoholism, prostitution, and drug trafficking, support medical care, help people in trouble, and especially the victims of natural catastrophes. To put Küng's explanation in a nutshell, the church must leave aside its inner problems or even the problems which arise from the diversity of Christian confessions; what the church should be doing these days is to focus on the issues which are external to its constitution. Thus, the church must find a way to get permanently involved in the problems of society, not in its own ecclesiastical issues.[15]

Should one look for a single phrase to summarize Küng's intentions for the church which see the church as a secularized institution of

---

[14] What Küng proposes here is by no means a piece of religious novelty. In the late 1880s, German Protestants had already proposed that the church should be more open to society and thus more aware of the problems of modern society. See Harry Liebersohn, *Religion and Industrial Society: The Protestant Social Congress in Wilhelmine Germany* (Philadelphia, PA: The American Philosophical Society, 1986), 5.

[15] Küng, *On Being a Christian*, 29-30.

today's lay society, this could be that the church must not only open itself to the secular world, but also fight for freedom in all possible respects.[16] It is interesting to notice that Küng does not criticize the alliance between the church and the state; what he opposes in fact is the alliance between the church and the state with the intention to protect the privileged. Certainly, Küng advocates the alliance but also the full cooperation between the church and the state but only if it is meant to support the underprivileged so that every human person enjoys total freedom in the world. Thus, the church must fight for freedom of conscience, freedom of religion, and against virtually anything that could impair human freedom.

Openness to the world and the fight for freedom takes the shape of a positive attitude which the church must assume if, as according to Küng, it desires to go successfully through the process of secularization. Consequently, the church should think positively about rethinking its service, preaching, and pastoral care from the perspective of the problems of today's world. The church should no longer be preoccupied exclusively with its members; the service, preaching, and pastoral care of the church must be extended and expanded to the entire world. The church should not live in fear of the world; this is why Küng recommends that the church rid itself of its former negativity which found expression in movements such as Counter-Reformation and Counter-Enlightenment. These ecclesiastical initiatives are anti-social in nature so must be dismissed; the church must embrace all the values of the world in order to be able to care for the world. The church must turn itself to all human beings and in doing so, it must cease to stay in the rearguard of humanity, in fear of novelty, and without any creative desire to discover the developments of our modern society. If the church is to become secular, it must concern itself with man, not with God; its primary focus is man's social problems: poverty, famine, drought, illnesses, lack of education, injustice, and tyranny of any kind.[17] The church must therefore turn into a social foundation which promotes a common morality for everybody, some sort of ethical code which Küng believes has the power to solve man's social problems in an effective way.[18]

---

[16] For the appropriation and implementation of secularization outside today's Western society based on a program which resembles Küng's proposals, see Abraham V. Thomas, *Christians in Secular India* (Cranbury, NJ: Associated University Presses, 1974), 121-122.

[17] In this respect, Küng comes very close to the liberation theology of Latin America, see David Lehmann, *Democracy and Development in Latin America: Economics, Politics, and Religion, in the Post-War Period* (Philadelphia, PA: Temple University Press, 1990), 121-122.

[18] Küng, *On Being a Christian*, 30-31.

12

Seeing Reality as It Is: Harvey Cox

Nature and Faith

The first aspect of Harvey Cox's theory of secularization resides in the very sharp distinction which he draws between secularization and secularism.[1] For Cox, secularism is an ideology and – like any ideology for that matter – it is a bad thing mainly because it seeks to take over any other perspective on life. In this respect, Cox argues, secularism functions like religion, in the sense that it claims to hold the truth itself, so that any other ideas about anything are wrong. Secularism is a menace since it endangers the realities of openness and freedom. As far as Cox is concerned, secularism blocks the whole process of secularization, which is defined as the opposite of secularism. While secularism is narrow, limited, and arrogant, secularization is supposed to be characterized by freedom and openness to the material reality of the world. Cox acknowledges that the roots of secularization are the social attempts to transfer ecclesiastical institutions into the patronage of public administration, but what has come to be described as secularization today is much more than that. The original pattern – namely the shift from the sacred to the secular – has remained the same, but a proper definition of secularization cannot be limited to social issues. This is why Cox's perspective on secularization includes social, political, cultural, and religious aspects.

In other words, secularization attempts to reduce the influence of religion in contemporary society in all the domains of public life. Cox is convinced that secularization is a process which began a long time ago and can be traced back even to the Bible itself. This is why secularization cannot be stopped and is consequently irreversible.[2] To be sure, secularization takes different shapes in different social, political,

---

[1] See also Andrea L. Parliament, *Secular Hope: What the Religious Right Really Wants and Why Liberal Democrats Should Support Them* (Bloomington, IN: iUniverse, 2010), 48-50.

[2] See Mark A. Torgerson, *An Architecture of Immanence: Architecture for Worship and Ministry Today* (Grand Rapids, MI: Eerdmans, 2007), 18.

cultural, and religious contexts; irrespective, however, of the particularities of these settings, secularization is always based on man's desire to diminish the influence of religion and, in doing so, to enhance the impact of non-religious ideas within contemporary society. From this perspective, secularization seeks to produce a worldview which sees reality as it is. The very constitution of the world, the materiality of nature, and the objectivity of the universe are all to be understood as they exist in reality, without any religious influence whatsoever.

As a result of such a program, secularization is a process which inevitably leads to what Cox calls "the disenchantment of nature"; in other words, secularization is supposed to help today's society acquire an understanding of reality which is not dominated by spirits, demons, magic, and bewitched unseen energies. All these pertain to religion in its wide range of forms and manifestations; secularization though attempts to investigate reality for what it is in order to produce a worldview which is non-religious and devoid of any patronizing spiritual influences. According to Cox, the religious worldview is magical predominantly because every major religion is based on the conviction that God and man pertain to the reality of nature. The great exception here seems to be what Cox calls "the biblical faith", which not only severs God from nature but also differentiates between man and nature.[3]

Cox seems to be quite fond of "the biblical faith" because it defines God and man in terms which point to no relationship with nature.[4] Neither God nor man is presented in the Bible as having powerful liaisons with the material reality of nature. Man indeed lives in nature, but his origin lies in God, while God himself exists beyond nature. In other words, man is somehow neutral when it comes to his actual relationship with nature. The biblical image of man, according to Cox, presents society with a man who is aware of his status, a man who does not revere nature and also does not destroy nature. In the Bible, man is connected with God and only lives in nature, which means that he carefully administers its resources.

As far as Cox is concerned, such an image of man is the first sign of secularization, because nature is no longer seen in magical terms. Biblical imagery, Cox writes, is not characterized by the myths of other religions. There are two exceptions to this rule – the serpent which tempted Eve and the donkey which spoke to Balaam – but they are

---

[3] Harvey Cox, *The Secular City* (London: SCM Press, 1967), 20-22.
[4] For details about the role of biblical faith in Cox's view of secularization, see William A. Beardslee, *A House for Hope: A Study in Process and Biblical Thought* (Philadelphia, PA: Westminster Press, 1999), 87.

certainly too few to place "biblical faith" among the other major religions of antiquity. This is why, for Cox, the Bible contains the seed of secularization: man is presented as independent from nature in the sense that his origin lies within the realm of God, and God himself is said to exist beyond the material reality of nature. In other words, nature is not considered divine in the Bible, and this is the first step towards seeing nature in non-magical terms.

Consequently, Cox argues that seeing nature as it is constitutes an "absolute precondition" for the progress of science. When it comes to science, though, it has to be said that it cannot develop without this non-magical understanding of nature. Science is a point of view and, in order for it to develop, it needs to be based on convictions which accept nature for what it is in reality. The endeavor to see nature in non-magical terms is characterized by Cox as "the disenchantment of nature", and when this comes true then one can see secularization in progress.[5] Thus, secularization leads to technology and urbanization, which both seek to rid society of traditional understandings of religion. As strange as it may sound, Cox is convinced that the secularizing task to remove religious traditionalism was performed not only by science and technology, but also by Christian missions and Communism. The latter two worldviews – Christianity and Communism – caused serious devastation amongst traditional religions in many parts of the world and, while Cox does not ascribe any negative connotations to either, he nevertheless points to the fact that both advanced the disenchantment of nature and, in doing so, actively promoted the never-ending process of secularization. This is why, as far as Cox is concerned, secularization is not promoted only by the non-religious institutions of human society; it is evident that throughout history secularization was spread with considerable degree of success even by the Christian church itself. Given its view of God which was borrowed from the "biblical faith" of Judaism, the Christian church continued to promote the separation between God and nature as well as the clear distinction between man and nature. In this respect, the Christian church is different from any traditional religions which see the sacred as pertaining to nature. The Christian church, however, has its own perspective on the sacred and when Christianity promotes its vision of the sacred to the detriment of the secular state, Christianity itself needs to undergo the same process of secularization. It is important to realize that, in Cox, secularization is a process, not a *status quo*. In other words, secularization happens as history goes by, so today's society has to find a way to

---

[5] Joseph Blenkinsopp, *Treasures Old and New: Essays in the Theology of the Pentateuch* (Grand Rapids, MI: Eerdmans, 2004), 37-38.

promote secularization in the present, even if this means that Christianity will have to give up some or all of its perspectives on the sacred.[6]

Politics and History

In order for Christianity to give up its perspectives on the sacred or at least minimize them so that they no longer influence society on a large scale, one needs to consider the secularization of politics, as seen in history. This imperative emerges as compulsory because – like any other segment of society – politics has not managed to escape the influence of religion.[7] For instance, in antiquity, Roman society promoted a kind of politics in which the emperor was not only the political ruler but also assumed the religious role of *pontifex maximus*. Such a position blended politics with religion, so that the official program of the Roman state included the promotion of religion as supported by the secular state, which obviously could not be considered secular any longer, at least not entirely. Whether or not religion was pursued personally as a result of the individual's convictions had no bearing on politics whatsoever; what was important resided in the fact that religion was formally supported by the state. The situation repeated itself centuries later when Christianity became the official religion of the Roman empire following Constantine's decision to recognize its right to exist among other Roman religions.

Resuming Cox's interest in the secularization of politics, one may wish to focus on his conviction that society cannot change for the better if religion is kept as a ruling entity. While Cox admits that there is no perfect union between politics and religion as contemporary states tend to differentiate between the responsibilities of each segment, there is nevertheless a powerful influence of religion in today's politics which – according to Cox – seems to prevent contemporary nations from achieving their fullest potential because of religious interference. Consequently, politics needs to be desacralized – very much like nature should be disenchanted – if the idea of social, political, economic, scientific, and any other kind of progress is to be achieved responsibly.[8] What Cox suggests here for the desacralization of politics is a shift in the place of God. It is quite evident that God is not a metaphysical reality or being for Cox; thus, God is only a concept – an extremely

---

[6] Cox, *The Secular City*, 23-24.
[7] See also Frank Lambert, *Religion in American Politics: A Short History* (Princeton, NJ: Princeton University Press, 2008), 193.
[8] See Carl J. Starkloff, SJ, "Renewing the Sacred Loop", 159-172, in Vine Deloria Jr. (ed.), *A Sender of Words: Essays in Memory of John G. Neihardt* (Salt Lake City, UT: Howe, 1984): 167.

powerful one at times – which can be allowed to exist, but not in nature and certainly not in politics. This is why Cox suggests that God could be kept and his influence could remain more or less intact in the realm of history.

It is Cox's conviction that while nature constantly repeats itself, history is not affected by repetition. So, as history tends to be linear, while nature is characterized by repetition, Cox recommends that God should be left within the sphere of history. This way, God's influence remains limited to the periods when the concept was indeed extremely influential and, because there is no repetition in history, there is no danger of God's influence becoming a reality again. This explains Cox's belief that secularization is irreversible: history is linear, it does not repeat itself, so it does not return to previous situations. As secularization happens in history, the influence of God in the past which was severely impaired by secularization is never to happen again, so secularization is basically free to develop into a program that will support the advance of science, technology, and progress in general. God must be kept in history, not in nature; if kept in nature, nature repeats itself and contemporary society runs the risk of having the idea of God return in a powerful way, with disastrous consequences for social development and scientific progress. With God connected to history, though, such a risk is eliminated and, as politics is a feature of history, not of nature, the secularization of politics can be achieved through a program of political desacralization.[9]

Cox is aware that the secularization of today's society through the desacralization of politics is not an easy thing to achieve.[10] Contemporary Western nations – European, those belonging to the Commonwealth, and the United States of America – are still very much influenced by some sort of religious politics despite the vast program of secularization that has been pursued in recent times. Secularization, however, is not a state of affairs; secularization is a process, and one can never say it has been achieved in a complete way. Significant steps were taken towards the implementation of secularization in the world; for instance, in medieval times, the fight between popes and emperors was a sign that politics should be liberated from religion (and also religion from politics for that matter), then Renaissance thinkers showed that religion has nothing to do with effective politics if the state is seriously oriented towards progress, and finally Marxism attempted – in a rather decisive as well as incisive way – to rid politics of religion. All these attempts to separate politics from religion are instances when

---

[9] Cox, *The Secular City*, 25.
[10] For details, see Paul Lakeland, *The Liberation of the Laity: In Search of an Accountable Church* (London: Continuum, 2004), 168-171.

history tried to take religion as far away as possible from the decision-making process of politics, but such endeavors have never been completely successful.

According to Cox, sacral politics continues to exist throughout the world and even in the most technologically advanced societies. Oaths taken with one's hand on the Bible – regardless of whether one is a president, judge, or other public official – especially in countries where the Bible, prayer, or religious Christian symbols have been banned from schools are reminiscences of sacral politics, and they do not seem to go away as easily as the promoters of secularization, Cox included, would like. It seems that despite his desire to keep religion away from politics, Cox is not a promoter of savage secularization. On the contrary, he appears to be quite resigned to the fact that religion will most likely never fade away from politics; but this does not mean that he would not like to see religion extinguished for good. Marxism attempted to promote an ideology according to which religion will eventually disappear; clearly, this was definitely not the case. As a careful observer of history, Cox does not hasten into preaching the death of religion and neither does he fight for its eradication. What he seems to favor is a state whose politics is not decisively influenced by religion. Whether or not religion or at least religious symbols will continue to be present within politics is not the most important aspect of contemporary society; what is important, however, has to do with the public awareness that religion needs to decrease in politics and indeed in the whole of society.[11] For as long as religion does not interfere with politics or with the affairs of the state and therefore scientific progress is not hindered because of it, religion may be allowed to be harbored by contemporary society. Its values, however, must be deconsecrated and stripped of their metaphysical content, so that religion is never enabled to make claims to absolute truth.[12]

Ethical Values and the World

The deconsecration of values – and here Cox points to religious values – turns secularization into a process of fundamental relativization. The idea of values includes a wide range of human insights about virtually everything: language, customs, and even science. Everything needs to go through the relativization of secularization, because this points to

---

[11] This can happen only if Christianity renounces its metaphysical convictions. See Elizabeth Shakman Hurd, *The Politics of Secularism in International Relations* (Princeton, NJ: Princeton University Press, 2008), 29-30.

[12] Cox, *The Secular City*, 26-30.

how the human being looks at things, and how he looks at things is the very aspect which must be secularized and relativized.[13] The idea of ultimate significance or final meaningfulness – a reference to the belief that God incorporates the best of man's values – must be detached from the realm of human interpretation. Contemporary society should produce people whose awareness of the world is no longer fostered with religious insights and absolute values. In doing so, the very notion of God should be extracted from human values – exactly as it was detached from the sphere of nature or the domain of politics. When nature, politics, and values are liberated from anything resembling the idea of God or the concept of divine will, then secularization has a real chance in today's world. Cox's perspective on secularization as the deconsecration of values calls for a dramatic reassessment of ethics, so the notion of good should no longer be left to religion. It is no longer religion that tells man what is good and what is bad; man himself needs to decide on the morality of his own individuality and how his personal existence relates to the world of humanity or the materiality of nature.

Thus, secularization leads to the destruction of ethical certainty but this should never trigger sheer nihilism. When secularization leads to nihilism, it produces just another ideology, which is neither desirable, nor good for society. This is why secularization should lead to relativization but only to the degree that the end-result is pluralism. In Cox, the purpose of secularization is not to annihilate values, but to make them more diverse. Expanding the range of human values is possible as long as they are kept within the realm of history. As in Cox history does not repeat itself, when values are relativized in the sense that they are made more diverse and kept away from the influence of religion, this situation can be maintained and even taken a step further provided values are seen as an integral part of history, not of nature. This is why Cox argues that the final product of secularization is historical relativism, which allows for the existence of ethical diversity and religious pluralism.[14] Like religion, values are quite unlikely to disappear. Ultimately, Cox seems to be sure that neither religion nor values are meant to disappear. Humanity seems to need both, but their claims to infallibility, to divinity, and absolute truthfulness should never be accepted other than in secularized, disenchanted, desacralized, and deconsecrated terms. This is why it is important for secularization to avoid nihilism and attempt to reinstate pluralism. Secularization is able to show that

---

[13] Darrel J. Fasching, *The Ethical Challenge of Auschwitz and Hiroshima: Apocalypse or Utopia?* (Albany, NY: State University of New York Press, 1993), 247.

[14] For a critical position on Cox's view of pluralism, see D.A. Carson, *The Gagging of God: Christianity Confronts Pluralism* (Grand Rapids, MI: Zondervan, 1996), 28-29.

God is dead – with evident consequences for how man understands nature, politics, and values – but the dead God of traditional religion should never be replaced by the non-God of nihilism. God, Cox argues, should be kept in religion, even in society, and politics as dead; when the traditional God exists as a dead God, a new meaning of religion, politics, and values is discovered in the sense that freedom and pluralism become the lenses which assist contemporary society in reading the world. Absolute claims to truth and supreme values are no longer legitimate in a secularized society; freedom to see the truth in a diverse and pluralistic fashion based on a wide range of human values has become the new standard of contemporary secularization.[15]

In other words, the deconsecration of values as a result of secularization implies a deep awareness that ethical values do not come from heaven. Cox underlines this aspect by pointing to the fact that politics and ethics should be placed on the same level. Thus, since man is aware that political constructs are not divine but deeply human, in the very same way man should realize and consequently accept that ethical values are human perspectives on the quality of things as they exist in the world. Whether something is good or bad is a personal, individual judgment which should not be inspired by traditional metaphysical convictions. Religion should not play any role in deciding the quality of the entities which exist in the reality of the world. This is why, in Cox, secularization as the process which strips values of their claims to absolute truth or goodness based on religious convictions should include a high degree of personal responsibility.[16]

As far as Cox is concerned, personal responsibility is achievable if pursued with what he calls "real maturity", an ingredient which is compulsory for a healthy social consensus. As for the social consensus, this is needed despite and, at the same time, because of the relativization and pluralization of values in contemporary society as a result of secularization. Maturity implies a deep awareness of man's capacity to liberate himself from the impression that values are ultimate. Such a conviction is, according to Cox, devoid of serious criticism and is consequently illusory. As a result of secularization, contemporary man should live responsibly and maturely based on the powerful and personal awareness that values should be embraced in all their plurality and diversity.[17] This is why, for Cox, secularization is a process which dis-

---

[15] Cox, *The Secular City*, 30-34.
[16] See also Eileen Flynn & Gloria Thomas, *Living Faith: An Introduction to Theology* (2nd edn, Lanham, MD: Rowman & Littlefield, 1989), 8.
[17] See Ronald D. Anderson, *Religion and Spirituality in the Public School Curriculum* (New York, NY: Peter Lang, 2004), 150.

places the reality of responsibility from a God that does not exist in reality to man himself who not only exists in reality, but is also completely and vigorously involved within its actuality. Man, not God, is the one who creates values, and this allows for pluralism, diversity, and freedom in the realm of ethics. What Cox does not explain here is how a non-secularized ethic is still possible as well as much alive in traditional communities which cling to a metaphysical understanding of God. Ultimately – and this is what Cox seems to understand quite well – secularization depends on how people succeed in embracing the idea of God and how far they are willing to go in clinging to or giving up belief in a metaphysically real God.[18]

---

[18] Cox, *The Secular City*, 34-36.

13

Putting an End to Religion: John Shelby Spong

Religion and Interiority

For John Shelby Spong, secularization refers to man's decision to terminate whatever religion meant throughout history. In his own words, "putting an end completely to the religious traditions of the past" seems the most effective way in which secularization can be enforced in our contemporary society, based on a thorough investigation of what religion should be for today's man, a categorical reconsideration of the significance of God for humanity, and a profound search of man's interiority and experience in the world.[1] The first step, which has to do with the investigation of religion and especially of the meaning of religion for today's society, can be considered a process which seeks to interiorize religion. Thus, the first aspect of secularization is the internalization of religion as a counterstrike against man's traditional perception thereof. Spong seems convinced that until our contemporary times, religion has always been perceived as an external reality in the sense that man established a connection with religion seen as a system that existed beyond each man's individuality. Religion was dictated from outside, as it were, so man's experience was shaped by doctrines, teachings, and rituals which had their own standing as totally independent from what happened with or within man. If secularization is to be implemented correctly and effectively, man must detach himself from seeing religion as an external system; religion therefore must become interiorized.[2] Man should internalize religion as an active spiritual reality of his own individuality. Religion should no longer impose certain doctrines on man; on the contrary, man should devise his own religion through accepting it as his own spirituality.

---

[1] For a criticism of Spong, see Michael Horton, *The Gospel Commission. Recovering God's Strategy for Making Disciples* (Grand Rapids, MI: Baker Books), 9.

[2] See also Walter Kania, *Healthy Religion: A Psychological Guide to a Mature Faith* (Bloomington, IN: AuthorHouse, 2009), 239.

In other words, Spong invites today's society to think of religion as the result of one's own intuition, knowledge, and desires; doctrines no longer come from outside in order to shape man's psychological constitution. On the contrary, it is what happens within man's internal psychological structure which determines the content of religion. Religion's quest has always been ultimate truth, but as far as Spong is concerned, ultimate truth cannot be imposed on anybody from a religious system which is permanently and fundamentally external to each human individual. If man wants not only to seek the ultimate truth these days but also to find it, then what he has to do is internalize religion; think of religion as his own, innermost reality. Doctrines and religious convictions should no longer originate in a system that has its own existence outside man's individuality; they should spring from man's internal, psychological depth. Nevertheless, in order to be able to turn traditional external religion into some sort of secularized internal spirituality, man has seriously to consider his anxiety about aging and death. For Spong, the knowledge of this particular anxiety, which is fundamental for the human being, is the first step in understanding religion and how it should be embraced today. Coping with the thought of one's aging and death is definitely not easy; it is in fact a real burden, which, in Spong, is described as "a heroic task and a universal responsibility".[3]

Having been aware of his life and death, man traditionally sought to provide his existence with meaning. Dying without any prospect of some sort of existence beyond this life seems meaningless, so Spong explains that religion turned out to be man's "coping device" in the face of death and meaninglessness. This is why religion was conceived as an external system; precisely because it offers man the hope that existence is possible beyond death. Fully convinced that contemporary society was able to prove that no existence is in fact possible once death occurs, Spong suggests that such realization corresponds with the end of religion as an external system. If religion no longer works as an external reality given its utter inability to provide man with meaning since there is no personal existence beyond death, what man has to do next is to move beyond religion. In doing so, religion *per se* is not abolished; it is only unmasked as a coping device in the face of death, so – because a coping device is no longer effective once recognized as a coping device – man should accept religion as an internal reality.

---

[3] John Shelby Spong, *Rescuing the Bible from Fundamentalism: A Bishop Rethinks the Meaning of Scripture* (New York, NY: HarperOne/HarperCollins, 1992), 247. See also John Shelby Spong, *Eternal Life: A New Vision. Beyond Religion, Beyond Theism, Beyond Heaven and Hell* (New York, NY: HarperOne/HarperCollins, 2009), 80.

As meaning did not come from outside, from religion seen as an external system, it means that the only other option left – which Spong considers valid in all respects – is searching for meaning inside the human being. Man must look inside himself and approach religion from the perspective of his own psychological depth.[4] Internalizing religion is, therefore, a powerful means to promote secularization, Spong argues, since religion was traditionally man's creation. Man must understand that it was he who created religion as an external doctrinal system which proved unable to solve his existential problems. Although external religion was meant to help man understand reality and his place within the reality of the world, this type of religion demonstrated man's inability to understand both reality as nature and his own reality as experience. In other words, accepting religion as an external doctrinal system is hiding from reality. Conversely, through the process of secularization, religion should be accepted as an internal set of beliefs, which assists man in discovering the true reality of external nature and of his own interiority.[5]

In our secularized society, man must understand what it means to be human. As far as Spong is concerned, being human is not ridding oneself of religion, but terminating what religion traditionally meant. It means turning religion from its ancient exteriority to its contemporary interiority. Externalized religion is utterly incapable of telling the modern man what to do and how to understand his existence in the world; only internalized religion – the religion which is based on man's own understanding and beliefs – can do that. This is why, for Spong, secularization begins with the reassessment of religion in the sense that religion should no longer be seen as external; in order to be relevant for man's contemporary quests for truth and meaning, religion must be internalized. In other words, it is compulsory for religion to originate in man's deepest thoughts and desires.[6]

God and Man's Reality

Spong's second step towards secularization is to lower God from his traditional transcendent position to the level of humanity. In other words, God cannot be accepted as a living being that exists beyond the reality of the world; what people should do these days is embrace God

---

[4] Robert Wilhelm, *Return to Soul: An Invitation to View the Soul* (Lincoln, NE: Writer's Showcase/iUniverse, 2002), 89.
[5] See also Jos C.N. Raadschelders, *Government: A Public Administration Perspective* (Armonk, NY: M. E. Sharpe, 2003), 68.
[6] Spong, *Eternal Life*, 80-83.

as part of their own reality.⁷ Lowering God is therefore a necessary process which is supposed to align the desires of the heart with the thoughts of reason. While the heart is still capable of telling man that God's existence could be possible, the mind refuses to accept such a tenet. Accepting what the heart tells man is succumbing to traditional religion, traditional theology, and the traditional way of seeing God as a transcendent, benevolent, and personal deity. Embracing what the mind tells man, namely that God's existence is pretty much impossible, is dealing with the religion of man's own experience, which – according to Spong – should become the norm of our secularized society. This points to the fact that lowering God from his traditional transcendence to the material reality of the world and the daily experience of humanity is a rational enterprise, a construct of the mind.

Spong argues that, since traditional religion cannot find a satisfactory way to reconcile human tragedy with the idea of a benevolent, transcendent God, it means that such religion is flawed and its corresponding idea of God is seriously impaired. If taken further, this line of reasoning ends with the conviction that God does not exist. If God is thought to be benevolent and human tragedy still unfolds throughout history on a daily basis, it means – or rather it must mean – that the existence of such God should be questioned in a very earnest way. Spong is convinced that God, the traditional and transcendent God of external religion, does not exist.⁸ For the secularized mind of today's society, God cannot and should not be conceived as a benevolent deity who gets involved in the lives of his creatures because that simply does not happen and human tragedy is full proof of that. Religious traditionalists may well display signs of what Spong calls "pious hope", which is in fact a form of denial – denial of the evidence that God does not exist – but for the mind of serious people who are willing to embrace the thoughts of reason while rejecting the desires of the heart such denial is not only futile, but also counterproductive.

This is why, for Spong, there is no God "above the sky", but this does not mean that man has to ditch the concept of God. The fact that God does not exist in a transcendent way does not mean that the notion of God has lost all meaning and must be thrown away. What today's man needs to do is make sure that the lowering of God deprives God of his traditional transcendence, externality of being, and "power" supernaturalism; in a word, the secularized individual of contemporary times should rid himself of whatever God has traditionally meant for

---

⁷ Emilio Gentile, *God's Democracy: American Religion after September 11* (Westport, CT: Greenwood, 2008), 30.

⁸ See also Gary D. Badcock, *The House where God Lives: Renewing the Doctrine of the Church for Today* (Grand Rapids, MI: Eerdmans, 2009), 15.

humanity in order to accept him as a human reality that depends on man's experience in the world.[9]

Thus, lowering God as part of the secularization process does not mean that God is dead. What has died is man's perception of what God used to be for him in the past, but this does not point to an actual death of God. Spong insists that one cannot say that there is no God as a result of lowering him from his traditional transcendence to the level of man's historical immanence and materiality. God, as a concept, continues to inform our religion based on our own experience; in other words, secularized people should wholeheartedly and wholemindedly accept what Spong calls "the reality of ... God-experience".[10] This is the meaning of secularization as the lowering of God: that God is defined as God-experience. The God of secularized persons is no longer the God of external religion which imposes doctrines of everybody; on the contrary, it is the God of one's own experience. In fact, it is one's experience that should be called "God", since it is based on experience that decisions are rationally taken for one's well-being. Secularized persons should be scientifically informed in the sense that their lives should be based on the knowledge of reality as existence in the material world. This is why traditional, external religion is a compendium of mythology, Spong argues, so lowering God to the level of humanity consists of unmasking such mythology for what it is. [11]Mythology does not convey truth and as experience is all about truth, mythology should be dismissed as incompatible with man's new image of God as experience.

Consequently, today's secularized religion based on the idea of God as experience should give up the idea of creation, God's kingdom, the virgin birth of Jesus, God incarnating himself in the person of Jesus of Nazareth, his resurrection from the death, his ascension to heaven, his return from heaven to judge humanity, the possibility of man's existence in heaven with God, the pouring out of the Holy Spirit, and virtually any doctrine which contains traces of supernaturalist convictions. In this respect, secularization – seen as the lowering of God to the level of human experience – is only the result of what Spong calls "the advance of knowledge". Scientific progress is the very fact which naturally imposes the shift from transcendence to experience. Externalism in religion is anti-secularistic, so the scientifically informed con-

---

[9] Spong, *Eternal Life*, 119-121.
[10] For details on the relationship between God and experience, see Jack Nelson-Pallmeyer, *Jesus against Christianity: Reclaiming the Missing Jesus* (Harrisburg, PA: Trinity Press International/Continuum, 2001), 16.
[11] See also Lawrence Meredith, *Life before Death: A Spiritual Journey of Mind and Body* (Atlanta, GA: Humanic Trade Group Publication, 2000), 38.

sciousness of today's people should turn the externalism of traditional religion into a movement of spiritual internalization and theological "down-climbing" with reference to the concept of God. Spong's beliefs are heavily influenced by Darwinism, hence his conviction that humans are animals "with bigger brains"; the realization of our biological structure and status is therefore not only the result of our scientific progress, but also the necessary precondition for the secularized lowering of God to the level of our daily experience in the material world.[12]

Experience and Objectivity

The third component of Spong's secularization process is linked with man's experience in the world, which needs to be investigated from the perspective of the newly acquired redefinitions of religion and God. Fathoming experience is thus not only a consequence of how man's secularized mind understands his relationship with religion and the idea of God; it is man's relationship with himself as the source of religion and the notion of God.[13] Experience in Spong is not informed by religion and God; it is the other way around; experience shapes both religion and God in a way which starts from within the human being and ends beyond his own individuality. In order to explain how experience should be understood in light of secularization, Spong points to the need to define how "human life has existed". In other words, man's existence, his actual, real, and personal existence coincides with the range of his biological life, which leads to the evident conclusion that there is not personal existence beyond one's biological life. Man exists as a person, so personhood defines man's life as his existence in the world. Personhood has played a crucial role in religion and especially in traditional Christian theology, according to which personhood defines the being of God as transcendent and benevolent towards humanity. As such affirmations are rejected by Spong, the secular translation of them points to the fact that, in traditional religion, personhood was attached to God as a result of man's desire to believe in God as external to his own, material, and physical existence in the world. Thus, according to Spong, traditional religion is the externalization of man's experience into the belief that God exists in a personal, transcendent, and objective way. In order for today's secularized people to understand religion properly, this argument needs to be reversed in the sense that man's religion should not be externalized, but rather internalized, which means that God is no longer man's objectivation of

---

[12] Spong, *Eternal Life*, 121-127.

[13] James A. Herrick, *The Making of the New Spirituality: The Eclipse of Western Religious Tradition* (Downers Grove, IL: InterVarsity Press, 2003), 68.

experience. It is rather man's turning his own experience towards the interiority of his psychological awareness; so experience turns to itself in order to find meaning for religion and God.

Consequently, and based on man's experience in the world, God cannot be conceived as a being any longer; secularization turns him instead in some sort of process which, to quote Spong, "calls" humanity "into being". In other words, God is the process – the natural, evolutionary Darwinian process – that produces the human being and also human individual experience.[14] God is a word, a mere concept which is attached to the active processes that cause the human individual to come into being; this way, experience is the result of materiality but in order to find meaning for itself, experience must understand materiality in a way which provides experience with some degree of significance. In order for experience to be meaningful, it has to be understood not only as the result of nature, but also as a reality which is characterized by self-consciousness. The materiality of nature produces experience and consequently the self-consciousness of that particular experience. Self-consciousness, though, is the utmost proof of personhood, so the juxtaposition of self-consciousness and personhood is what makes experience relevant to the individual human being because it explains human life as an integral part of the material world.[15]

It has been shown that, according to Spong, experience causes the human person to step outside his individuality, but not in order to discover an external form of religion and a transcendental God. Experience needs to take a step beyond one's individuality only to be able to look at one's individuality in a more objective way. In other words, one has to step outside oneself to have a good look at oneself and, in doing so, to understand one's own experience in a meaningful way. In stepping beyond his individuality, man is supposed to comprehend his biological life in a way that allows him to understand the naturalness and materiality of his existence. Man's personhood cannot be detached from the material world in which he lives, so experience should also be seen as thoroughly connected with materiality and nature. What Spong suggests here is that man "must recognize the biological drive to survive", which despite placing human beings amongst the animal kingdom still points to man's capacity to evaluate his life self-consciously as experience in the world.[16]

---

[14] For details of how Darwinism determines the reading of the Bible in Spong, see Ann Monroe, *The Word: Imagining the Gospel in Modern America* (Louisville, KY: Westminster John Knox Press, 2000), 25.

[15] Spong, *Eternal Life*, 154-155.

[16] On self-consciousness in Spong see Edgar J. Burns, *Foundations of a Global Spiritual Awakening* (Bloomington, IN: AuthorHouse, 2003), 119-120.

Given man's self-consciousness, he should reevaluate religion and God from this experiential perspective, especially because that self-consciousness comes together with creativity, rationality, emotivity, the capacity to love others and also to sacrifice for others. These features are the result of man's self-consciousness as they originate in his experience. So, in Spong, they all should become features of man's religion. Certainly, religion should come from man's experience and so should the concept of God; when this happens, man is able to understand religion as an exploration of the meaning of God seen through the lens of the human being. Thus, religion is no longer about understanding God, but about understanding man.[17]

For Spong, this whole process through which man seeks to understand himself consists of man's stepping outside himself in order to be able to step back inside himself; in other words, experience begets religion as trust in man, and *this* religion ascribes meaning to experience. Spong sees religion in terms of a journey that man is supposed to take in order to understand God, but since God is man himself, religion is man's attempt to comprehend himself, not an external and transcendent God "in the sky". Secularization is looking for God "in the world", in man's experience, so fathoming experience becomes necessary for the implementation of secular thinking in today's society. At the same time, secularization is man's attempt to picture his physical existence in the world of matter. Meaning comes from this realization and, according to Spong, from this realization only, because only a religion that turns man towards himself can fully account for what the mind tells humanity today, namely that God exists in the world, not beyond it. Secularization means, in the end, that God should no longer be accepted "as other", but rather as the individual human self.[18]

---

[17] This means that religion should embrace humanity in the totality of its manifestations, including homosexuality and lesbianism, which is evidently contrary to traditional theology. For details about Spong's endorsement of homosexuality, see Patrick Allitt, *Religion in American since 1945: A History* (New York, NY: Columbia University Press, 2003), 237.

[18] Spong, *Eternal Life*, 155-157.

14

Absorbing the Sacred into the Profane: Don Cupitt

Religion and Humanism

Don Cupitt's first contact with the reality of secularization came from his firsthand experience with the working class. As a young parish priest in the area of Manchester, he was fully aware of the way workers led their lives and how they understood their existence in the world. While acknowledging that the idea of secularization was first connected with the attempts to promote the interests of the working class in the world, which led to a dramatic replacement of the role of religion in society, Cupitt also extends the use of the concept over the necessity to change "education, morality, and practical living" from the perspective of lay concerns, not ecclesiastical ideas. He also identifies a more recent influence on the concept of secularization which has to do with the promotion of a distinct way of life that was influenced by instrumental and utilitarian patterns of thought. In other words, one can speak of secularization when the influence of the church – or, by extension, religion – decreases to the point that it is replaced by a totally lay understanding of man's life and existence in the world.[1] In this respect, secularization is the perspective of the world on all the aspects of man's life. As Cupitt puts it, secularization happens when the sacred is "absorbed into the profane".

What seems to be specific to Cupitt is his conviction that secularization should be connected with the reality of the Industrial Revolution, when the working class appears to have lost their faith in what used to be perceived as the then European Christianity.[2] A clear "switch" took place in society, when the traditional importance given to God and religion began to wane in favor of a new interest in the immediate concern of people for their daily, mundane, and physical needs. In

---

[1] See also Anne Glyn-Jones, *Holding up a Mirror: How Civilizations Decline* (Bowling Green, OH: Imprint Academic, 1996), 401-402.
[2] See Leslie Francis, Adrian Thatcher, "Christian Education", 264-281, in Leslie Francis & Adrian Thatcher (eds.), *Christian Perspectives on Education* (2nd edn, Leominster: Gracewing, 1998): 278.

other words, the shift from God to man, from divinity to humanity is in fact a transfer of preoccupation which started with religion and ended up with humanism. This essential replacement of religion with distinctly human concerns did not happen right away; it took generations before society's main interest could be described in terms of secularism, so the process of secularization can be said to have existed at the same time with the respect people still showed to what Cupitt calls "Jesus and religion".

At the end of the day and as a European phenomenon, secularization was meant to aim at the church's domination over society as a whole; this is why Cupitt sees secularization as an enterprise which was supposed to inculcate within people the idea that the church "was not for them". When the conviction that the church no longer represents one's interests, concerns, and ideals, one can legitimately claim that secularization has been rendered effective. With this in mind, Cupitt tries to push secularization back in history as far as he can; in this respect, he insists that at least in England the vast majority of people who claimed to have been practising Christians two centuries ago when the country was still considered predominantly religious were not as faithful to Christianity as was traditionally thought. As far as Cupitt is concerned, the working class who lived during the Industrial Revolution was driven more by religious "speculation and ... superstition" than by orthodox Christian beliefs.[3]

Another very significant aspect about secularization in Cupitt is revealed by his conviction that the actual process of secularization which reached a salient peak during the Industrial Revolution took place because people were socially displaced. As Cupitt explains, as the progress of science was being practically implemented in the construction of new machines for the increase of production, people were needed to operate them, so many left their homes in villages and came to towns. What happened in fact was not only a social relocation, but also a social displacement.[4] Masses of people who had been accustomed to "an agricultural society" were suddenly forced to face a social order which did not prove to be so appealing after all. Their traditional ways of life – and also their traditional ways of thinking, and by this Cupitt means their distinctly Christian upbringing – were replaced by a new reality that engulfed their entire existence. Consequently, when people relocated socially, they realized they had been rooted out from their

---

[3] Don Cupitt, *The Sea of Faith: Christianity in Change* (Cambridge: Cambridge University Press, 1984), 24-25.

[4] For a critical assessment of Cupitt and displacement theories of secularization in general, see John Bowker, "World Religions: The Boundaries of Belief and Unbelief", 210-217, in Lynne Broadbent & Alan Brown (eds.), *Issues in Religious Education* (London: Routledge, 2002): 214.

old lives in order to be relocated in a totally new environment. This seems to have caused a deep sense of displacement which was not predominantly social – although this aspect cannot and should not be ignored – but rather existential. Since their former lives had been dominated by the church and a religious pattern of life, what they came across in towns was not what they expected. The church was no longer there for spiritual guidance; the "authority of God and tradition" was simply choked by the authority of the people they worked for.

This is why Cupitt expresses his belief that during the Industrial Revolution people went through a real breakdown which forced them to reconsider their spiritual allegiance. God was no longer available through the agency of the church, so belief in him grew weaker with each generation of workers. The influence of the church in industrialized places was far from being powerful, so the need to believe in God as a supernatural being was replaced by disbelief or simply by a sense of existential estrangement which rendered belief useless.

Man's old personal and communitarian struggle for salvation was also replaced by a new fight, this time for salvation from the domination of capitalist institutions. Cupitt's Marxist approach to secularization reveals his understanding of it as a long process which erased the influence of the church from the lives of people in order to have it replaced by the Marxist overarching perspective of the world.[5] To be sure, the new social reality as drafted by the Industrial Revolution assisted Europe in switching from religious belief to worldly preoccupations. The spiritual world of traditional Christianity was pushed aside by the natural world of industrial capitalism, so man's faith in God turned into a powerful feeling of natural awareness.

In many respects, the old religious patterns survived in the new secularized world but were given new meanings; for instance, the idea of the church was stripped off its ecclesiastical connotations only to be replaced by the community of workers, and the socially oppressed worker was now being seen through the old perspective of the suffering Christ. The "brotherhood of believers" – a key reality for all the people living in the pre-industrial agricultural society – was being read as the solidarity of the working class; all in all, Cupitt sees secularization as the shift from religion to humanism through the mediation of the Industrial Revolution in all its social, psychological, and existential complexity.[6]

---

[5] For a critical approach to Cupitt's understanding of Marx, see Denys Turner, "Religion: Illusions and Liberation", 310-338, in Terrell Carver (ed.), *The Cambridge Companion to Marx* (Cambridge: Cambridge University Press): 331.
[6] Cupitt, *The Sea of Faith*, 26-27.

The Church and the World

For Cupitt, secularization involves the totality of processes which attempt to reduce the influence of the church in particular, and of religion in general, for the benefit of the lay state and its non-theological understanding of the world. This means that all the duties held by the church – and Cupitt especially underlines the church's "rights and privileges" – should be attributed to "non-religious agencies". In other words, the power of the church should be given to the power of the state and, if not to the state itself, then to institutions which function within the state, which is considered thoroughly secular in nature.[7] This is why secularization can be conceived in terms of a "program"; as Cupitt puts it, the religious dimension of man's existence needs to be eliminated by the non-religious state. Such a program cannot be carried out unless the institutions which Cupitt alludes to, namely those which are supposed to demote religion in today's society, are run by people of similar convictions. This is why it seems that, in Cupitt, secularization is not something which just happens in history; religion does not just happen to be replaced by a non-religious way of thinking. What happens in fact is that secularization is something which is being carried out as a clear intention of some people to diminish the influence of religion in today's society. Cupitt uses words like "confident", "well-organized", and "self-conscious" when he describes "secular power", which is supposed to destroy religion in a methodical way. What may have begun as a historical process which just happened as time went by can in fact become a clear intention of people who see the necessity of secularization for today's society – such as Cupitt himself. He admits that secularization began with the appearance of religion itself; in the case of Christianity, one can speak of secularization from the moment of its manifestation as an institutionalized religion.

According to Cupitt, Christianity was initially a "religion of redemption", which means that it was based on the eschatological hope that the end of history will come and a new beginning will start as the world is literally terminated. The fundamental Christian hope to see the end of evil, God's righteous judgment, and everlasting life with God brought with it a very low appreciation of this life, Cupitt believes, so any attempt to bring secularization to fruition must involve a high esteem for this life, for man's existence in the world, and not for expectations beyond it – which for Cupitt seem both unrealistic and unreasonable. Cupitt is convinced that the church was forced to face the real truth that the original Christian expectation of redemption for

---

[7] See also Robert Protherough & John Pick, *Managing Britannia: Culture and Management in Modern Britain* (Exeter: Imprint Academic, 2002), 141-142.

eternal life in another world was never going to happen.[8] This is why the end of history grew to be understood as being "delayed", so once a concept received a different interpretation from its original understanding, all religious concepts can and indeed should undergo the same process. The very process which changes the original meaning of religious concepts into connotations which speak of this world, not of the one to come, can be counted among man's attempts to advance the program of secularization.[9]

Everything appears to move towards secularization in the end, Cupitt seems to point out, because once progress and prosperity emerge within humanity, society becomes much more relaxed. There is a "softening" of virtues, in the sense that the traditional virtues of religion – and of Christianity in particular, which Cupitt deems "barbarian" – turn into a totally different spectrum of expectations. As such, contemporary society is characterized by a higher degree of civilization which is no longer based on the predominantly male virtues of traditional religion. As far as Cupitt is concerned, today's society features a range of virtues which can be seen as "more feminine". Thus, the effemination of virtue is a sign of secularization, most likely because today's society is ready to leave aside its ancient devotion to the maleness of Christ. The life and person of Christ, his sufferings, the stress placed on the importance of his wounds and the spilling of his blood are all part of the "barbarian", specifically male-oriented, values of traditional religion; these days, though, such values become useless, so our society seems ready to discard them completely. This is why a more feminine approach to moral values seems not only the right thing to do but also the natural path which appears to have been taken by humanity as a result of progress and prosperity.[10] All this happened because traditional religion believed in a supernatural God – at least this was the creed of Christianity – and the perception of Christ as God, as part of the Trinitarian Godhead, was a distinctly integrative part of the initial core values of such religion.

Through progress and prosperity, these traditional values and the specific belief in a supernatural God were simply replaced by a sheer interest in what happens with humanity. As a result, the beauty of the world and of humankind became the area of interest for society in general, and the immediate consequence has been the acceleration of

---

[8] See also Philip Kennedy, *A Modern Introduction to Theology: New Questions for Old Beliefs* (London: I.B. Tauris, 2006), 28.

[9] Cupitt, *The Sea of Faith*, 27.

[10] See also Beverley Clack, "God and Language: A Feminist Perspective on the Meaning of God", 148-158, in Stanley E. Porter (ed.), *The Nature of Religious Language: A Colloquium* (London: Continuum, 1996): 158.

what can already be seen as secularization. What followed was the replacement of religious ethics with non-religious morality, so the ethical pattern of today's society is the "moral autonomy of the secular man". In other words, secularization also entails the autonomy of morality which is thought to have been liberated from the constrictive morality of religious values.

Criticism against traditional religious values brought with it an equally sharp criticism of issues such as original sin, gender affiliation, and sexuality. Cupitt underlines that original sin is no longer believed in today, the subjection of women is heavily criticized, the traditional understanding of nakedness, homosexuality, and contraception is also being targeted as obsolete. To be sure, by reversing Cupitt's argument, secularization is based on the specific promotion of autonomous individual morality, the emancipation of women from any religious constraints, the proliferation of nakedness in all its forms, which goes hand in hand with the open defense of homosexuality. The last but not the least important aspect has to do with contraception, which, at least in Cupitt's understanding, seems to have been ignored or banned by the church. In a word, secularization has to do with the well-being of humanity and specifically with the well-being of each human individual as informed by one's individual understanding of the world. This is why secularization is an attempt to rid humanity of its pre-scientific and consequently its pre-industrial view of the world as subordinate to divinity.

Such a perspective on the world is essentially mythical, Cupitt believes, so secularization is a program of intense demythologization of the pre-scientific perspective on the world.[11] When religion is replaced by science, myths become images of the actual world, so the reality of the world is what should inform contemporary society, not the mythical imagery of the divine which lies behind religion. Myths are associated with lack of truth and, by extension, religion is a phenomenon which disseminates lies. By contrast, secularization is the process through which myths, lies, and religion are all eliminated, so today's society is able to rest on the trustworthy mechanism of our material world. The world as man is able to see it without any mediation from the church or religion appears to be the very marrow of Cupitt's idea of secularization.[12]

---

[11] Stephen Prickett, *Narrative, Religion, and Science: Fundamentalism versus Irony, 1700–1999* (Cambridge: Cambridge University Press, 2002), 208.
[12] Cupitt, *The Sea of Faith*, 27-31.

Rationality, Mythology, and Meaning

In Cupitt's thought secularization does not seem to develop into a war against religion; it is more an attempt to push religion into some sort of private existence. For as long as religion is no longer the center of public life, Cupitt seems to be content with the achievements of secularization. As a matter of fact, Christianity – as a religion – proved to be the very origin of secularization. Its distinction between laity and clergy, Cupitt suggests, led to the very sharp delineation of the sacred from the secular. Although his analysis is based on the situation of the main Christian confessions, he seems to accept that some religious movements themselves – such as Dissenters and Separatists within the Church of England – were active manifestations of secularization at least from the standpoint of their intentions to cancel out the distinction between clergy and laity. Any movement which tries to diminish the influence of religion in general over society is considered a significant part of the whole process of secularization. From this perspective, secularization intends to reclaim all the fields of human activity from the control of the church. As the church itself, Cupitt alleges, kept for itself only the field of theology, while other fields were somewhat ignored, they were still under the influence of the church. Their reclaim by contemporary society seems to be an act of normality. Thus, politics, economics, technology, and science grew independent from the church, so nowadays they seem to function outside the boundaries of traditional religion.[13]

Again, Cupitt refers to Western society while no indication is given concerning the situation in other major world religions; nevertheless, Western secularization – as Cupitt sees it – could be a model for other secularizing attempts in other parts of the world. This appears to be the case due to his conviction that religion should lose its public influence in society to the point that even private life benefits from the same secularizing activities. Cupitt is hopelessly optimistic about the extent of secularization in Western society because, as he points out, traditional religion seems to have lost its capacity to convince people of the truthfulness of supernatural beliefs. When this actually happens in society and supernatural convictions are rooted out from private and public consciousness, secularization has achieved one of its main goals. This is why people no longer attend church services, so the actual need to encounter the sacred has been severely diminished in our contemporary society. Something dramatic has recently happened due to pro-

---

[13] See also Amanda Dackombe, "T.S. Elliot's Brown God", 108-121, in Andrew Dix & Jonathan Taylor (eds.), *Figures of Heresy: Radical Theology in English and American Writing, 1800–2000* (Brighton: Sussex Academic Press, 2006): 118.

gress and prosperity, and this is the fact that man's trust has shifted from a supernatural God to his own powers and capacities.[14] The means of life are no longer considered as being provided by God himself; on the contrary, daily existence and especially its welfare seems to be viewed as the result of man's working activities. Secular rationality focuses on what man can do, on his actual achievements for the immediate benefit of his own personal and communitarian existence in the world, so any reference to the objective reality of another world beyond the confines of this one is not only irrational but also futile for the purposes of man's longing for welfare and prosperity.[15]

An important aspect of Cupitt's idea of secularization has to do with the recognition that religion continues to exert a considerable influence in the world, and even amongst Western secular societies. While religion has lost almost all its influence in today's hi-tech society, one cannot say religion has been extinguished. This is why secularization – at least how Cupitt sees it – should admit that the continuance of religion in the world can only be explained through man's "religious needs and impulses". While religion has lost its overall influence in society, in the individual life of men and women religion appears to have maintained its capacity to impose patterns of thought which are neither rational nor secular. The reality of death and man's actual insignificance compared to the vastness of the universe causes man to think in religious terms and hope beyond all reasonable hope in some sort of deity which is supposed to have supernatural features. In other words, man still seeks for meaning in a world of natural materiality whose main characteristic – at least from the perspective of the human being – is sheer indifference.

At the end of the day, it seems that in Cupitt secularization is the other facet of religion; religion and secularization are two avenues which attempt to explain human life. The former does it "from above" with reference to a supernatural God, while the latter moves "from below" as it searches for natural causes for everything which happens within the world.[16] What really counts – and Cupitt seems to push the scales in favor of secularization – is that today's people be consistent in their beliefs. The religious should be religious to the end, while secularists should cling to secularization with obstinate diligence. It is impossible to combine the two, so religion and secularization are

---

[14] This new reality, Cupitt believes, is expressed in linguistic terms, so it is language which regulates man's perception of religion, regardless of whether he accepts supernaturalism or secularism. See Chris A.M. Hermans, *Participatory Learning: Religious Education in a Globalizing Society* (Leiden: Brill, 2003), 94.

[15] Cupitt, *The Sea of Faith*, 31-32.

[16] See also Ziauddin Sardar, *Postmodernism and the Other: The New Imperialism of Western Culture* (London: Pluto Press, 1998), 247-248.

mutually exclusive. It is indeed true that each should acknowledge the existence of the other, as well as the specific attempts to explain reality, but a combination of the two is beyond any actual possibility. Holding to a scientific worldview excludes belief in religion and its supernatural tenets; this is why, for Cupitt, secularization goes against religion although it acknowledges its permanence in the world.

Cupitt believes that scientific explanations are far better than their religious counterparts, so he is convinced that "by and large" people seem to have adopted this worldview. From this perspective, secularization is what Cupitt calls a "cultural change" which, while it does not destroy religion, shows that religious ideas need to be given up as outdated.

In other words, secularization should be unmasking religion as mythological thinking and it is Cupitt's conviction that mythological thinking is not clear thinking. Even though based on unclear thinking such mythological beliefs can nevertheless be held if they confer meaning to one's life; they should not be held as objectively true but, for the sake of someone's individual and personal existence, religious beliefs can be accepted as good.[17] In Cupitt, secularization should take this aspect into account, so while it is the process which uncovers religion's mythological content, it should also accept the validity of religion for existential, specifically individual, purposes. In other words, secularization is based on man's scientifically informed rationality which, despite its attempts dramatically to reduce the influence of religion in the world, can still accept that religious mythology has the capacity to convey some degree of existential meaningfulness to the individual lives of some people.[18]

---

[17] For the validity of the truth contained in myths as understood by Cupitt, see Susan Sellers, *Myth and Fairy Tale in Contemporary Women's Fiction* (New York, NY: Palgrave Macmillan, 2001), 32.

[18] Cupitt, *The Sea of Faith*, 32-35.

15

Recognizing the Indispensability of Religion: Mark C. Taylor

The Power of Religion

Mark C. Taylor is convinced that secularization implies a very serious and earnest study of religion.[1] As secularization designates a process which focuses on the importance of the world itself for whatever is meaningful for humanity in general, man's understanding of the world – Taylor argues – is far from being complete without a proper perspective on what religion is and how it influences the human being in history. In fact, man's understanding of the world is not only incomplete without religion; it is actually deficient without it, since religion explains not only how history developed to this day, but also how man understood the world and himself through the lens of religion. This is why Taylor insists that there is no understanding of the world without an understanding of religion. This stems from his conviction that religion is endowed with an extraordinary power which manifests itself throughout history; in other words, religion generates historical events which have a clearly distinct, powerful, and sometimes destructive impact on the actuality of the world. Thus, if perceived as a phenomenon which focuses on the development of the world, secularization must learn not only how to include religion within its spectrum of interests but also how competently to study religion as a world or secular phenomenon.

Taylor believes that the power of religion is as strong as it can get within today's society. This goes hand in hand with actual or practical manifestations of religion which translate into conflictual and consequently dangerous events that affect large portions of the world. Through secularization, today's world has to learn that religion is no longer a phenomenon confined to religious institutions such as the

---

[1] For details about the definition of religion in Taylor, especially seen as an elusive human reality, see Carl Olson, *Religious Studies: The Key Concepts* (Oxford: Routledge, 2011), 10.

church, the synagogue or the mosque.[2] What happens today is that religion manifests itself beyond the limits of traditional religious settlements into the daily routine of contemporary society. As Taylor puts it, religion is in the street and in the "airways", and the messages it leaves behind are not devoid of dangerous conflicts with fatal consequences.

As far as Taylor is concerned, these days religion seems to run out of control, so the process of secularization should not dismiss religion as fading away because this is simply not the case: religion makes its presence felt in a powerful way, and this is why secularization not only has to include religion within its preoccupations but also study religion as earnestly as such endeavor can be performed. Taylor admits that the traditional perspective on secularization involved the conviction that secularization is the result of modernization and, as modernization sought to play down the role of religion in society, it was taken somewhat for granted that secularization should continue the program of modernization in the sense of taking religion down from its dominant role in the past to a non-role in the present. Thus, secularization not only went hand in hand with modernization; it was also connected with the idea of progress. The more societies grow scientifically, economically, and socially, the more religion is rooted out and thus rendered useless. For Taylor, however, this is neither what happened nor what happens in our society. Religion has never left the scene and even though downplayed theoretically, it has always continued to manifest itself one way or another. What secularization should do, therefore, is appropriate religion as its object of study and, in doing so, correctly evaluate its role, importance, and manifestation in society.[3]

For Taylor, secularization – at least as it appears to have developed in the West – is not a process which seeks to oust religion from society or from its position in society; on the contrary, secularization is a religious phenomenon, a whole process which should be utterly concerned with understanding religion in the best possible way. Religion is a fact or, as it were, a conglomerate of factual realities which simply exist in the world in a wide variety of forms, beliefs, and manifestations, so ignoring religion as a fact of today's society is extremely detrimental to the actual life of our society. Since religion simply exists in the world and should be acknowledged as such, a proper understanding of secularization should focus on religion as well as on what lies be-

---

[2] See also Lyn McGreden, *Luminous Moments: The Contemporary Sacred* (Hindmarsh, SA: ATF Press, 2010), ix.
[3] Mark C. Taylor, *After God* (Chicago: The University of Chicago Press, 2007), xiii.

yond religion.⁴ Religion has its promoters and secularization has its defenders; both parties though should be aware of each other and of the fact that religiousness and non-religiousness are at the same time realities which inform the actual existence of human beings in the world. Nevertheless, because non-religiousness may go unnoticed and thus be taken for granted, religiousness and religion in general could also be taken lightly, in the sense that their influence on society could be inadvertently misinterpreted. This is why secularization should not only focus on religion itself; it should bring under closer scrutiny the whole complexity of today's society as it unfolds in various fields which fall under the powerful impact of religion.

Secularization should thus be a process of tireless research of fields such as philosophy, literature, and art, then architecture, politics, and economics, but also science and technology. These were all listed by Taylor in an attempt to prove that none has escaped the influence of religion.⁵ To this day, all these domains of human interest have been inculcated with religious aspects, so secularization should resolutely perform serious research into all of them in order to understand how religion works in each. As a matter of fact, Taylor's secularization is a constant attempt to spot religion everywhere in the world. A proper recognition of religion is not only the result of secularization; it is first and foremost the actual purpose of secularization. Religion must be pursued everywhere in the world, in the places and domains where its influence can be felt in any particular way. Moreover, secularization should also focus on identifying religious influences especially where manifestations of religion usually go unnoticed. In other words, it is Taylor's belief that "religion is often most influential where it is least obvious", so secularization must include the diligent concern to spot religion where its presence is felt the least. Thus, secularization is the process which acknowledges the key importance of religion in the actuality of man's life and the present configuration of today's society.⁶

---

⁴ A good discussion about the search for universal human values beyond religion, also with reference to Taylor, can be found in Max L. Stackhouse, "Christian Ethics, Practical Theology, and Public Theology in a Global Era", 99-112, in Michael Welker & Friedrich Schweitzer (eds.), *Reconsidering the Boundaries between Theological Disciplines. Zur Neubestimmung der Grenzen zwischen den theologischen Disziplinen* (Münster: LIT Verlag, 2005): 109.
⁵ This is an indication of the fact that man has been in a constant, uninterrupted search for meaning in all the aspects of his life. See, for details, Ronald T. Michener, *Engaging Deconstructive Theology* (Aldershot: Ashgate, 2007), 102.
⁶ Taylor, *After God*, xiii-xiv, 2.

Immanence and Transcendence

Having established that secularization implies a detailed study of religion, Taylor moves on and offers a distinct methodology for this enterprise. To start with, he mentions that secularization is the result of modernization, but in religions terms, modernization cannot be detached from Protestantism.[7] For Taylor, Protestantism should be described better in terms of a religious and theological revolution. Thus, the study of religion is a must, provided that the knowledge of what Protestantism did and meant for theology and religion in general is included in it. At the same time, for the truly secularized person, awareness of Protestantism is mandatory as one develops a sense of religion as manifested throughout history.

In Taylor, though, the study of Protestantism should be coupled with an equally important research of Judaism.[8] Both Protestantism and Judaism are religions but for Taylor they are more than just religions. When he comes to present them, Taylor actually shows that they are religious revolutions. Protestantism revolutionized Catholicism, while Judaism revolutionized Near-Eastern religions. What Taylor notices beyond this observation is that both Protestantism and Judaism are characterized not only by a revolutionary spirit, but also by a profound desire to reform the contexts in which they appeared. So what can be said about Protestantism as a reformation of Catholicism can also be affirmed about Judaism as a reformation of Near-Eastern religions. Secularization must take into account the revolutionary and reformatory character of Protestantism and Judaism because in doing so, it raises awareness about the idea of transcendence as attached to the God of both Protestantism and Judaism. While the God of Protestantism was omnipotent, the God of Judaism seems to be a divine invasion of the world.

What Taylor wants to underline here is that since both images of God are transcendent, they are defined as such by opposition to the world which is dominated by "immanent natural forces deemed divine". In other words, what Protestantism and Judaism achieved in revolutionizing and reforming religion in their specific historical contexts, was to promote a transcendent image of God in a world composed of elements which had been ascribed too much "divinity". It is clear thus that, according to Taylor, the notion of divinity and also the concept of God are words which speak of what humanity believed to

---

[7] See also Clayton Crockett, *Radical Political Theology: Religion and Politics after Liberalism* (New York, NY: Columbia University Press, 2011), 147.

[8] For the connection between Judaism and Christianity, see Mark C. Taylor, *Erring: A Postmodern A/Theology* (Chicago, IL: University of Chicago Press, 1987), 55.

have been sacred. On the one hand, there is an immanent perspective on God which suggests that divinity is to be found within the natural elements of the world, while on the other hand, one can clearly notice the transcendental perspective on God which implies that God exists beyond the created reality of the natural world.

Either way, the idea of God is present in the reality of religion and it does not really matter which religion is selected for study. What is important for Taylor is to establish that religion is dominated by these two perspectives on God – transcendent and immanent – and secularization is the process which acknowledges that religion exists in the world as a movement between transcendence and immanence.[9]

A crucial aspect which derives from Taylor's understanding of religion as a swing between transcendence and immanence has to do with how religion develops throughout history. Religion is not a static reality; it is essentially dynamic and it is not only the fact that one can single out this movement from transcendence to immanence as the marrow of religion;[10] it is also the realization that there is a natural understanding of religion, which is coupled with a metaphysical understanding of religion. While natural religion is what humanity produces on an ordinary basis with reference to (or perhaps concerning?) the idea of divinity, images of God, and doctrines, metaphysical religion is the result of what humanity comes up with in extraordinary circumstances. Thus, natural religion seems to be the common state of religion while metaphysical religion is the exceptional state of religion. Natural religion begins in the immanence of the world, like Near-Eastern religions and Catholicism, with a "theology" which is oriented towards humanity and its capacities. In a totally different way, metaphysical religion, like Judaism and Protestantism, is based on a theology which draws heavily on a divine reality that exists beyond humanity and its capacities.

As the process which deals with the earnest study of religion, secularization must be aware of the dynamics between nature and metaphysics, but also between immanence and transcendence. Secularization also implies that transcendence and immanence are contrasting views, so their distinct perspectives on God are mutually exclusive although they both represent religion in its historical development. The contrasting nature of immanence and transcendence is given by the fact that while immanence is based on a monistic view of God, transcendence promotes a dualistic view of God. According to the monism of immanent religion, the words "God", "self", and "world"

---

[9] Taylor, *After God*, 133.
[10] See also William C. Placher, *The Domestication of Transcendence: How Modern Thinking about God Went Wrong* (Louisville, KY: Westminster John Knox Press, 1996), 11.

15. Recognizing the Indispensability of Religion: Mark C. Taylor

speak of the same reality; in other words, what really counts is the materiality of nature which can be referred to as either God, or self, or world. On the other hand, the dualism of transcendent religion works with the idea of the "radical Other". God is no part of the world as in monistic religions; God is separate from it and works from outside the world. Taylor, though, believes that regardless of whether one works with the monism of immanence or with the dualism of transcendence, the idea of God is practically sentenced to disappearance. The concept of God literally disappears in both cases as it vanishes within the materiality of the world according to monism and as it detaches itself from the world so categorically that no connection with its reality is possible according to dualism. Thus, in monism God is too present in nature, while in dualism God is absent from nature. Secularization presupposes such awareness because religion is the totality of events, theories, and doctrines which find themselves moving between monism and dualism, immanence and transcendence, God in the world and God outside the world.[11]

In modern times, secularization still needs to recognize this movement and Taylor identifies four distinct stages of the development of religion based on the shift from immanence to transcendence and then from transcendence back to immanence. First, there is the development of religion from deism to romanticism and idealism which is characterized by the movement from transcendence to immanence. Second, from liberalism to neo-orthodoxy one can easily see an upward course from immanence to transcendence. Third, when the transition from neo-orthodoxy to the "death of God" movement is taken into account, one understands that religion has relapsed from transcendence to immanence. Fourth, "the death of God" is followed by neo-fundamentalism as a movement from immanence to transcendence.

It is vital to note here that while Taylor works with both transcendence and immanence in religion, his understanding of religion is heavily shaped by modernism. His perspective on secularization thus follows the pattern of modernism which, while acknowledging the complex reality of religion with its ideas of transcendence and immanence, sees religion as a phenomenon that unfolds in the world, in the natural reality of the material world.[12]

---

[11] See also Steven M. Emmanuel, *Kierkegaard and the Concept of Revelation* (Albany, NY: State University of New York Press, 1996), 30.

[12] Taylor, *After God*, 133-134.

The Necessity of Cyclicality

Since in Taylor secularization cannot be properly understood without a concept of religion which includes both transcendence and immanence as cyclical contrasting views within the historical development of religion, it should be helpful to illustrate how the movement from one to the other actually takes place. It has been shown that immanence goes hand in hand with a monistic understanding of God, while transcendence is attached to a dualistic view of divinity. Since for Taylor religion is an extremely complex reality which unfolds in history by means of "symbols, myths, and rituals", secularization must take into account the fact that the historicity of religion is the key to a reasonable understanding of it. Symbols may refer to images of God, which are put together in myths, and myths – once performed over a considerable period of time – result in rituals. The triad which encompasses symbols, myths, and rituals is a key component of religion regardless of whether one refers to its immanent or transcendent manifestations.[13]

According to Taylor's perspective on religion, secularization presupposes a clear awareness of how immanent and transcendent religion works in history, so he exemplifies each type. Thus, in immanent religions based on monistic understandings of God, human life cannot be detached from the idea of a "divine prototype".[14] As the drive of religion is to find meaning and purpose for man's existence in history, monistic immanent religions are based on the conviction that only a repetition of the divine prototype can provide human life with the much-desired meaning and purpose. In these religions, the idea of meaning does not depend on temporality or historicity; meaning is somewhat naturally rhythmic in the sense that it occurs based on various events which end up being relevant for man. This is why monistic immanent religions lack a sense of progress. Since meaning cannot be found in temporality, relevance for man's life does not exist in the cyclicality of history. There is no expectation of meaning and relevance in the future because the future itself is prefigured in the past. Nothing new happens, since the future is only a reiteration of the past, so another feature which is lacking in monistic immanent religions appears to be creativity. The idea of creativity cannot be attached to either

---

[13] For details of what constitutes the reality of religion as a phenomenon, see Jorge N. Ferrer & Jacob H. Sherman, "Introduction. The Participatory Turn in Spirituality, Mysticism, and Religious Studies", 1-80, in Jorge N. Ferrer & Jacob H. Sherman (eds.), *The Participatory Turn: Spirituality, Mysticism, Religious Studies* (Albany, NY: State University of New York Press, 2007): 4.

[14] See also Graham Ward, "Postmodern Theology", 322-338, in David Ford (ed.), *The Modern Theologians: An Introduction to Christian Theology since 1918* (3rd edn, Oxford: Blackwell, 2005): 327.

divinity or humanity. Change is only factual in the sense that it happens; it is not a necessity which can produce hope or expectations for meaning in the future precisely because the future has already happened in the past. There is no desire for novelty in such religions, so the constant repetition of old realities is the only aspect which can turn immanence and divine monism into something meaningful. Monistic Gods, though, exist in immanence, in the materiality of nature, so the whole idea of "beyond-ness" does not exist. This is why monistic religions are fatalistic, because there is no novelty which expects humanity "round the corner" in time. It is not meaningful to look for what lies beyond immanence because there is no concept which explains such a possibility. The only relevance that can be identified within such religions has to do with perpetuating what has already been established.[15]

Dualistic transcendent religions are completely different. When explaining how they work, Taylor uses the example of Judaism, which is deeply rooted in the conviction that a transcendent God enters the reality of the natural realm. Thus, God is seen as the "radical Other", which not only emerges within the materiality of this world, but is described as being the originator, the creator of the world itself. So, divinity is no longer to be sought in nature because there is no such thing as a God who exists in nature. In dualistic transcendent religions, such as Judaism, God exists by definition beyond nature; nature itself is the result of God's work, so man's hopes and expectations suddenly become temporal and historical because the revelation of God happens in history. God can be "met" here and now; history is the playground of God as he discloses himself to humanity.[16] Meaning has nothing to do with this world, but rather with the realm in which God himself exists; God, the reality which exists beyond the world, is the very source of meaning.

Such an understanding of God within dualistic transcendent religions introduces a series of what Taylor calls "structured oppositions", such as God and the world, one and the many, creator and creature, history and nature, revelation and reason, inward and outward, chosen and not chosen, faithful and unfaithful. These become possible because God is not at the disposal of each man and woman. Since God is not to be found in the world, as in monistic immanent religions, it means that

---

[15] Taylor, *After God*, 137.
[16] For an interesting discussion about God in Taylor's thought, see Mary-Jane Rubenstein, "The Unbearable Withness of Being: On the Essentialist Blind Spot of Anti-ontotheology", 340-349, in Creston Davis, John Milbank & Slavoj Žižek (eds.), *Theology and the Political: The New Debate* (Durham, NC: Duke University Press, 2005): 341.

God must be looked for beyond the world, but access to him is no longer available to everybody, at least not from the beginning. God interacts with his people in dualistic transcendent religions, which means that some actually enter a relationship with God, while others do not. Secularization should take note of this fundamental feature of religion, although the objective reality of the interaction between God and his people is not real. One can speak about God interacting with people but this is only a mythological conviction. In reality, the process of secularization should take into account this "supposed historical interaction of God and his people" as a key feature of dualistic transcendent religions. It is the interaction between God and people that confers meaning on man's existence. If in monistic immanent religions, the meaning of man's life is "retrospective and archeological", so it is anchored in the past, in dualistic transcendent religions meaning is "prospective and teleological" because man is supposed to develop a continuous interaction with God. As people seek to pursue a relationship with a transcendent God, a growing realization takes shape, and this is that the harder man tries to reach the transcendent God, the tougher it gets.

In other words, the more man wants to get closer to the transcendent God, the further away he appears to be in relationship with humanity to the point that he eventually becomes totally absent.[17] The transcendent God ends up being completely absent from the world, which sets the stage for the reemergence of monistic immanent manifestations of religion. As this movement is cyclical, secularization should lead to an acute awareness that while images of God change throughout history from monism to dualism and from immanence to transcendence in a cyclical way, what remains as a constant reality in the world is the existence of religion itself.[18]

---

[17] See also Michael S. Horton, *Lord and Servant: A Covenant Christology* (Louisville, KY: Westminster John Knox Press, 2005), 9.

[18] Taylor, *After God*, 138-140.

16

Cultivating a Civil Religion: Vito Mancuso

The Reevaluation of Atheism

Vito Mancuso, who might be called the "bad boy" of today's Catholic theology in Italy, defines secularization as a process which needs to lead to a civil religion or a lay theology, which in turn has to produce an equally lay morality. Mancuso cannot rid himself – or his theology for that matter – of the concept of God, so his understanding of secularization has to include God one way or another. He even speaks about his trust in God, although his view of God is far from being associated with traditional theology. To be sure, Mancuso's concept of God is non-transcendental and even anti-traditional; God appears to be merely a concept which supports a certain conviction in human values such as goodness, justice, and peace, so God must be searched for in nature.[1]

In his thought, secularization – and its corresponding idea of God – is explained through what he calls the "significance of atheism, incarnation, and the trinity". With reference to the first aspect, the significance of atheism, Mancuso points out that a proper understanding of atheism needs to be based on a correct understanding of God.[2] What Mancuso has in mind here is his belief that atheism and one's trust in God are not mutually exclusive. In fact, accepting atheism today goes hand in hand with one's adherence to the concept of God; the only problem here is to define God in a way which fits today's atheistic trend of our lay society. In other words, one's belief in God is acceptable provided that God is seen in atheistic terms. One cannot get rid of God; God is a concept which has been on man's minds and lips forever. This is why there is no need to detach humanity from it; the very essence of

---

[1] Roberto Verolini, "The Soul and Its Destiny: Readings and Dialogues on Science, Philosophy, and Religion – a Meeting with Vito Mancuso and Orlando Franceschelli", 431-450, in Anna-Teresa Tymieniecka (ed.), *Analecta Husserliana. The Yearbook of Phenomenological Research*, vol. IC: Existence, Historical Fabulation, Destiny (Dordrecht: Springer, 2009): 433.

[2] See also Frank Schaeffer, *Patience with God: Faith for People Who Don't Like Religion or Atheism* (Cambridge, MA: Da Capo Press/Perseus Books, 2009), 44.

a human being is interwoven with the idea of God, which in turn has to do with redefining God as a concept based on our secularized perception of God. This secular outlook must include today's atheistic drive; God, in other words, must not be seen as existing "above" humanity, in a realm which is not only objectively real, but also superior to man's. Atheism is one's belief in a God who is no longer accepted as transcendent, so this kind of atheism can be accepted since it professes man's conviction that there is a reason attached to the concept of God which in turn provides man's being with significance.

To be sure, for Mancuso, belief in God as non-transcendent defines some sort of "correct" or "proper" atheism because it is based on a rational, eternal foundation for the reality of being. The wrong kind of atheism is one's belief that there is nothing rational or eternal attached to the reality of being, and when Mancuso discusses the issue of being, he evidently points to the human being. Thus, "wrong" atheism begins with man's hope, which is expressed in his life, but then abruptly ends in nothingness. By contrast, the "correct" atheism stems from man's hope as seen in one's life, which does not end in nothingness but rather becomes one with the reality of "being". In Mancuso's terms, "wrong" atheism is expressed through the following triad: hope – life – nothingness, while "correct" atheism has to do with an equally important "trinity": hope – life – being. What Mancuso wants to covey here is that while both hope and life are fundamental components of man's existence, the reality of one's existence does not end with the moment of death. One's personal existence continues beyond death and while it is no longer characterized by personal awareness, it includes features like personal character and the idea of being. One's being, as it were, continues after death; if not in a way which includes personal awareness and life, certainly as personal "being" and the idea of being here includes one's personality beyond death.[3]

This is a clear reevaluation of atheism, which goes hand in hand with a dramatic reassessment of the concept of God. At the same time though it also implies a redefinition of one's trust in God, but for as long as the idea of being is kept intact, atheism as one's belief in a non-transcendent God makes perfect sense. Mancuso's atheism brings God down to earth because the very foundation of God is the being itself – evidently, the human being – and all its most mysterious depths.[4] Our

---

[3] Vito Mancuso, "La religione civile che manca all'Italia", in *La Repubblica*, 13 January 2009. Accessed online as http://ricerca.repubblica.it/repubblica/archivio/repubblica/2009/01/13/r2-la-religione-civile-che-manca.html, on March 14, 2011. See also Corrado Augias, Vito Mancuso, *Disputa su Dio e dintorni* (Milan: Mondadori, 2009), 227-230.

[4] An excellent explanation of atheism can be found in Thomas Molnar, *Theists and Atheists: A Typology of Non-Belief* (The Hague: Mouton, 1980), 179-180.

secularized society and its overarching lay consciousness needs not be atheistic in the sense that man should lose hope by giving in to nothingness. What man should be doing these days when secularization and laicization become evident in the world is to believe in a God who makes sense of our being; a concept which explains why and how man exists in the material world. Man has to understand that he exists as a being; he lives as a being in the materiality of history, he dies as a being within the same reality of history, and then he continues to exist as a being beyond his personal death. When God is brought down from his traditional transcendence to the eternal rationality of being – man's existence in the material world as a particularization of the concept of being – then belief in such a God can help humanity not only accept death but also the possibility of existence beyond the end of life. Divinity is not a reality beyond humanity; divinity is a reality within humanity.[5]

Moreover, divinity is a reality within the materiality of humanity, the world, and whatever exists in the universe. Divinity exists in absolutely everything; divinity exists in the totality of physical phenomena. Divinity is powerfully, inextricably, and indelibly linked with the reality of materiality especially since each being exists as energy in the world. If man is seen as being and energy, and energy is the source of phenomena, the human being itself is the manifestation of energy as actual, material phenomenon in the material world. Divinity, therefore, is the material, physical, and objectively real principle which lies at the very foundation of humanity as a conglomerate of beings that exist as particularizations of energy in the materiality of nature.

For Mancuso, belief in God is belief in life, while belief in life – and especially in human life – presupposes belief in justice, the justice of life which translates as "the relational logic" of existence. As far as Mancuso is concerned, God is existence itself; to be precise, God is the existence of being, and existence is based on both necessity and freedom. One's belief in necessity and freedom – as they exist in the materiality of the world – account for belief in God, because the concept of God as the foundation for being includes not only the necessity of being, but also its freedom. This is why personal existence as being is possible beyond the end of life; necessity and freedom go beyond one's actual life into that kind of existence which makes being possible despite the reality of death.[6]

---

[5] See also Joseph A. Magno & Victor LaMotte, *The Christian, the Atheist, and Freedom* (New York, NY: Precedent, 1973), 34.
[6] Augias, Mancuso, *Disputa su Dio e dintorni*, 230-232.

The Reconsideration of Incarnation

The second concept which explains Mancuso's understanding of secularization is incarnation; for the purposes of exactitude, he specifies the meaning of incarnation. It is not the traditional incarnation of God's Son or God's Logos in the historical person of Jesus of Nazareth as in traditional theology; incarnation is a concept which helps Mancuso make the necessary correlation between his understanding of God as a concept that explains non-transcendence and the eternity of being as energy on the one hand, and the factuality of man's life as revealed by his mundane existence in the materiality of the universe. Man lives in the world, which means that man relates to the world one way or another; in Mancuso, this calls for a serious reconsideration of the notion of incarnation.[7] As a matter of fact, the relationship between humanity and the world can be expressed in terms of positivity and negativity; either way, though, the relationship between man and the world does exist and in order for Mancuso to explain it he needs to define the significance of the idea of incarnation. When man experiences a relationship with the world he or she may encounter what Mancuso calls a "perfect identification with the meaning of the world". In other words, man is able to feel himself "at home" within the material reality of the world. Other times, however, man's experience of the world and consequently his relationship with the world is not sheer positivity, but rather an acute sense of negativity, because while one's confidence in the world may spell positivity the corresponding experience of it can in fact be utterly negative. When this happens, man no longer feels comfortable in the materiality of the world; what man feels and experiences in such a state of negativity can be defined as alienation, a sense of estrangement which makes man perceive the world as anything but his "home". In other words, the world makes no sense to the human being at times and when this feeling of alienation settles within man's innermost corners of his being, he or she perceives the materiality of his surrounding environment as devoid of truth.

The concept of truth is crucial at this point because, in Mancuso, it defines man's experience in the world.[8] The world must be perceived as characterized by truth if one desires to experience it in a positive way. Truth must be seen, felt, and expressed in the material world in a way which speaks of the world's rationality. When the world makes

---

[7] See also John Hick, *The Metaphor of God Incarnate: Christology in a Pluralistic Age* (2nd edn, Louisville, KY: Westminster John Knox Press, 2006), 91-92.

[8] For an interesting discussion of the relationship between truth and the world, see Michael Gelven, *Truth and Existence: A Philosophical Inquiry* (University Park, PA: Pennsylvania State University Press, 1990), 18-20.

sense, the rationality of the world makes sense because truth is there and can be perceived in some particular way. The world makes sense rationally when truth makes sense in an equally important way, namely rationally; without truth and without its rationality there is no meaning attached to the reality of the material world. This is why the concept of incarnation is of such paramount importance to Mancuso: because it makes truth available to humanity in the materiality of the world. Man must identify himself with the world, he must understand the world as his own home in order for the world to make any sense whatsoever; this desire though cannot be achieved unless truth is somewhat incarnate in a physical, material, perceptible way.[9]

When it comes to the incarnation of truth, Mancuso makes a valid point when he shows that regardless of the actual incarnation of truth in the material world, man's experience of truth and consequently of the world is permanently ambivalent. In other words, man will always have a dualistic experience of truth despite its incarnation in the world; some will perceive the truth of the world in a positive way, while others will sense the same in negative terms.[10] This is why Mancuso writes that, from the perspective of the truth's incarnation in the world, the relationship between the self – the individual self – and the world ranges from complete identification (sheer positivity) to total estrangement (utter negativity). What Mancuso wants to say is that man's perception of the world and especially of the meaning of his own existence in the world can sometimes be explained on the basis of the objective materiality of the world (when this happens, man's experience of the world is positive); other times, however, the world as it is, its material constitution and physical characteristics are not sufficient to offer a good enough answer for man's sense of alienation (in such cases, man's experience of the world is negative). As Mancuso puts it, sometimes man is happy with the world's immanence; when this is not satisfactory, man thirsts after transcendence.

Regardless of whether or not man wants immanence or transcendence to explain the meaning of his existence in the world, what is rationally at man's disposal to investigate is the actual materiality of the world. The word exists as matter, and this begs for the very concept of incarnation to express the meaning of man's existence in terms which point to materiality, physicality, and immanence. Without materiality,

---

[9] Augias, Mancuso, *Disputa su Dio e dintorni*, 232-233.
[10] See also Mark Stelzer, "A New Ecclesial Reality and a New Way of Doing Theology: Heralding a New Pentecost", 13-26, in Peter C. Phan & Diana Hayes (eds.), *Many Faces, One Church: Cultural Diversity and the American Catholic Experience* (Lanham, MD: Rowman & Littlefield, 2005): 24.

its reality and the concept of incarnation which is able to convey it in a meaningful way, the individual self cannot relate itself to the reality of the world.

This is why, Mancuso believes, Christianity found the perfect way to speak of a transcendent God as being wholly present in a man, Jesus of Nazareth. While the transcendent God is beyond man's reach and today is not relevant as a meaningful concept for man's material experience of the world, the person of Jesus of Nazareth is within man's horizon and possibilities.[11] In Jesus, the concept of a transcendent God is incarnate in a meaningful way; what we have to understand these days is that the transcendent God is not ontologically real because it makes no sense based on the rationality of the world as matter and energy. The ontology of being presupposes not only the idea but also the reality of matter. This is why God cannot be transcendent; he has to be material and Jesus, who is said to have been the incarnation of God, can capture the meaning of incarnation in a way that satisfies the rationality of today's secularized society. Jesus is the plenitude of divinity in Mancuso, so he is the "singular event" which is capable of reconciling immanence with transcendence. The two concepts blend in one single event, and as the event is "produced" by matter and energy, Mancuso is convinced that Jesus – the actual person who lived in Palestine and is considered the embodiment of God's Logos in Christianity – not only is but also defines the incarnation of the concept of God for the lay consciousness of our contemporary secularized society.[12]

The Redefinition of the Trinity

The third element which throws light on Mancuso's idea of secularization is the redefinition of the trinity. One should know from the start that Mancuso's idea of God and his understanding of incarnation as material instances of humanity demolishes the traditional perspective on the trinity as the mode of being pertaining to a transcendental God whose objective existence in himself is stronger than material evidence. There is nothing transcendental in Mancuso's idea of trinity; to be sure, the trinity is merely a concept which illustrates the secularized way in which he sees God and incarnation.[13] When it comes to inves-

---

[11] This can lead to extremist, naturalistic incarnational Christologies which support homosexuality and lesbianism as "gifts from God" since the incarnation of Jesus speaks about our materiality in the world as a divine reality. See Michael S. Piazza, *Holy Homosexuals: The Truth about Being Gay or Lesbian and Christian* (rev. edn, Dallas, TX: Sources of Hope, 1997), 76-77.

[12] Augias, Mancuso, *Disputa su Dio e dintorni*, 233.

[13] An interesting discussion of the relationship between transcendence and non-transcendence as applied to God as trinity can be found in David Bentley Hart, *The*

tigating the trinity, and the traditional divine persons who make it up, the Father, the Son, and the Spirit are not important, not even as concepts. The identity of each person as constitutive for the trinity is far from having any relevance whatsoever. What is important within the concept of trinity is not the person or the identity of the person; it is the relationship between the persons of the trinity.[14] For Mancuso, the trinity is important because it does not point to one single person, but to many. The trinity, therefore, is a way of underlining the significance of what lies beneath the multiplicity of persons. It is not the human being which is of utmost importance for Mancuso; on the contrary, it is the reality of humanity which can be found in each human being and, at the same time, in all human beings. This is why the concept of trinity does not speak about the identity of the three persons who make up the trinity; what is really crucial is to see the importance of the one and unique substance, the divinity of the three persons, which takes precedence over their actual identity. The unicity of substance lies at the root of the development of persons; divinity is more important than the persons of the trinity, while humanity is far more significant than the individuals of the human race. It is true that Mancuso uses traditional trinitarian language which explains the primacy of relationship over personhood, in the sense that the Father is the Father due to his relationship with the Son and the Spirit, and this is true for each person of the trinity. Nevertheless, Mancuso's use of traditional language of trinitarian theology has nothing to do with classical Christianity.

For Mancuso, speaking of the trinity as Father, Son, and Holy Spirit is only a theoretical or conceptual exercise. In doing so, he theoretically discusses the relevance of the idea of trinity which needs to undergo a serious redefinition in today's secularized society, so what we need to do is bring divinity at the very practical level of man's existence in history. In order for the concept of trinity to be properly understood in accordance with today's secularized lay consciousness, it must be connected with the reality of the material world. As man exists in history, and his existence is physical, the reality of matter cannot and should not be detached from whatever meaning one ascribes to the concept of trinity.[15]

Beauty of the Infinite: The Aesthetics of Christian Truth (Grand Rapids, MI: Eerdmans, 2003), 165-166.

[14] See also Anne Hunt, *What Are They Saying about the Trinity?* (Mahway, NJ: Paulist Press, 1998), 45.

[15] Augias, Mancuso, *Disputa su Dio e dintorni*, 233-234.

In other words, the theoretical side of the concept of divinity must find some expression in the practical reality of man's material existence in the world. For Mancuso, this is an indication of the necessity that man's relationships should be sincere and total.[16] The more man's relationship with other individuals shares the characteristics of sincerity and completeness, the more one is able to speak of true "Christian" identity. So, it is not that Christian identity dictates the sincerity and completeness of human relationships as in traditional theology. Such an understanding would not do justice to Mancuso's perspective on the trinity. For him, identity is always preceded by relationship, so it is the completeness and sincerity of human relationships which indicate whether or not a certain human being is "Christian" or not. Evidently, the meaning of "Christianity" can therefore be extended to people who do not consider themselves Christians; if, regardless of one's religion, one cultivates sincere and complete relationships in one's life, then one is automatically "Christian" since the quality of one's relationship determines its identity.

In Mancuso, relationship means some kind of investment because the idea of risk is what guarantees its success. Thus, the trinity discloses man's capacity to risk one's personal investment in others; once this happens, the final result is already there. In Mancuso's words, "the more I empty myself, the more I am filled", "the more I lose myself, the more I am able to find myself", "the more I spend myself, the more I get as a result", and this is what he himself calls "the dynamism of Wall Street trinitarianism". This is why he points to the fact that the concept of the trinity should not be totally disconnected from the reality of the logic of economics; the risk and the courage to invest are surely the prerequisite for any success. This is the practical side of the trinity; trinity speaks of relationships and relationships mean investment. The men and women of today's secularized society must understand that the traditional concept of trinity does not tell them anything about a transcendent God; on the contrary, it points to the quality of the relationships that they should be investing in others.[17] That comes before finding one's identity; according to Mancuso, the real disclosure of one's identity is the result of the courage – and the corresponding risk – to invest in a practical relationship.

---

[16] For a possible connection with Chinese religions, see Chün-Fang Yü, "Chinese Religions on Population, Consumption, and Ecology", 161-174, in Harold Coward & Daniel C. Maguire (eds.), *Visions of a New Earth: Religious Perspectives on Population, Consumption, and Ecology* (Albany, NY: State University of New York Press, 2000): 166.

[17] See Thomas J. Norris, *The Trinity. Life of God, Hope for Humanity: Towards a Theology of Communion* (Hyde Park, NY: New City Press, 2009), 140.

The idea of trinity imposes on today's lay consciousness the belief, as well as the conviction, that the significance of the human being resides in peace and joy; true, significant relationships cannot be devoid of either peace and joy, so when these are present in one's life, they are also conveyed to others, so they eventually define the quality of relationships which exists amongst a group of people who actively share peace and joy. This is why, in Mancuso, the trinity points not only to the quality of human relationships but also to the content of the human life as it unfolds throughout the materiality of history. Certainly, Mancuso's trinity is not about God as in traditional theology; it is about man and his existence in the world, which should be constantly characterized by "good-will", freedom, goodness, and justice.[18]

---

[18] Augias, Mancuso, *Disputa su Dio e dintorni*, 234-237.

Viewing Secularization Today:
A Synthetic Conclusion

In the twentieth and twenty-first centuries the idea of secularization has always been promoted in religious thought as an attempt to appease the power of traditional ideas about God as well as their influence in society. Such enterprises led to the dissemination of a determined program of radicalization of religious thinking by presenting the traditional image of God (as otherworldly, supernatural, and ontologically real in his transcendent-metaphysical existence) through the lens of notions which pertain exclusively to the physical reality of the world. God was no longer seen as an omnipotent being who exists beyond the materiality of the universe, but only as a linguistic/psychological device which expresses man's capacity to think spiritually despite his essential material constitution as a being who lives in the physical world. Consequently, the discourse about God and religion, as well as religion itself, were detached from their non-material spirituality as connected with an extra-mundane reality in order to be incarcerated within the matter of the visible world. Regardless of whether the importance of religion was recognized or not, contemporary religious radicalism is determined to restrict the use of religion to the sphere of anthropology, while traditional theology – as religious thinking about God in terms of a different ontology from that of the human being – is dismissed as unreal and even irrational. These humanizing tendencies of contemporary religious radicalism have been briefly investigated through the sixteen chapters of this book with a view to underlining the specific features of each author's perspective on secularization.

Hence, as indicated in Chapter 1, *Bloch*'s Marxist understanding of secularization modifies the idea of religion in the sense that it no longer sees it as promoting a God that exists as an ontological and transcendent being; in Bloch, religion speaks of man's capacity to venture beyond his own historical, natural, and material self. Man is able to transcend himself in a dialectical way; in other words, man is capable of thinking about his capacity to transcend himself without mentioning the objective reality of any divine transcendence. Thus, man is able to understand the idea of transcendence and also think of it critically, rationally, and dialectically, which means that he is also able to understand transcendence – or what traditional religion understands by transcendence – as an image of what he can become in the future. In Bloch's words, this expectation about the future possibilities which await the human being in the future and traditionally explained through the notion of divine transcendence is "a hypostatized anticipation of being-for-itself". Secularization, though, seems to be present in traditional religion despite the latter's insistence on the metaphysical character of God. This is why, Bloch points out, the element of *humanum* became increasingly present with reference to the idea of God and this has to do with the fact that the future is unknown and the only way to access the reality of the future is to live the present as human beings.[1] The process of secularization showed that traditional references to God were in fact interpretations of what Bloch calls the "human mystery". God, a utopian image of man, is described by Bloch as being both the "familiar" and the "Utterly Different", two concepts which simultaneously point to man's humanity and the idea of divinity which is traditionally believed to be transcendent and ontologically real. As a result of the process of secularization, however, the traditional God, seen as omnipotent and savior becomes an "interpretative projection of the *homo absconditus* and his world",[2] which indicates that God is mere a concept, a hermeneutical tool which allows humanity to speak about itself in a spiritual way.[3]

In the specific case of Christianity, Bloch sees a powerful anthropologization when Christ is projected against the image of the old Adam; thus, while the latter speaks of man in his natural condition, the former introduces an element of hope in man's future seen as possibilities that have not yet been actualized in history. Hence the eschatological expectation of the "fullness of Christ", which points to what man could become in the future; secularization, though, shows that belief in Christ must be understood through the lens of what Bloch calls an "anthropological critique of religion". Without such an enterprise, Christian hope becomes superstition and mythology, a kind of hope which is "nonsensically unreal" but it is nevertheless believed to be real. This is why, as a result of the anthropological critique of religion

---

[1] For details, see James P. Mackey, *The Critique of Theological Reason* (Cambridge: Cambridge University Press, 2000), 295-296.

[2] Bloch's perspective on *homo absconditus* is confirmed by David J.A. Clines, *The Theme of the Pentateuch* (2nd edn, Sheffield: Sheffield Academic Press, 2004), 121.

[3] Bloch, *The Principle of Hope*, vol. III, 1288-1289.

which is the result of secularization, God becomes the "hypostatized ideal of the human essence which has not yet become in reality". In other words, Bloch is convinced that God can be described as an actualization of the human soul, which goes hand in hand with the actualization of God's world – which is actually man's world – in the specific case of paradise.[4] In Bloch, God cannot be conceived as ontologically real and transcendent; such an understanding of God would be unscientific and mythological because it has nothing to do with what man perceives to be his reality. In the end, Bloch's secularization shows that God should not be conceived as existing above this world for the simple reason that he has never been there anyway. What really counts is man's hope, but hope must not be understood in the traditional sense of religion as dependent on a transcendent and ontologically real God.[5] If it is to be true, scientific, and demystified, man's hope must be confined within the boundaries of physical reality as hope in man's future and in all the real possibilities that can become actualized in the world. In other words, as Bloch himself indicates, the concept of God can reach its achievement "as an ideal" only if dissolved in anthropology. This is the final lesson of secularization: God makes sense if explained as man's ideal about himself and his existence in the physical reality of the history and the world.[6]

Chapter 2 demonstrated that in *Herbert Marcuse* secularization is seen as an attempt to analyze society in a critical way, with the specific purpose of taking it a step further towards progress. Secularization presupposes the fact that society has reached a certain stage of understanding which recognizes the need to reorient human life from mythological beliefs to rationalized insights, although this can end in a return to metaphysics (not in a traditional, mystified way, but in a way which leads at least to a reconsideration of the concept).[7] This is why, for Marcuse, secularization is described as the destruction of certain values, the values of the past which were held dear by pre-industrialized societies. Industrialization brought with it the desacralization of mystified values and customs because the focus of man's attention shifted from beliefs in meta-historical realities to trust in the immediate historical setting as the only reality of man's existence. In other words, industrialization reoriented man's attention from whatever was said to lie be-

---

[4] See also Cvetka Tóth, "The Hermeneutics of Utopia and of Hope in the Bible", 1619-1634, in Jože Krašovec (ed.), *The Interpretation of the Bible. The International Symposium in Slovenia* (Sheffield: Sheffield Academic Press, 1998): 1626-1630.

[5] See Richard Bauckham, *The Theology of Jürgen Moltmann* (London: T&T Clark/Continuum, 1995), 44.

[6] Bloch, *The Principle of Hope*, vol. III, 1290.

[7] Peter M.R. Stirk, *Critical Theory, Politics, and Society: An Introduction* (London: Continuum, 2005), 52.

yond history to the historical reality of man's experience. As part of the secularization process, industrialization made a thorough and constant use of reason in order to provide humanity with a pacified existence, which also allowed for a redefinition of metaphysics (and transcendence) from the perspective of art. Within Marcuse's idea of secularization, metaphysics is possible as a concept which sums up man's unseen characteristics – such as the will – provided that they are explained on the basis of man's historical reality, not with reference to metahistorical aspects. Marcuse's idea of secularization is part of his broader critique of society, which is supposed to move towards progress, from sub-rational convictions associated with myths to rational experiences connected with demystified perspectives on life. When society moves from a certain sub-rationality to a more rationalized understanding of existence, Marcuse believes that progress has been achieved. Nevertheless, progress is reached only when liberation and pacification of man's existence are the products of secularization and industrialization.[8] These are compulsory because man's needs must be met, and civilization emerges where man's basic needs are turned into a decent life beyond the limit of subsistence. When man finds satisfaction in the fulfillment of his needs through the liberalism and democracy which arise from the industrialization of society, secularization has reached a point of progress towards liberation and pacification.[9]

In order for society to benefit from secularization, liberation must be understood as an attempt to translate its rationality into what Marcuse calls "historical practice".[10] If the program of secularization and industrialization does not become tangible in a historical sense, then the demystification of past, specifically pre-industrialized customs and values, was – if not in vain – at least a failed attempt to conquer nature in order to transform it into civilization.[11] While quite optimistic about how secularization and industrialization could work in theory through the promotion of liberalism and democracy, Marcuse seems a bit pessimistic concerning the practical implementation of his critical theory of society. This is why he underlines that beyond what can be practically achieved through secularization, there is always the realm of those who are not affected by it. Some societies do benefit from industrialization, liberalism, and – perhaps even more important – democracy,

---

[8] See also Timothy W. Luke, *Ecocritique: Contesting the Politics of Nature, Economy, and Culture* (Minneapolis, MN: University of Minnesota Press, 1997), 147.
[9] See also Marcuse, *One-Dimensional Man*, 254.
[10] For details, see Victor Margolin, *The Politics of the Artificial: Essays on Design and Design Studies* (Chicago, IL: University of Chicago Press, 2002), 238.
[11] Keekok Lee, *The Natural and the Artefactual: The Implications of Deep Science and Deep Technology for Environmental Philosophy* (Lanham, MD: Lexington Books, 1999), 155.

but for those who live outside the reach of democracy the satisfaction of their needs is certainly not met. For a wide variety of reasons, such persons refuse to engage in the "game" of secularization and industrialization, which for Mancuso could be a sign of a dramatic change for modern society. In his words, "the beginning of the end of a period" could be the right phrase to convey the fact that secularization – despite its efforts to civilize nature through industrialization, liberalism, and democracy – is not the only program that works in the reality of practical life. This is why Marcuse writes – on a rather gloomy note – that there is no indication of a "good end" for what can be perceived today as secularization, industrialization, and the current attempts to turn nature into civilization. Despite the contemporary level of progress, scientific discoveries, and the complexity of military defense, the perspective of a clash between industrialized societies and "barbarian", agrarian, and sub-rational communities still looms on the horizon; it still presents itself as a possibility which explains the current *status quo* through the lens of chance. The present is here and now, while the future is there and then, so there is a gap between what society experiences today and what the world can see in the future, and secularization is unable to bridge it effectively. Certainly, though, Marcuse's view of secularization – as part of his critical theory of society – is essentially negative in the sense that, while preaching the necessity of social change through industrialization, the end-result is far from being certain, so it remains within the wide spectrum of contingency.[12]

Rahner's idea of secularization – detailed in Chapter 3 – is best explained through its connection with demythologization, which aims at Christology in order to enrich anthropology. In this respect, the traditional image of Jesus Christ as a divine-human being, the incarnate *logos* of God, becomes a way to picture the human being as the God-Man.[13] In other words, incarnation no longer refers to the actual fact of God's Son becoming man; incarnation shows that man is able to embrace the material reality in which he lives. The traditionally divine attributes of Jesus Christ are transferred to the human being in general, so when traditional theology says that God self-communicates, Rahner understands that man is the one who self-communicates. Likewise, when traditional theology speaks of God's transcendence and his capacity to move beyond himself into creating the universe, Rahner wants to underline that such language refers to man's capacity of self-

---

[12] Marcuse *One-Dimensional Man*, 256-257.
[13] John J. O'Donnell, *Karl Rahner: Life in the Spirit* (Roma: Editrice Pontificia Università Gregoriana, 2004), 128-129.

transcendence.[14] Consequently, there is a powerful connection between Christology and anthropology in Rahner, which – owing to his understanding of secularization – no longer reveals the traditional relationship between God and man (seen as independent ontological realities) but rather man's relationship with himself and with the materiality of nature, which he is capable of conscientiously appropriating in a spiritual way. This is possible because Rahner is convinced that spirit and matter are one and thus designating one single reality, namely that of nature. Given this belief, the traditional teaching about Jesus' hypostatic union, which speaks about the unity of divinity and humanity in a single person, is deciphered as an image of man, who incorporates materiality and spirituality as indicative of the uniqueness of material reality. Rahner has a hard time detaching himself from traditional theology, so in order to express his secularized convictions he maintains a terminological adherence to traditional Christianity while modifying only the content of traditional concept. Perhaps the most evident example of such an attempt is the notion of hypostatic union.[15]

While traditionally ascribed to Christology, the idea of hypostatic union becomes an essential part of Christian anthropology in Rahner.[16] Thus, he explains that the hypostatic union can be understood in a dual way. For instance, the hypostatic union can be accepted as a singular instance which refers to what Rahner calls "the highest conceivable event", most likely an indication of the paramount importance of incarnation in traditional theology. In this respect, the hypostatic union is confined to Christology and expresses the Christian traditional belief in the unity between divinity and humanity in the person of Jesus Christ, the incarnate *logos* of God who assumed human flesh in order to redeem humanity. At the same time, however, the hypostatic union can also be seen as an intrinsic reality which defines human existence in general. Thus, the hypostatic union is not meant to single out Christ as the only person in the world who can be described as both divine and human. On the contrary, in Rahner's secularized understanding of Christology, the hypostatic union is supposed to go beyond traditional Christology into a Christian anthropology that sees Jesus as representative for each human being. In this sense, the hypostatic union is not meant to put divinity and humanity together, but to explain the materiality of humanity in a spiritual, even divine, way. Jesus is only the

---

[14] For further details, see Allen G. Jorgenson, *The Appeal to Experience in the Christologies of Friedrich Schleiermacher and Karl Rahner* (New York, NY: Peter Lang, 2007), 147-148.
[15] Rahner, *Foundations of Christian Faith*, 200-201.
[16] See also Tatha Wiley, *Thinking of Christ: Proclamation, Explanation, Meaning* (London: Continuum, 2003), 92.

human being in whom God's self-communication understood as man's self-transcendence became fully realized. According to Rahner, if that was possible with Jesus, then it is possible with every human being. This is why Rahner underlines that the reality of grace, which is manifested in all men and women, and the image of the hypostatic union, which is traditionally ascribed to Jesus Christ, must be taken together as pointing to the uniqueness of God's salvation, which in Rahner is described as God's self-communication.[17] It is clear, therefore, that God's self-communication as salvation is correctly understood as man's capacity to self-transcend his own being and, at the same time, enter an active relationship with himself and the world. Rahner's secularized perspective on the hypostatic union unveils his conviction that salvation is no longer to be found in a transcendent God, but rather in man, whose self-transcendence coincides with God's self-communication based on the uniqueness of the unity between spirit and matter.[18]

Chapter 4 showed that *Eliade's* understanding of secularization was based on his conviction that desacralization and rationalization are the two main forces which make secularization work in an effective way. His main thesis though has to do with the fact that secularization cannot completely detach religion from the inner psychological structure of the human being, which continues to manifest itself in a religious way although unconsciously. Thus, secularization is a process which attempts to reduce the impact of religion within modern industrialized societies, but this does not mean that religion can be totally extracted from the experience of the secularized man, whose unconsciousness takes over the role of religion in building meaningfulness and values. In order to prove this point, Eliade gives two examples of philosophies, which – while attempting to eradicate religion – ended up promoting religious patterns within the very structure of their secularized approach to human existence. First, Eliade mentions communism, which – as a particularization of Marxism – speaks about the soteriological role of the proletariat.[19] Thus, the soteriological role of Christ replaces the soteriological role of the working class, which allows Eliade to speak about the mythological structure of communism, but also about its eschatological meaning since communists and Marxists were convinced that a time would come when social tensions were appeased. According to Eliade, what Marx did in trying to rid society of religion was nothing but to enrich the ancient myth of the savior which is so

---

[17] Jeannine Hill Fletcher, *Monopoly of Salvation? A Feminist Approach to Religious Pluralism* (London: Continuum, 2005), 60.

[18] Rahner, *Foundations of Christian Faith*, 202-203.

[19] See Dennis Ford, *The Search for Meaning: A Short History* (Berkeley, CA: University of California Press, 2007), 42-43.

evident within Judaism and Christianity. The working class replaces Christ, the war between the good and the bad is now waged between laborers and employers, a pair which can be compared with Christ and the Antichrist.[20] As Christians were convinced that Christ would eventually emerge as triumphant, so were laborers who were unshaken in their belief that their opponents would end up being crushed. In line with communism and Marxism, Eliade mentions nudism or the movements for sexual freedom – which are essentially anti-religious – as examples of ideologies which unconsciously share the nostalgia of a lost paradise, so their manifestations are triggered by the desire to restore the state of humanity before the fall, when there was no breach between sexual pleasures and consciousness. In fact, what they want to achieve is the cancellation of the idea of sin, which lies at the foundation of religion as conscious belief in a trans-human reality.[21]

Second, Eliade writes about psychoanalysis, which retains the religious idea of initiation.[22] Religiously, human existence is based on initiation, and psychoanalysis is an unconscious secularized attempt to explain man's experience in the world in a meaningful way. Thus, the patient is asked to delve deep into his or her being, then he is demanded to live his past once again, so that he is better equipped to confront his traumas. This looks like the religious attempt to descend into the inferno, which is meant to help man confront his fears in order to make sense of his existence. Psychoanalysis, though profoundly secularizing and secularized at the same time, maintains this religious pattern in an unconscious way, because it tries to assist modern man in his quest for significance and meaningfulness in the material world of nature. In traditional religions, man was required consciously to fight anything which could trigger his innermost fears; in modern psychoanalysis, the patient must fight his or her unconsciousness, which is the very source of fear but is able to help him interpret his anxieties.[23] Either way, the purpose is for the human individual to become fully responsible and open to spiritual as well as cultural values. This is why,

---

[20] See also David Cowart, *History and the Contemporary Novel* (Carbondale, IL: Southern Illinois University Press, 1989), 84.

[21] Eliade, *The Sacred and the Profane*, 186-187.

[22] Espen Dahl, *In Between: The Holy Beyond Modern Dichotomies* (Göttingen: Vandenhoeck & Ruprecht, 2011), 38.

[23] The process is based on the rediscovery of the "archaic man", which is modern man's forgotten self, based on the interpretation of religious symbolism. See, for example, Tatsuo Murakami, "Asking the Question of the Origin of Religion in the Age of Globalization", 7-26, in Jennifer I.M. Reid (ed.), *Religion and Global Culture. New Terrain in the Study of Religion and the Work of Charles H. Long* (Lanham, MD: Lexington Books, 2003): 19-20.

in Eliade, secularization includes religion as a necessary component of human life in the world. Religion can be acted upon, its influence can be reduced, and its impact can be diminished; what is crucially important though is the fact that an effective approach to secularization must be based on the recognition that religion is vital for the human being. Whether or not man deals with religion in a conscious or unconscious way is not important; it is crucial, though, that secularization should never lose sight of the pervasive character of religion as well as of how it manages to infiltrate the deepest corners of the human mind despite all secularizing efforts to eradicate it.[24]

In Chapter 5, *Schillebeeckx's* attempt to define secularization ends with his conviction that desacralization is perhaps the best term to define it, mostly because it involves reshaping the traditional concept of God from an atheistic, agnostic, and profane perspective.[25] Secularization though is doubled by an equally important process, which Schillebeeckx calls "a tendency towards sanctification" and has to do with the rediscovery of a new religious dimension of humanity. While Schillebeeckx mentions the widespread Pentecostal movements as proof of this "tendency towards sanctification", what he means by it appears to be just another facet of secularization. The tendency towards sanctification intends to rediscover God from a totally new perspective, which involves the idea of absolute freedom and transcends the present time of our contemporary society. What it is important to realize here is that the transcendence which Schillebeeckx ascribes to the concept of God as rediscovered by the current tendency towards sanctification is not ontological, as in traditional theology, but rather temporal. God transcends the present time of our society, from which he is absent and towards which he is silent, but is to be rediscovered in the future. God, therefore, is our future, the absolute future of humanity; one could even say that God is our temporal future, when man's quest for perfection in science, technology, culture, and any other major field of human existence will reach unprecedented levels that could help man find meaning for his existence in the world.[26] This is why, in Schillebeeckx, secularization may mean desacralization and even the removal of religion from man's life; but rediscovering God in a brand new way,

---

[24] Eliade, *The Sacred and the Profane*, 186-187.

[25] For a critical perspective on Schillebeeckx's idea of secularization as desacralization which is seen as unconvincingly inclusivistic and confusing when it comes to identifying the world with "implicit Christianity", see John Wilkinson, "Introduction", vii-xvi, in Jacques Ellul, *The Meaning of the City*, trans. Dennis Pardee (Grand Rapids, MI: Eerdmans, 1993): xii.

[26] For details of Schillebeeckx's belief in the primacy of future over the past, see Liam Bergin, *O Propheticum Lavacrum: Baptism as Symbolic Act of Eschatological Salvation* (Roma: Editrice Pontificia Università Gregoriana, 1999), 199-200.

in a way which exemplifies a tendency for sanctification is nevertheless a clear token that religion is not to be given up altogether. The new God of our secularized society is not only absent and silent; he is also present in our future, in our expectations of total freedom and gratuity. All these expectations will be met in the future; the present time is quite far for providing us with such an image of God. The future, though, lies ahead and is open to infinite possibilities which can become real one day.[27]

Total freedom and gratuity may indeed be the active and present realities of man's life in the future; this is why describing God from their perspective is not only a logical enterprise given the contemporary attitude to secularization but also a desired goal which can turn into something real in the temporal future of man's historical development. Schillebeeckx's idea of God, as it results from his analysis of secularization as desacralization and sanctification as man's hope for seeing God as man's future, appears to be a concept which does not define religion as an "attitude towards 'God', but an attitude towards the *totality* of reality".[28] In other words, God is a concept which speaks of all reality. Trusting God is trusting our reality; trusting God in a new way is trusting our future reality or trusting what can be achieved in the future as part of man's reality. Secularization is therefore not restricted to the present time of our society; it is extended and in fact it comprises even the tendency for sanctification which Schillebeeckx sees as complementary to secularization. Trusting God as man's temporal future and the future reality of what humanity can achieve scientifically, technologically, and culturally at a later state of its history is the quintessence of Schillebeeckx's idea of secularization. There is, though, a final test for secularization and this has to do with meaning. The purpose of secularization is to find meaning for humanity, for the most part in the present; one can see, though, that the future is not excluded. Man can find a way to lead a meaningful life in the present but what he should also be doing is to understand that the concept of God can also extend to his temporal future when and where a greater meaning is waiting to be discovered. This world must be seen as part of man's future, which in Schillebeeckx is nothing less than God's grace itself.[29] Trusting God and his grace are realities of the present society and secularization is able to show them to contemporary men and women by God's ab-

---

[27] Schillebeeckx, *World and Church*, 88-89.

[28] See also Val Webb, *Like Catching Water in a Net: Human Attempts to Describe the Divine* (London: Continuum, 2007), 67.

[29] For a perspective which defends Schillebeeckx's understanding of grace, especially in his later theology, see Roger Haight, SJ, *The Future of Christology* (London: Continuum, 2005), 112.

sence and silence. At the same time, however, man must understand that the key for a meaningful understanding of life lies in the future, which seems to be the plenitude of God's grace. In Schillebeeckx's secularized perspective on God, God's being is not an objective and personal reality. In other words, God's being is not a being; it is man's realization that his future is capable of providing him with the plenary meaning of his existence in the world.[30]

Hick's notion of secularization – explained in Chapter 6 – focuses on the attempt to push Christianity beyond what he calls fundamentalism. In Hick, Christian fundamentalism is belief in Jesus as God, so in order for Christianity to become secularized and hence relevant for today's consciousness, the direct connection between divinity and the human person of Jesus of Nazareth must be abolished. Secularization in Hick starts with a clear attempt to detach the image of Christ as God from the historical person of Jesus, but this cannot be achieved unless Hick manages to convince his readers that today's Christian teaching about Christ is marked by utter confusion. It is as if the Christian church or churches were ignorant about what they hope to preach as the very core of their message, which is Christ. Hick suggests that what churches should be preaching these days is not Christ as God – which is a reminiscence of Western imperialism as well as an open offense to other religions – but Jesus the man, the founder of Christianity. For as long as Jesus is seen as a man and his personal existence in the world has nothing to do with any claims to divinity, the church should feel free to say whatever is useful for its internal purposes. Outside its own backyard, though, the church should be willing and able to go beyond its "fundamentalism",[31] namely its belief in Jesus as God, and proclaim a mythical Christ which offends nobody. In other words, Hick's program of secularization targets the traditional doctrine of incarnation and, by extension, anything else which seems either unreasonable or supernatural.[32] For instance, the six days of creation, creation of Adam and Eve as individual beings and the first ever humans, the actions of the snake in the Garden of Eden – the Garden of Eden itself for that matter – should all be read in a mythological key in order for them to make sense today. These myths are supposed to illuminate people's lives in a meaningful way, but they have no historical character. This is why Hick explains that when the church professes its belief in the Son of God, who reportedly came down from heaven and assumed human

---

[30] Schillebeeckx, *World and Church*, 89-90.

[31] For Hick's definition of fundamentalism, see Tim S. Perry, *Radical Difference: A Defense of Hendrik Kraemer's Theology of Religions* (Waterloo, ON: Wilfried Laurier University Press, 2001), 16.

[32] Charlene P.E. Burns, *Divine Becoming. Rethinking Jesus and Incarnation* (Minneapolis, MN: Augsburg Fortress, 2002), 26.

flesh for our salvation, this is only a story and one should be able to recognize the myth behind it. The myth itself is crucially important because it speaks of how important the idea of God is for humanity and how human beings are ready to believe in unreasonable things only to find spiritual comfort for their lives.[33]

Hick, however, appears very optimistic as he expresses his conviction that biblical fundamentalism is on the verge of being totally overthrown, especially because of its offensive character in supporting Jesus as the only way to salvation.[34] The whole process of ridding the church of fundamentalism coincides with secularization, and the church must become aware of the new situation. Although the process of secularization started at least a couple of centuries ago, the church is still unable – Hick contends – to face the necessity of having fundamentalism taken out of the church. He is convinced that the church itself is incapable of placing together the traditionalist and the secularizing tendencies from within its manifold denominations. Secularization implies not only overthrowing fundamentalism; such an enterprise is based on a liberal understanding of the Christian message, so liberalism is the key to successful secularization. The church, though, Hick shows, cannot accept both fundamentalism or traditionalism and liberalism or secularism within the same ecclesiological boundaries, so the two currents still find themselves at odds with each other. In the final analysis, however, Hick is not very concerned about what happens to the church and whether the church is willing to embrace liberalism or not. Regardless of what the church does, Hick is convinced that the relevance of Jesus for contemporary society does not have to come from within the church; Jesus can be explained without the theology of the church, so the traditional mediation of the church with reference to the proclamation of the message of Jesus is no longer needed in Hick's view. Jesus is a religious figure that can produce a great impact on the world in the future, very much as he has already done, and this is because Jesus is no longer the sole property of the church. Jesus may well be the church's contribution to the world, but he can still be relevant without the church. For Hick, Jesus is a "man of universal destiny" who belongs to the world, not only to the church. If detached either from the fundamentalist or traditionalist image of the divine Christ or from the church itself, Jesus can be meaningful to all major religions.[35] Hick's

---

[33] Hick, "Jesus and the World Religions", 183-184.
[34] See Robert M. Bowman Jr. & J.E. Komoszewski, *Putting Jesus in his Place: The Case for the Deity of Christ* (Grand Rapids, MI: Kregel, 2007), 19.
[35] Terrence Merrigan, "Postmodernity and Sacramentality: Two Challenges to Speaking about God", 106-111, in Lieven Boeve & John C. Ries (eds.), *Sacramental Presence in a Postmodern Context* (Leuven: Peeters, 2001): 110.

blatant optimism is coupled with his conviction that God will continue to enter the world in the future and the image of Jesus will also play its crucial part in this divine involvement in the historical lives of all human beings. This is why secularization in Hick can also be explained as man's continuous expectation to see God at work in the future, as an attempt to see the possibility of acquiring meaning for one's life in a time which is different from the present.[36]

In Chapter 7, *Paul van Buren's* thought revealed a hermeneutic of suspicion both with reference to the idea of God and to the reality of the universe. The only reality which humanity can be sure of is human experience in the world. The world itself exists, as it were, "beyond" the reality of humanity in the sense that – regardless of whether humanity is aware of it or not – the world, the universe in its entirety, continues to exist as material reality. What van Buren wants to establish in his theology is the fact that a connection should be made between the reality of the existence and experience of the human being on the one hand, and the reality of the existence of the universe on the other. Such a relationship can be achieved through the concept of hope, which should develop into a living reality for humanity. Hope, though, cannot function properly without the idea of God, so, in van Buren, God is able to sustain – at least partially – the human desire for hope.[37] At the same time, however, for van Buren hope tends to be even more important than God himself because, while God could be understood as a notion that could collapse in itself, hope should be able to survive such an event. Van Buren builds on the biblical image of God who is said to be "all in all" – evidently a sample taken from the apostle Paul's theology – but God and the world may well come to an end.[38] Contemplating this possibility, van Buren produces a rather confusing piece of theology because, while using biblical language, the meaning of each concept is clearly not confined within the limits of traditional theology. As such, God has nothing to do with metaphysics; his being cannot be conceived in transcendent, metaphysical, and ontologically real terms. Nevertheless, God is said to be the creator of the world – another confusing rendering in van Buren – taking into account that everything can eventually disappear and even God himself may share this fate. As a salient feature of his program of secularization,

---

[36] Hick, "Jesus and the World Religions", 184.

[37] Hope is a central theme for the radical theology of the 1960s. See Douglas J. Hall, "*Honest to God* in North America", 145-162, in John A.T. Robinson, *Honest to God*, with essays by Douglas J. Hall and Rowan Williams, 40th anniversary edition (Louisville, KY: Westminster John Knox Press, 2002): 149.

[38] For details of what van Buren means by the phrase that God is "all in all", see also James H. Wallis, *Post-Holocaust Christianity: Paul van Buren's Theology of the Jewish-Christian Reality* (Lanham, MD: University Press of America, 1997), 141.

van Buren's hermeneutic of suspicion becomes incarnate when he explains that the meaning of the hope that God should be all in all may have escaped even the apostle Paul himself. In other words, man's hope for a better, more righteous, and peaceful world based on the idea of God cannot be fully erected on a certain meaning of the biblical text. The text itself is open to various interpretations, so the authors of the books of the Bible – such as the apostle Paul – may have had a totally different understanding of whatever they said than contemporary society.[39]

Van Buren is convinced that what humanity should be doing these days is to look closely at the "final vision" proposed by the apostle Paul, which – according to van Buren – lacks any "christological reference". This is an indication that secularization left an indelible mark on van Buren's theology, in which Christ is no longer useful for the interpretation of the very "last things"; the only idea which can be helpful in this respect seems to be that of God. In van Buren though, God is not personal; God is neither a supernatural (or, even less so, a natural) being, nor a living entity which acts in conjunction with humanity. God is only a notion which gives some shape to the idea of hope; this is why in van Buren when God is said to reign what one should hear is, in fact, that hope reigns.[40] This is why van Buren's "Way" is the ultimate concern of the human being; not how people should walk the Way, but the Way itself. As final proof of secularization, van Buren postulates the ultimate validity of man's experience in the world. This is what counts in reality, the "Way" or human existence in itself.[41] How this is lived in the actual fact, in nature, is a different story. For as long as people walk the Way in hope, human experience can be meaningful with or without the idea of God. What makes the real difference is life itself, and it is life which searches for meaning either in the notion of God or in life itself. For van Buren, hope – sometimes associated with God, other times totally dissociation from such notion – is the only reality that makes human life worth living.[42]

In *Hamilton's* thought – analyzed in Chapter 8 – secularization is nothing but seeing religion from a different angle to traditionalism. With specific reference to Christianity as a religion, secularization

---

[39] Van Buren, *Discerning the Way*, 199-200.

[40] For details about the optimism of the "death of God" movement, especially with reference to the possibilities of life in this world, see James H. Moorhead, *World without End: Mainstream American Protestant Visions of the Last Things, 1880-1925* (Bloomington, IN: Indiana University Press, 1999), 198.

[41] See also Walter Brueggemann, *Interpretation and Obedience: From Faithful Reading to Faithful Living* (Minneapolis, MN: Augsburg Fortress, 1991), 132.

[42] Van Buren, *Discerning the Way*, 200-201.

teaches contemporary society that people need to embrace the legacy of Christianity within a totally different mindset. As Hamilton explains it, traditional Christianity has always worked with two "intellectual spaces", and it was the reality of these two aspects that provided it, as well as its believers, with comfort. This is perhaps why Christianity lasted for so long in its traditional format: precisely because belief and unbelief were easily distinguishable as well as different from each other. Belief had its rules and manifestations, and unbelief could be also easily identified. The mere fact of knowing that Christianity existed as a religion between the two realities, belief and unbelief, provided Christianity with constancy and consistency. Nevertheless, times have changed recently and the change has been notoriously dramatic. Contemporary society is no longer interested in seeing, accepting, and promoting the power of religion, which includes Christianity, so the process of secularization forces modern people to think of Christianity in a brand new way. This is why, as Hamilton indicates, belief and unbelief may not remain the only two valid intellectual spaces for religion in general and for Christianity in particular.[43] Consequently, contemporary society – as influenced by secularization – is no longer at ease with seeing Christianity in traditional terms, which means, above all, that the idea of truth cannot be attached to Christianity in its traditional acceptance any more.[44] This is not to say that Christianity is unveiled as treacherous, full of deception and lies. On the contrary, Christianity can be seen as true, but not with reference to its traditional values. As a result of this new perspective, the traditional God of Christianity is better seen as dead and Jesus as not being accessible today through history, which also means that the Gospels should not be read as history, but rather as literary fiction. Hamilton seems to be convinced that between the traditional polarity of belief and unbelief, a third aspect – which pertains to secularization – could be inserted: something which is neither belief nor unbelief. Hamilton himself considers his theological position as swinging between the two, so he describes himself as both believer and unbeliever at the same time.[45]

When Christianity ceases to be true in the traditional sense because of secularization, a new standard of truth needs to be found, otherwise no speech about Jesus would make any sense. The secularized world of today does not believe in Jesus and, even more so, does not feel any

---

[43] See also Alistair Kee, "Death of God", 105-106, in Gordon S. Wakefield (ed.), *The Westminster Dictionary of Christian Spirituality* (Philadelphia, PA: Westminster, 1983): 105.

[44] For a critical perspective on Hamilton's idea of truth and how it should be understood in radical theology, see Bruno Forte, *The Essence of Christianity*, foreword by Geoffrey Wainwright (Grand Rapids, MI: Eerdmans, 2003), 131.

[45] Hamilton, *A Quest for the Post-Historical Jesus*, 8-9.

need to believe in Jesus, which does not cancel out Christianity's importance for contemporary society.⁴⁶ Jesus, though, is the central figure of Christianity as a religion; the very status of Christianity depends on Jesus, so in order for Christianity to last within a secularized society, the discourse about Jesus – as well as the talk about God – must be seriously reconsidered. This is why Hamilton speaks about God in terms of death; God is dead for contemporary people, but God as a concept has never been expelled from human language. God is very much alive as part of language, although he is dead if considered only from the traditional perspective of his divine ontology. Our society may no longer be willing to believe in God as a being; this, though, does not imply that God, the word God, the idea of God, should simply vanish. Without God, without the notion of God, the very basis of morality is shattered and on the verge of disappearance; chaos is just inches away from bursting into secularized society unless God is somehow kept within human language in a meaningful way. God, the concept not the being, symbolizes the very existence of human virtue as the foundation of morality, so human talk about God must never be extinguished. God may be perceived as dead, but in the radical theology of Hamilton's idea of secularization, a dead God could make more sense for human morality than a living one.⁴⁷ In other words, the dead God of today's secularization – which is in fact the notion of God, not the being of God – is much more helpful than the living God of traditional theology, Hamilton believes, for the daily concerns of our contemporary, industrialized, technologized, and scientifically informed society.⁴⁸

In Chapter 9, *Vahanian's* idea of secularization was equated not only with the process which led to the death of God and the era of post-Christianity, but also with the awareness that today's society was able to put behind it both the traditional idea of God and the Christianity which promoted it.⁴⁹ In other words, secularization leads to a time in human history when Christianity is seen as a mere religion among many; this is the true and most beneficial result of Christianity – a result which corresponds to the legacy that Christianity itself left for today's society – if one is to accept Vahanian's conclusions. This indi-

---

⁴⁶ See also Werner Ustorf, *Robinson Crusoe Tries Again: Missiology and European Constructions of "Self" and "Other" in a Global World 1789–2010* (Göttingen: Vandenhoeck & Ruprecht, 2010), 194.

⁴⁷ See also Harold Fromm, *The Nature of Human Being: From Environmentalism to Consciousness* (Baltimore, MD: Johns Hopkins University Press, 2009), 209-210.

⁴⁸ Hamilton, *A Quest for the Post-Historical Jesus*, 10-11.

⁴⁹ See Barry L. Callen, *Discerning the Divine: God in Christian Theology* (Louisville, KY: Westminster John Knox Press, 2004), 122.

cates that post-Christianity is a time when religiosity has not been done away with; on the contrary, secularization may have led to seeing Christianity as a religion and its God as a dead God, but religiosity has not ceased to influence man's existence at all. According to Vahanian, Christianity itself turned into religiosity – very much like secularism became an equally religious type of bigotry – and when this happened, Christianity ceased to be Christianity. In Vahanian's words, "religiosity is apostasy from Christianity", mainly because Christianity ceased to proclaim the virtues of faith, hope, and love, while turning instead into sheer moralism.[50] When Christianity reached the stage of moralism, it began to impose itself on other beliefs and displayed claims to ultimate truth; all in all, Christianity placed itself on higher ground compared with other religions and even saw itself as the only valid religion. Such an attitude of rigorist moralism transformed Christianity into a religion of blatant offense – with respect to other religions – and from this perspective, secularization is nothing but the attempt to reposition Christianity where it belongs, namely among other religions of equal validity, importance, and claims to ultimate truthfulness. In doing so, however, Christianity cannot simply be taken from its self-imposed higher position; humanity needs to go historically over or beyond the period when Christianity was seen as the most important or the best religion in the world. In other words, humanity must leave Christianity behind in order to see it as a religion among other religions.[51]

What secularization did according to Vahanian is see Christianity through the lens of a dramatically altered concept of God; the living God of traditional Christianity no longer served its purpose and the offensiveness of Christianity's claims to absoluteness in terms of truth and existential meaningfulness were no longer in line with contemporary society. The utter transcendence and otherworldliness of God in traditional Christianity needed to be replaced by an immanent view of God and an immanent God is, in fact, a dead God. In Vahanian, killing God was a heritage that proved to be deeply embedded in the very marrow of Christianity itself. As such, traditional Christology contains within itself the very essence of the death of God since the death of Christ was thought to turn man into a deified being. When man is raised above his own natural, material, and normal condition, and praised as if he had turned into something beyond his evident condition, what happened in Western culture – Vahanian contends – was a

---

[50] See also Ralph K. Hawkins, *A Heritage in Crisis: Where We've Been, Where We Are, and Where We're Going* (Lanham, MD: University Press of America, 2001), 129-130.
[51] Vahanian, *The Death of God*, 228-229.

transfer from "radical monotheism" to "radical immanentism".[52] Christianity's belief in the deification of man killed the transcendent God; God is dead because his intention to deify man was part of Christianity's doctrinal essence. Secularization is merely the process which notices this crucial transfer from transcendence to immanence in Christianity, a transfer which placed Christianity where it belonged, namely among other world religions. Secularization, though, continues to acknowledge man's deep religiosity because the death of God did not necessarily bring meaning to man's existence.[53] This is why Vahanian's perspective on secularization may be optimistic when it comes to listing the results of secularization itself, but it is quite pessimistic when it comes to what radical immanentism has to offer instead of Christianity's supernatural transcendentalism. The recognition of the death of God may be a fact – even a historical, cultural, and theological fact – but this does not change the equally visible reality that the contemporary world has not detached itself from religion, so its quest for meaning continues to be a constant feature of humanity, and secularization must take this aspect into full and responsible account. In the end – and this aspect is crucial for Vahanian's idea of secularization – the whole process of secularization must accept that man understands himself, his life, and existence in the world by defining himself against the reality of God seen in terms of infinitude, transcendence, and otherworldliness.[54]

In *Altizer*, whose ideas were the subject of Chapter 10, the need for the secularization of religion and especially the secularization of the Christian religion with its transcendent and ontologically real God comes from what he sees as the sheer opposition between flesh and the spirit. The "apocalyptic war between *sarx* and *pneuma*" is the very thing which triggers the necessity of secularization because, as Altizer points out, these opposites must come together in what can be considered a unique characteristic of Christianity seen in non-religious terms. The antagonism between *sarx* and *pneuma* is nothing but the dualism between matter and spirit, but Altizer does not see the two realities as being in conflict.[55] The conflict between flesh and spirit can only be

---

[52] See also Stephen Schwarzschild, "The Lure of Immanence – The Crisis in Contemporary Religious Thought", 61-82, in Manachem M. Kellner (ed.), *The Pursuit of the Ideal: Jewish Writings of Steven Schwarzschild* (Albany, NY: State University of New York Press, 1990): 69.

[53] For the absence of meaning in contemporary society, Tony Pipolo, "*Winter Light* and *The Silence*", 114-120, in Mary L. Bandy & Antonio Monda (eds.), *The Hidden God: Film and Faith* (New York, NY: The Museum of Modern Art, 2003): 116.

[54] Vahanian, *The Death of God*, 229-231.

[55] See also Francesco Zaccaria, *Participation and Beliefs in Popular Religiosity: An Empirical-Theological Exploration among Italian Catholics* (Leiden: Brill, 2010), 178.

appeased in a secularizing way which begins with a dramatic reinterpretation of Christology. To be sure, the traditional image of Christ as both divine and human must be left behind in order for the new secularizing tendency which speaks of the human Jesus in divine terms to emerge as victorious. Altizer is not bothered by the unity between humanity and divinity in Jesus Christ; what disturbs him is that the divinity ascribed to Jesus is connected with the transcendence of God. When God is seen as transcendent and hence ontologically real, humanity and divinity are separated by a huge chasm despite their unity in Jesus Christ. So, what secularization should do is rid Christianity of God's transcendence and ontological objectivity, which inevitably leads to the affirmation of what he calls the death of God; in the case of Christianity, the death of the Christian God.[56] This can be achieved once the traditional meaning of incarnation and crucifixion as historical events is shifted from historical reality to a non-historical and existential connotation. Thus, Jesus died but never rose again, so his incarnation and crucifixion have no existential meaning for human beings as actual events; they can only speak meaningfully to man's contemporary experience as existential images of the divine which succumbs in humanity and, in doing so, the spirit becomes meaningful to matter, to the actual reality of the flesh.[57]

Altizer's death of God and particularly the death of the Christian God is rather a dissolution of God in the sense that God becomes unknowable. What it is important to realize here is that God does not simply become unknowable; he becomes unknowable as God.[58] This can only happen in the material reality of history, so secularization is the process through which God becomes dead in history. The dissolution of God in history – which is, in the end, the dissolution of spirit in matter – is probably the most important feature of history because it establishes the precedence of history over theology or religion.[59] Religion cannot be done away with; it continues to exist, but it exists in history and is interpreted within history. Secularization is a process which gives spiritual meaning to man's historical existence and experience in the world, and the death of God as a representation of the descent of the spirit into the historical reality of matter is the key aspect

---

[56] William J. Leffler II & Paul H. Jones, *The Structure of Religion: Judaism and Christianity* (Lanham, MD: University Press of America, 2005), 57.

[57] Thomas J.J. Altizer, *The New Gospel of Christian Atheism* (Aurora, CO: Davies, 2002), 19-25.

[58] For a good analysis of the unknowability of God and transcendence, see Laura Quinney, *William Blake on Self and Soul* (Cambridge, MA: Harvard University Press, 2009), xiii.

[59] See also Sophia Heller, *The Absence of Myth* (Albany, NY: The State University of New York Press, 2006), 192-193.

which is able to confer meaning to man's life in contemporary society. Traditional religion is useless today especially when attached to a transcendent image of God; Altizer though is willing to believe that religion can be revived if totally open to secularization. Thus, Christianity can be relevant today if, once secularized, it is no longer perceived as a religion but rather as a process which explains how the idea of the spirit can be brought down to earth, in the material reality of man's experience in history. In order for it to be relevant today, Christianity must cease to exist as a distinct religion, so the only option left for it is to transcend its own religious boundaries and unite itself with the world. Such a transformation – which is in fact a disintegration – of Christianity through which Christianity becomes one with the world, the church becomes one with society, and theology becomes one with philosophy, is the essence of secularization as the process which extracts divinity from the realm of transcendence in order to make it meaningful for man's immanent experience in the materiality of nature.[60]

In Chapter 11 it was shown that *Küng* wanted the church not only to open up to secular society, but also to become a secular society. This is why he points out that the church must work hand in hand with secular society, so the people of the church must cooperate with the people of lay convictions. Thus, theologians on the one hand must engage in constructive work with atheists, Marxists, liberals, and secular humanists on the other.[61] Such interaction should not be a rarity in today's world, because each party should seize the opportunity to work for the improvement of our society in a lay-minded approach to social involvement. The fate of Christianity is dependent on the fate of humanity and not so much the other way around. This is why being a Christian these days, Küng believes, is being a man, a secular man with a lay consciousness.[62] Being a Christian today no longer means believing in God, but believing in man; being a Christian today no longer has anything to do with working for God, but rather with working for man. Being a Christian today means believing and promoting the mor-

---

[60] See also Thomas J.J. Altizer, *Living the Death of God: A Theological Memoir*, foreword by Mark C. Taylor (Albany, NY: State University of New York Press, 2006), 120; Thomas J.J. Altizer, *The Genesis of God: A Theological Genealogy* (Louisville, KY: Westminster John Knox Press, 1993), 45-46.

[61] For a view which does not share Küng's optimism, see James Arthur, Liam Gearon & Alan Sears, *Education, Politics, and Religion: Reconciling the Civil and the Sacred in Education* (London: Routledge, 2010), 23-24.

[62] For details about the secularization of consciousness, see Kurt Bowen, *Christians in a Secular World: The Canadian Experience* (Montreal: McGill-Queen's University Press, 2004), 17.

al values of humanity, not those of traditional divinity. It is clear that, in Küng, church and society are not opposed but rather complementary realities. Being a Christian is being a secular person of lay convictions, so Christianity and humanism or even Christianity and secularism are neither opposing concepts, nor contrary social – or perhaps even religious – experiences. As Küng puts it, Christians can be humanists and humanists can be Christians, which – on a larger scale – means that Christians can be atheists, Marxists, liberals, and lay humanists, while atheists, Marxists, liberals, and lay humanists can be Christians.[63]

This is a radical definition of Christianity and a fundamental deflection from traditional Christian doctrines; this, however, is not important for Küng. What really counts for him is that Christianity should be understood nowadays as radical humanism; a fundamental redefinition of Christianity from a sheer social point of view.[64] One of Küng's greatest desires is that Christians should learn how to practice humanism. He even seems somewhat embarrassed that Christians are not entirely capable of professing some sort of quality humanism since post-Christian humanists – such as liberals, Marxists, and various positivists – appear to have been better at this job. It is evident that Küng wants to liberalize every aspect of Christianity, so he is not content to see only the social implication of the church secularized; what he wants is that doctrines, church governance, finances, and everything else be permeated by the lay consciousness of today's society. In other words, the greatest challenge for Christians nowadays is to live as secularists, humanists, and lay persons. According to Küng, a true Christian today is a person who no longer believes in the God of traditional theology, but in the man of contemporary society.[65] This should be the case because Christianity and secularism have been existing together in Europe for a long time; ancient Greek philosophy and modern Enlightenment thought are both manifestations of secularism, but neither has escaped the influence of Christianity, while Christianity was challenged by both. This is why Christianity not only has to live together

---

[63] Küng, *Christ sein*, 23.

[64] For an interesting discussion of whether secularization should be described as radical humanism, see Miguel Vatter, "Introduction: Crediting God with Sovereignty", 1-28, in Robert Gooding-Williams (ed.), *Crediting God: Sovereignty and Religion in the Age of Global Capitalism* (Bronx, NY: Fordham University Press, 2011): 15-17.

[65] Hence the idea of social solidarity, because belief in man means belief in the shared values of humanity. See also Gábor V. Orosz, "Human Dignity and Genetics in a Postsecular Age: Habermas' Ideas Concerning Pre-Implantation Genetic Diagnosis and Enhancement in the Context of Theological Tradition Hermeneutic Age", 167-178, in Péter Losonczi & Aakash Singh (eds.), *Discoursing the Post-Secular: Essays on the Habermasian Post-Secular Turn* (Vienna: LIT Verlag, 2010): 168.

with secularism; Christianity has to work together with secularism and, if possible, the two should merge into one single movement which could be capable of providing today's society with a new morality for the improvement of human life. Very much like traditional theology, Küng is concerned with human life, but being a Christian today means improving one's life through giving up the ontologically real God of traditional theology while embracing the material and spiritual reality of today's secularist religious philosophy.[66]

Chapter 12 proved that secularization depended on the use of the word "God", which in *Harvey Cox* had a pre-Christian origin. The word itself presents no problem whatsoever, but the way it is used in contemporary society can create substantial trouble, which could hinder scientific progress because of religious connotations that create a specific image of God in people's minds. Cox takes it for granted that Christianity is on the verge of disappearing, so the word "God" should no longer be used with specific metaphysical meanings. Reading Cox, it seems that the best solution for contemporary society would be to detach itself from Christianity. This religion, which traditionally uses the word "God" in a way which presents God in metaphysical, transcendent, ontological, and personal terms, should be treated as an "enclave" and – as Cox suggests – left behind.[67] He does not mention, though, what such an enterprise entails; where and how could Christianity be left behind is an issue that Cox does not address. He seems to presume – quite wrongly – that Christianity can be treated as a monolithic block of faith which, once identified as such, can be literally placed outside or behind our contemporary secularized society. Cox also presumes – again, quite wrongly – that metaphysical discourse about God no longer makes sense. In his thought, today's society is secularized and the process of secularization cannot be stopped. He may be right that secularization cannot be stopped, but he is wrong in saying that metaphysical talk no longer makes sense in today's society. Contemporary society includes people who, despite the general secularizing tendency of the world, still believe in a God who exists as a personal, metaphysical, and transcendent being. For such people, specifically for Christian believers, a metaphysical God not only makes sense, but also provides them with a set of values which are ultimate and final. Cox, though, is convinced that Christianity is a reality from the past and, if traces of it are still to be found today, they will soon belong to the past as irrelevant for the secularized present. Thus, if the

---

[66] Küng, *Christ sein*, 22-23.
[67] See also Martin E. Marty, *Modern American Religion*, vol. III: *Under God, Indivisible: 1941-1960* (Chicago, IL: University of Chicago Press, 1996), 472.

word God is still to be used today in a relevant way, it should no longer make reference to metaphysical insights but become part of the general culture of today's secularized society. In other words, the word God can make sense only if used in cultural, not religious, terms.[68] For Cox, this is compulsory given that – as he plainly states –metaphysical language about God is not only anachronistic, but also separatist. In this former sense, the word God turns Christianity into a religious ghetto, which is irrelevant and unimportant for today's secularized consciousness.[69]

According to Cox, Christianity must be integrated into secular culture. The rites and myths of Christianity – and of other religions for that matter – should be explained in a non-religious way so that the inclusion of religion in contemporary culture be achieved effectively.[70] Religion should no longer be allowed to function as an instrument of human segregation. In other words, religion should not be permitted to teach that what happens in nature depends on a reality which exists beyond nature. Religion, Cox contends, should be for everybody; everybody should see religion as a way to understand the world, not what lies beyond it. He urges that action should be taken, so that the future of religion and the future of contemporary society should be shaped in a non-religious way.[71] In doing so, though, he does not say what exactly should be done in this respect and neither does he draft the steps that could be taken in order for secularization to succeed. He does mention that responsibility and action are fundamental characteristics of secularization but the actual steps – beyond merely argumentative aspects such as the disenchantment of nature, the desacralization of politics, and the deconsecration of values – that need to be followed so that secularization works effectively are not detailed. The only thing that can be done in this respect seems to be to make people aware of their historicity. The fact that humans are "creatures ... embedded" in history while their existence is in no way shaped by any other reality that lies beyond history appears to be the only aspect that can, in Cox's view, elevate secularization over religion.[72]

---

[68] See also David L. Weaver-Zercher, "Theologies", 5-38, in Philip Goff & Paul Harvey (eds.), *Themes in Religion and American Culture* (Chapel Hill, NC: The University of North Carolina Press, 2004): 32.

[69] Cox, *The Secular City*, 244, 246, 248.

[70] See also George M. Thomas, *Revivalism and Cultural Change: Christianity, Nation Building, and the Market in the Nineteenth-Century United States* (Chicago, IL: University of Chicago Press, 1997), 26-27.

[71] In other words, God lies "ahead" of humanity in man's historical future. See Judith M. Buddenbaum & Debra L. Mason (eds.), *Readings on Religion as News* (Ames, IA: Iowa State University Press, 2000), 277.

[72] Harvey Cox, *Many Mansions: A Christian's Encounter with Other Faiths* (London: Collins, 1988), 211-212.

As seen in Chapter 13, for *Spong* secularization is the end of religion as we know it. God is not other; God is humanity, the totality of human beings, and — if one wants to take the argument further towards particularization — the individual human being. If secularization is to work properly even in religion, religion should no longer be seen as external and a promoter of a supernatural God; religion is internal, it belongs to and investigates the depth of personal psychology, so God is deprived of his traditional transcendence and exteriority in order to be accepted as immanent and characterized by the specific interiority of each human individual. The human being is fundamentally self-conscious, but one's self-consciousness is — at least today, in our secularized society — totally alienated from the idea of God as supernatural being.[73] Man's heart may be ready to believe in a supernatural God, but his mind refuses to do so. Consequently, man alienates himself from his own being because he refuses to believe that the premises of traditional theology can be wrong. Man wants to believe in a supernatural God, but he cannot, so he looks for "some form of atonement" which is meant to give him peace with himself and thus cancel the deep feeling of alienation. In order to do that, man must accept that traditional religion is wrong and its doctrines are flawed. When this happens, religion becomes a reality which no longer praises the majesty of a supernatural God, but rather the "grandeur and the potential of humanity". This leads to a dramatic redefinition of all the things man has known so far about religion and in doing so, man goes beyond religion — at least in its traditional form.[74] What today's secularized religion should do is search for meaning in the reality of "being", which is in fact the actuality of man's being in the world. As Spong puts it, man's identity is part of God's being, hence man and God are placed at the same existential and ontological level. Man is God and God is man since the reality of being speaks about both but reality can only be one. Since God cannot be perceived by the senses, the only reality man is left with is his own reality.[75]

Consequently, the God about whom religion has been speaking all along is in fact man. Each human being, though, needs to realize that self-consciousness is a reality which, although present in all men and women, is distinct in terms of depth and realization from person to

---

[73] For man's sense of alienation and the role of self-awareness in Spong, see Stanley A. Fry, *A New Vision of God for the 21st Century: Discovering the Essential Wesley for Pastors and Other Speakers* (Lincoln, NE: iUniverse, 2005), 117.

[74] This includes, most prominently, the traditional doctrine of the atonement. See Ron Miller, Laura Bernstein, *Healing the Jewish-Christian Rift. Growing Beyond Our Wounded History* (Woodstock, VT: SkyLight Paths Publishing, 2006), 120-121.

[75] Spong, *Eternal Life*, 205-208.

person. Some people are more self-aware than others, so their self-consciousness will reach new levels of profundity. An example is Jesus of Nazareth, whose unique self-consciousness led many to declare his full divinity. Jesus was understood as God's Logos and Christ, the very son of God because he was uniquely aware both of himself and of the relationship he claimed to have had with God. Spong is convinced that Jesus' uniqueness and the profoundness of his self-consciousness turned him into a being who had the capacity to transcend "all human limits". His sheer ability to go beyond what was considered "regular" or "normal" for others has been told for centuries under the narrative of the resurrection.[76] There is no such thing as resurrection *per se*; resurrection should be understood as Jesus' ability to rise above the normality of human self-consciousness in a way which prompted others to consider him God incarnate.[77] This is why Jesus has always been a model for humanity, because – as Spong says – each person can see in Jesus what he or she can become. Christ is so fully human that people believed him to be fully divine. If each person does the same, namely tries his or her best to be fully human by living in love and freedom, then divinity is within the reach of everybody. Everything God is supposed to be and has been believed so far can be found within the human being. This means that even eternity is part of man's life in the world. God is in me, which points to the fact that God cannot be said to "be" as much as he can be said to "mean". Evidently, as God is no longer seen as a being and even if he is defined as a being, he is connected with and explained through man's being, but God is therefore a mere concept which defines a reality. This is why God cannot be said to "be"; God does not exist first and foremost. What can be said to "be" is the human being. Consequently, humanity can and perhaps should be explained in terms of divinity, so the new secularized religion is no longer about the God of traditional theology seen as a supernatural being; it is all about man and his natural existence in the world.[78]

For *Cupitt*, whose thought was systematized in Chapter 14, secularization comes with the awareness that the sacred, as understood in Christianity, has not yet come and, even more importantly, is not

---

[76] For more information about Spong's view of Jesus' resurrection, see James H. Charlesworth, "Resurrection: The Dead Sea Scrolls and the New Testament", 138-186, in James H. Charlesworth, C.D. Elledge, J.L. Crenshaw, H. Boers & W.W. Willis Jr. (eds.), *Resurrection: The Origin and Future of a Biblical Doctrine* (London: T&T Clark/Continuum, 2006): 167-168.

[77] For Spong's re-interpretation of the resurrection in bodily terms, see also Caleb O. Oladipo, *The Will to Arise. Theological and Political Themes in African Christianity and the Renewal of Faith and Identity* (New York, NY: Peter Lang, 2006), 186, n. 6.

[78] Spong, *Eternal Life*, 208-212.

going to come as promised by traditional theology. When man realizes this fundamental truth, then he also admits that he must cope without it. Cupitt, though, is more optimistic than that, in the sense that man can do without the sacred, so – by extension – he can manage very well without religion. With reference to Christianity, he points out that the Kingdom of God, which was promised so assiduously in Holy Scripture and the church's tradition is not going to show up, so man finds itself in the position to create a substitute for it. In other words, secularization is the process through which man replaces religion with what Cupitt calls "secular materials". In Cupitt, secularization owes a lot to the dramatic reinterpretation of the doctrine of incarnation.[79] It is in fact a radicalization of Christology, which is meant to bridge the traditional gap between divinity and humanity. This is why secularization implies the interconnection between humanity and divinity in the concept of Christ, which eventually leads to the disappearance of divinity in the material reality of humanity. God vanishes in the world as a result of secularization, so there is no need for contemporary people to think in terms of the distinctiveness between God and humanity. God is humanity and humanity can be described as divine; all in all, there is one single reality which bears the characteristics of both humanity and divinity. This unique reality, though, is in the world; it is the world with its material specificity. Consequently, secularization implies a transfer of characteristics from divinity to humanity and vice versa. The sacredness of God should no longer be searched for outside the world, but in the world and specifically in the human being.[80] For Cupitt, there is no sacredness outside the human being, so whatever is sacred exists in the world and is practically manifested in the human being. Man is the full measure of the divine, and this is the very essence of secularization.[81]

With the dispersion of divinity into humanity comes the loss of identity. Religion and implicitly the very concept of God lose their traditional identity as supernatural realities. Religion no longer proclaims a God which exists beyond the world; the realization of the dispersion of divinity into the world and the actuality of man's existence helps man to understand that redemption depends on this new understanding. Whoever wishes to be redeemed must nowadays

---

[79] Details of Cupitt's understanding of incarnation can be found in Herbert McCabe, *God Matters* (London: Continuum, 2005), 60-61.
[80] Linda Woodhead, "Theology: The Trouble It's In", 173-186, in Gavin Hyman (ed.), *New Directions in Philosophical Theology. Essays in Honour of Don Cupitt* (Aldershot: Ashgate, 2004): 176.
[81] Don Cupitt, *Is Nothing Sacred? The Non-Realist Philosophy of Religion: Selected Essays* (New York: NY: Fordham University Press, 2002), 66.

change his or her view of God from supernaturalism to materialism. God is still valid and useful as a concept provided that it helps us cope with our materiality. Such dramatic reassessment of the concept of God is possible only when man is ready to accept God's existence as non-realist. In other words, God as a supernatural being does not exist in reality; God exists only as a concept in man's mind, which means that his existence is profoundly non-realistic.[82] This is a clear indication of the fact that secularization goes hand in hand with religion, but not with traditional religion. Religion can be said to accompany and even support secularization if its understanding of God is based on non-realist convictions. A persistence of religion is possible within secularization provided that doctrines are reconsidered from a thoroughly human perspective. Thus, one can even speak of a secularized religion whose doctrine of revelation promotes the idea that God is disclosed in the human being or, as Cupitt puts it, God is "hidden in human form". Clearly, in Cupitt, God is no longer the concrete God of traditional theology which pictures him as an objectively real and personal being, but rather the "Abstract Sacred" of today's rationalistic and scientific way of thinking.[83] From this perspective, secularization is the critical acceptance that, as a human system of thought, religion is fictional and mythological, so what man understands by the concept of God should not point to a reality beyond the world, but to the world itself, to the human being, and to his complex existence in the materiality of nature.[84]

In *Taylor's* understanding of religion – presented succinctly in Chapter 15 – secularization is the awareness which sees religion as a cyclical movement between transcendence and immanence. It is crucial to apprehend the fact that, either way, God is supposed to disappear from religion, so religion works with a concept of God which is based on his remoteness, rather than his closeness. For Taylor, secularization has to do with accepting religion based on the idea of God's absence regardless of whether one deals with immanent religions anchored in monistic images of God or with transcendental religions resulting from dualistic perspectives on God. So, in Taylor, the idea of God's disappearance defines not only the movement from immanence to transcendence and from monism to dualism, but also the very core principle of religion. God can be present as in monistic immanent religions or he can be absent as in dualistic transcendent religions; ei-

---

[82] See also Grahame Miles, *Science and Religious Experience: Are They Similar Forms of Knowledge?* (Eastbourne: Sussex Academic Press, 2007), 230.

[83] See Dennis Lines, *Spirituality in Counseling and Psychotherapy* (London: Sage, 2006), 38.

[84] Cupitt, *Is Nothing Sacred?*, 67-70.

ther way God slowly but surely disappears from religion because in monistic immanent religions he is too present in the world, while in dualistic transcendent religions he is too absent. When God is too present, people get used to him; when he is too absent, people forget about him. This is how, in Taylor, both the concept of God's presence and that of God's absence eventually lead to the fact of God's disappearance from religion.[85] Secularization, therefore, must take into account the reality of God's disappearance and think of religion in both atheistic and theistic terms. Taylor's idea of secularization has enough room left for both, so irrespective of one's approach to God, the reality of religion is preserved and duly acknowledged throughout the world for as long as the concept of God is used in any way. Thus, in Taylor, what is important has to do with how one deals with the idea of God; whether God is seen as present in theistic terms or is accepted as absent in a specifically atheistic way is not important. Religion is present in the world and manifests itself in today's society with or without God's presence.[86] What needs to be there in one's approach to religion is the very concept of God, and this is what turns a certain discourse into active religion. Secularization must embrace this fact that religion works with the concept of God, which is used in wide variety of ways. This is why religion is in fact man's religious imagination which informs culture.[87]

Today's secularization should be aware of the power that can be exerted by man's religious imagination over culture by the impact of its "critical reflections" and "constructive arguments". Thus, for Taylor, for as long as religion leads to constructive criticism, it must be embraced as a fundamental human characteristic. This is in fact what secularization should be doing in contemporary society. Religion works with symbols, and symbols create relations; this is how cultures are created and religion is part of the construction of human culture.[88] Secularization should accept the role of religion in building human culture and also promote it in today's society. The acknowledgment and promotion of religion through secularization needs, however, to meet an important standard, and this is to take religion beyond what Taylor calls "the confines of the church, university, and museum". In

---

[85] Amy Hungerford, *Postmodern Belief: American Literature and Religion since 1960* (Princeton, NJ: Princeton University Press, 2010), 18.
[86] For details about how God's presence or absence determine the meaning of religion, see Jill Robbins, *Altered Reading: Levinas and Literature* (Chicago, IL: Chicago University Press, 1999), 35.
[87] Taylor, *After God*, 181.
[88] See also Russell R. Manning, *Theology at the End of Culture: Paul Tillich's Theology of Culture and Art* (Leuven: Peeters, 2005), 188-189.

order for religion to be useful today, it must go beyond its traditional contexts, which for Taylor seem to be rather theoretical. It is as if he is suggesting that religion is irrelevant if kept in the church and universities. The reference to museum deciphers his understanding of traditional religion as a theoretical construct which has no relevance or impact in today's practical, scientific, and technological society. This is why secularization is the process which turns religion from theoretical insights into practical realities. Thus, once extracted from its traditional theoretical background represented by the church, universities, and museums, religion is free to manifest itself practically in the much more active domains of politics, economy, and technology.[89] Such an understanding of religion presents the world with a twofold expectation: on the one hand, there is the threat of global collapse since religion can take a wrong turn if used fanatically in combination with modern science; on the other hand, though, there is what Taylor dubs "the only hope that remains", which is preserved within the very idea of "creative emergence". If religion develops alongside today's society by embracing the contemporary scientific outlook on man's existence, if it is able to embrace both theism and atheism as equally important and relevant perspectives on God's disappearance, then secularization has fulfilled its purpose.[90]

Chapter 16 explained that, for *Mancuso*, secularization is nothing but bringing God to the level of humanity. It is a whole process through which the traditional God of Christianity, the one whose personal existence transcends the whole universe seen as his creation, is lowered to the material reality of our physical world and subjective consciousness.[91] Whatever happens in the world with human beings is in fact what happens with God as well. As far as Mancuso is concerned, this is the civil religion or the lay theology which results from today's process of secularization, but the very same way secularization begets civil religion or lay theology, one notices that civil religion itself produces a certain type of ethics that professes the same justice for all. Mancuso's secularization thus ends with a call for justice, the kind of justice which applies equally to God and the human being. To be sure, however, God is the human being, at least from the perspective of what Mancuso calls "being"; the energy which runs through the universe and gets particularized in ordained phenomena such as the human being

---

[89] For the religious nature of contemporary society in Taylor, see Morten T. Højsgaard, "Cyber-religion: On the Cutting Edge between the Virtual and the Real", 50-64, in Morten T. Højsgaard & Margit Warburg (eds.), *Religion and Cyberspace* (Oxford: Routledge, 2005): 61.

[90] Taylor, *After God*, 185.

[91] Steve Bruce, *God is Dead: Secularization in the West* (Oxford: Blackwell, 2003), 208-209.

itself. Beyond the materiality of the human being itself, God is nothing but a concept which reminds humanity of the need for justice, goodness, and peace as the necessary results of the process of secularization. When man rids himself of the transcendent God of traditional theology and embraces his divinity within the reality of the physical nature, the origin of divinity and consequently of spirituality is matter itself. Once one acknowledges this reality, one is no longer afraid of criticism and freedom, as Mancuso himself confesses. He insists that having realized that God needs to be brought to the level of humanity so that the same justice is applied to God and humanity, his faith increased as an "exercise of criticism and freedom". Secularization is thus the process through which God is brought to the level of humanity as a result of criticism applied to the traditional concept of God in freedom.[92] Man must acquire for himself the freedom which allows him to approach God in a critical way; the result is man's capacity to think of God in civil or lay terms, which in turn provides him with common lay ethics for every single human being. Such a realization pushes the individual self beyond the boundaries and influence of the church; Mancuso himself says that since his liberation from the traditional understanding of God, he is a free human being, who has no *missio canonica* – a reference to the fact that traditional Catholics must follow the doctrine of the church whenever they teach theology – no willingness to defend the church or to act as subordinate to anybody at all. Secularization is professing one's own thinking in total freedom; this is the dogma of the secularized man, namely the freedom of research in all fields, "from molecular biology to theology".[93]

Secularization is therefore the fight for complete freedom in all fields with a view to helping man understand his being and God as part of the world.[94] Humanity, all human beings for that matter, should live for life, for the improvement of their own individual lives as well for the benefit of the lives of others. The secularized mind of today's human being must understand that one's fight for life – and consequently for peace, justice, and goodness – is bound to be victorious and such an endeavor takes one's life beyond itself and even beyond one's death into the pure reality of being as energy. Secularization happens when our lay consciousness understands that God must exist within humanity; the concept of God should relentlessly inform man's materiality and

---

[92] Heinrich Fries, *Fundamental Theology*, trans. Robert J. Daly, SJ (Washington, DC: The Catholic University of America Press, 1996), 207-209.
[93] Augias, Mancuso, *Disputa su Dio e dintorni*, 247-248.
[94] See Stanley J. Grenz & Roger E. Olson, *Twentieth Century Theology: God and the World in a Transitional Age* (Downers Grove, IL: InterVarsity Press, 1992), 165.

his very existence. God cannot be cancelled out by humanity; he can only be brought to the level of humanity. As a concept, God can never be extinguished and should never be cast away because it represents the very essence of man's existence in the world. Religion, therefore, must continue to speak about man's spirituality but only if it explains man's existence in close connection with the world and, of course, if God as a concept is confined by a spirituality which is not detached from materiality. Secularization presupposes that the religions of the world remain right and valid in themselves because they all point to the same spiritual reality of man's material existence in the world.[95] In order to do this, Christianity – and any other world religion for that matter – must preach the reality of love, the only proof that the concept of God is still valid and helps humanity understand its existence in the material world as an attempt to spread the ethics of goodness, justice, and peace. For any secularized person, all these are embodied in the life of Jesus of Nazareth, the man who showed that God is within the reach of every human being when, based on love, a common morality for all is searched for in justice and peace.[96]

---

[95] See also D.H.-W. Gensichen, "World Community and World Religions", 27-37, in J.S. Pobee (ed.), *Religion in a Pluralistic Society. Essays Presented to Professor C.G. Baëta* (Leiden: Brill, 1976): 30.

[96] Augias, Mancuso, *Disputa su Dio e dintorni*, 249-254.

Bibliography

Abdul-Masih, Marguerite. *Edward Schillebeeckx and Hans Frei. A Conversation on Method and Christology*. Waterloo, ON: Wilfrid Laurier University Press, 2001.
Agger, Ben. *The Discourse of Domination. From the Frankfurt School to Postmodernism*. Evanston, IL: Northwestern University Press, 1992.
Allen, Douglas. *Myth and Religion in Mircea Eliade*. London: Routledge, 2002.
——— , *Structure and Creativity in Religion. Hermeneutics in Mircea Eliade's Phenomenology and New Directions*. The Hague: Mouton, 1978.
Allitt, Patrick. *Religion in American Since 1945. A History*. New York, NY: Columbia University Press, 2003.
Rego, Aloysius, OCD. *Suffering and Salvation. The Salvific Meaning of Suffering in the Later Theology of Edward Schillebeeckx*. Louvain and Grand Rapids, MI: Peeters Press and Eerdmans, 2006.
Altizer, Thomas J.J. *Living the Death of God. A Theological Memoir*, foreword by Mark C. Taylor. Albany, NY: State University of New York Press, 2006.
——— , *The Contemporary Jesus*. Albany, NY: State University of New York Press, 1997.
——— , *The Genesis of God. A Theological Genealogy*. Louisville, KY: Westminster John Knox Press, 1993.
——— , *The Gospel of Christian Atheism*. Louisville, KY: Westminster, 1966.
——— , *The New Gospel of Christian Atheism*. Aurora, CO: The Davies Group, 2002.
——— & William Hamilton, *Radical Theology and the Death of God*. Indianapolis, IN: Bobs-Merrill, 1966.
Anderson, Ronald D. *Religion and Spirituality in the Public School Curriculum*. New York, NY: Peter Lang, 2004.
Arthur, James, Liam Gearon & Alan Sears, *Education, Politics, and Religion. Reconciling the Civil and the Sacred in Education*. London: Routledge, 2010.
Asa, Robert. "Classic *Star Trek* and the Death of God. A Case Study of '*Who Mourns for Adonais?*'," in Jennifer E. Porter & Darcee L. McLaren, eds. *Star Trek and Sacred Ground. Explorations of Star Trek, Religion, and American Culture*. Albany, NY: State University of New York Press, 1999: 33-60.
Augias, Corrado & Vito Mancuso. *Disputa su Dio e dintorni*. Milan: Mondadori, 2009.
Badcock, Gary D. *The House where God Lives. Renewing the Doctrine of the Church for Today*. Grand Rapids, MI: Eerdmans, 2009.

Bauckham, Richard. *The Theology of Jürgen Moltmann.* London: T&T Clark/Continuum, 1995.
Baum, Gregory. *The Twentieth Century. A Theological Overview.* London: Continuum, 1999.
Beardslee, William A. *A House for Hope. A Study in Process and Biblical Thought.* Philadelphia, PA: Westminster, 1999.
Bent, Charles N., SJ. *The Death of God Movement. A Study of Gabriel Vahanian, Paul van Buren, William Hamilton, and Thomas J. J. Altizer.* Mahwah, NJ: Paulist Press, 1967.
Bentley Hart, David. *The Beauty of the Infinite. The Aesthetics of Christian Truth.* Grand Rapids, MI: Eerdmans, 2003.
Bergin, Liam. *O Propheticum Lavacrum. Baptism as Symbolic Act of Eschatological Salvation.* Rome: Editrice Pontificia Università Gregoriana, 1999.
Birkeland, Inger J. *Making Place, Making Self. Travel, Subjectivity, and Sexual Difference.* Aldershot: Ashgate, 2005.
Blenkinsopp, Joseph. *Treasures Old and New. Essays in the Theology of the Pentateuch.* Grand Rapids, MI: Eerdmans, 2004.
Bloch, Ernst. *The Principle of Hope,* vol. III. Cambridge, MA: The Massachusetts Institute of Technology Press, 1995; originally published as Ernst Bloch, *Das Prinzip Hoffnung.* Frankfurt am Main: Suhrkamp, 1959.
Bloesch, Donald G. *A Theology of Word and Spirit. Authority and Method in Theology.* Downers Grove, IL: InterVarsity Press, 1992.
Boer, Roland. *Criticism of Heaven. On Marxism and Theology.* Leiden: Brill, 2007.
Boggs, Carl. *The End of Politics. Corporate Power and the Decline of the Public Sphere.* New York, NY: Guilford Press, 2000.
Booker, M. Keith. *The Post-Utopian Imagination. American Culture in the Long 1950s.* Westport, CT: Greenwood, 2002.
Borgman, Erick. *Edward Schillebeeckx. A Theologian in His History,* trans. John Bowden. London: Continuum.
Borowitz, Eugene B. *Exploring Jewish Ethics. Papers on Covenant Responsibility.* Detroit, MI: Wayne State University Press, 1990.
Bottici, Chiara. *A Philosophy of Political Truth.* Cambridge: Cambridge University Press, 2007.
Bowen, Kurt. *Christians in a Secular World. The Canadian Experience.* Montreal: McGill-Queen's University Press, 2004.
Bowker, John. "World Religions. The Boundaries of Belief and Unbelief". In: Lynne Broadbent, Alan Brown, eds. *Issues in Religious Education.* London: Routledge, 2002: 210-217.
Bowman, Robert M. Jr. & J.E. Komoszewski. *Putting Jesus in his Place. The Case for the Deity of Christ.* Grand Rapids, MI: Kregel, 2007.
Braaten, Carl E. "The Crux of Christianity's Case. The Resurrection of Jesus". In: Michael Shahan, ed. *A Report from the Front Lines: Conversations on Public Theology. A Festschrift in Honor of Robert Benne.* Grand Rapids, MI: Eerdmans, 2009: 23-34.
Braiterman, Zachary. *(God) after Auschwitz. Tradition and Change in Post-Holocaust Jewish Thought.* Princeton, NJ: Princeton University Press, 1998.
Brenkert, George G. *Political Freedom.* London: Routledge, 1991.
Bruce, Steve. *God is Dead. Secularization in the West.* Oxford: Blackwell, 2003.

Brueggemann, Walter. *Interpretation and Obedience. From Faithful Reading to Faithful Living*. Minneapolis, MN: Augsburg Fortress, 1991.
Buddenbaum, Judith M. & Debra L. Mason, eds. *Readings on Religion as News*. Ames, IA: Iowa State University Press, 2000.
Burns, Charlene P.E. *Divine Becoming. Rethinking Jesus and Incarnation*. Minneapolis, MN: Augsburg Fortress, 2002.
Burns, Edgar J. *Foundations of a Global Spiritual Awakening*. Bloomington, IN: AuthorHouse, 2003.
Callen, Barry L. *Discerning the Divine. God in Christian Theology*. Louisville, KY: Westminster John Knox Press, 2004.
Caputo, John D. "Spectral Hermeneutics: On the Weakness of God in the Theology of the Event". In: John D. Caputo & Gianni Vattimo, *After the Death of God*, edited by Jeffrey W. Robbins. New York, NY: Columbia University Press, 2007: 47-88.
Carson, D.A. *The Gagging of God. Christianity Confronts Pluralism*. Grand Rapids, MI: Zondervan, 1996.
Chapelle, Daniel. *Nietzsche and Psychoanalysis*. Albany, NY: State University of New York Press, 1993.
Charlesworth, James H. "Resurrection: The Dead Sea Scrolls and the New Testament". In: James H. Charlesworth, C.D. Elledge, J.L. Crenshaw, H. Boers & W.W. Willis Jr., eds. *Resurrection. The Origin and Future of a Biblical Doctrine*. London: T&T Clark/Continuum, 2006: 138-186.
Cheetham, David. *John Hick. A Critical Introduction and Reflection*. Aldershot: Ashgate, 2003.
Clack, Beverley. "God and Language. A Feminist Perspective on the Meaning of God". In: Stanley E. Porter, ed. *The Nature of Religious Language. A Colloquium*. London: Continuum, 1996: 148-158.
Clements, Keith W. *The Theology of Ronald Gregor Smith*. Leiden: Brill, 1986.
Clines, David J.A. *The Theme of the Pentateuch*, 2nd edn. Sheffield: Sheffield Academic Press, 2004.
Cooper, John C. *The "Spiritual Presence" in the Theology of Paul Tillich. Tillich's Use of St. Paul*. Macon, GA: Mercer University Press, 1997.
Cowart, David. *History and the Contemporary Novel*. Carbondale, IL: Southern Illinois University Press, 1989.
Cox, Harvey. *Common Prayers. Family, Faith, and a Christian's Journey through the Jewish Year*. New York, NY: Houghton Mifflin, 2001.
——, *Many Mansions. A Christian's Encounter with Other Faiths*. London: Collins, 1988.
——, *The Secular City*. London: SCM Press, 1967.
Cox, James L. *A Guide to the Phenomenology of Religion. Key Figures, Formative Influences, and Subsequent Debates*. London: Continuum, 2006.
Crockett, Clayton. *A Theology of the Sublime*. London: Routledge, 2001.
——, *Radical Political Theology. Religion and Politics after Liberalism*. New York, NY: Columbia University Press, 2011.
Crowley, Paul G. *Rahner beyond Rahner. A Great Theologian Encounters the Pacific Rim*. Lanham, MD: Rowman & Littlefield, 2005.

Cupitt, Don. *Is Nothing Sacred? The Non-Realist Philosophy of Religion: Selected Essays*. New York: NY: Fordham University Press, 2002.

———, *The Sea of Faith. Christianity in Change*. Cambridge: Cambridge University Press, 1984.

Dackombe, Amanda. "T.S. Elliot's Brown God". In: Andrew Dix & Jonathan Taylor, eds. *Figures of Heresy. Radical Theology in English and American Writing, 1800-2000*. Brighton: Sussex Academic Press, 2006: 108-121.

Dahl, Espen. *In Between. The Holy beyond Modern Dichotomies*. Göttingen: Vandenhoeck & Ruprecht, 2011.

Davis, Stephen T. *Encountering Jesus. A Debate on Christology*. Louisville, KY: Westminster John Knox Press, 1988.

Deane-Drummond, Celia. *Ecology in Jürgen Moltmann's Theology*. Lewiston, NY: Edwin Mellen Press, 1997.

Dych, William V. *Karl Rahner*. London: Continuum, 2000.

Eliade, Mircea. *The Sacred and the Profane: The Nature of Religion*, trans. Willard R. Trask. New York, NY: Harcourt, 1987.

Emmanuel, Steven M. *Kierkegaard and the Concept of Revelation*. Albany, NY: State University of New York Press, 1996.

Fasching, Darrel J. *The Ethical Challange of Auschwitz and Hiroshima. Apocalypse or Utopia?* Albany, NY: State University of New York Press, 1993.

Ferrer, Jorge N. & Jacob H. Sherman. "Introduction. The Participatory Turn in Spirituality, Mysticism, and Religious Studies". In: Jorge N. Ferrer & Jacob H. Sherman, eds. *The Participatory Turn. Spirituality, Mysticism, Religious Studies*. Albany, NY: State University of New York Press, 2007: 1-80.

Fiddes, Paul S. "The Quest for a Place which Is 'Not-a-Place': the Hiddenness of God and the Presence of God". In: Oliver Davies & Denys Turner, eds. *Silence and the Word. Negative Theology and Incarnation*. Cambridge: Cambridge University Press, 2002: 35-60.

———, *The Creative Suffering of God*. Oxford: Oxford University Press, 1988.

Flannery, Edward H. "The Cross in Jewish-Christian Relations". In: Alan L. Berger, Harry J. Cargas & Susan E. Nowak, eds. *The Continuing Agony. From the Carmelite Convent to the Crosses at Auschwitz*. Lanham, MD: University Press of America, 2004: 235-248.

Flynn, Eileen and Gloria Thomas. *Living Faith. An Introduction to Theology*, 2nd edn. Lanham, MD: Rowman & Littlefield, 1989.

Ford, Dennis. *The Search for Meaning. A Short History*. Berkeley, CA: University of California Press, 2007.

Forte, Bruno. *The Essence of Christianity*, foreword by Geoffrey Wainwright. Grand Rapids, MI: Eerdmans, 2003.

Fountain, J. Stephen. "Postmodernism, A/Theology, and the Possibility of Language as Universal Eucharist". In: Stanley E. Porter, ed. *The Nature of Religion Language. A Colloquium*. Sheffield: Sheffield Academic Press, 1996: 131-158.

Frame, Tom. *Losing My Religion. Unbelief in Australia*. Sydney: University of New South Wales Press, 2009.

Francis, Leslie & Adrian Thatcher. "Christian Education". In: Leslie Francis & Adrian Thatcher, eds. *Christian Perspectives on Education*, 2nd edn. Leominster: Gracewing, 1998: 264-281.

Freundorfer, Rosemarie. *Dein Reich Komme. Das Zentrum in Rosemary Radford Ruethers Theologie.* Münster: LIT Verlag, 2004.

Fries, Heinrich. *Fundamental Theology*, trans. Robert J. Daly, SJ. Washington, DC: The Catholic University of America Press, 1996.

Fromm, Harold. *The Nature of Human Being. From Environmentalism to Consciousness.* Baltimore, MD: Johns Hopkins University Press, 2009.

Fry, Stanley A. *A New Vision of God for the 21st Century. Discovering the Essential Wesley for Pastors and Other Speakers.* Lincoln, NE: iUniverse, 2005.

Furet, François. *Marx and the French Revolution.* Chicago, IL: University of Chicago Press, 1988.

Geivett, R. Douglas. *Evil and the Evidence for God. The Challenge of John Hick's Theodicy.* Philadelphia, PA: Temple University Press, 1993.

Gelven, Michael. *Truth and Existence. A Philosophical Inquiry.* University Park, PA: Pennsylvania State University Press, 1990.

Gennaro, Stephen and Douglas Kellner, "Under Surveillance: Herbert Marcuse and the FBI". In: Harry Dahms, ed. *Nature, Knowledge, and Negation.* Bingley: Emerald, 2009: 283-314.

Gensichen, D.H.-W. "World Community and World Religions". In: J.S. Pobee, ed. *Religion in a Pluralistic Society. Essays Presented to Professor C.G. Baëta.* Leiden: Brill, 1976: 27-37.

Gentile, Emilio. *God's Democracy. American Religion after September 11.* Westport, CT: Greenwood, 2008.

Geoghegan, Vincent. *Ernst Bloch.* London: Routledge, 1996.

Glass, Marty. *Yuga. An Anatomy of Our Fate. A Companion to Spiritual Practice.* Hillsdale, NY: Sophia Perennis, 2001.

Glyn-Jones, Anne. *Holding Up a Mirror. How Civilizations Decline.* Bowling Green, OH: Imprint Academic, 1996.

Gowan, Donald E. *Theology in Exodus. Biblical Theology in the Form of a Commentary.* Louisville, KY: Westminster John Knox Press, 1994.

Granter, Edward. *Critical Social Theory and the End of Work.* Farnham: Ashgate, 2009.

Grenz, Stanley J. & Roger E. Olson. *Twentieth Century Theology. God and the World in a Transitional Age.* Downers Grove, IL: InterVarsity Press, 1992.

Griffiths, Brian. "The Business Corporation as a Moral Community," in Parth J. Shah, ed. *Morality of Markets.* New Delhi: The Academic Foundation and the Centre for Civil Society): 205-218.

Grigg, Richard. *Gods after God. An Introduction to Contemporary Radical Theologies.* Albany, NY: State University of New York Press, 2006.

Haight, Roger, SJ. *The Future of Christology.* London: Continuum, 2005.

Hall, Douglas J. "*Honest to God* in North America". In: John A.T. Robinson, *Honest to God*, with essays by Douglas J. Hall and Rowan Williams, 40th anniversary edn. Louisville, KY: Westminster John Knox Press, 2002: 145-162.

Hall, Lindsey. *Swinburne's Hell and Hick's Universalism. Are We Free to Reject God?* Aldershot: Ashgate, 2003.

Hamilton, William. "Dietrich Bonhoeffer". In: Thomas J.J. Altizer & William Hamilton, *Radical Theology and the Death of God*. Indianapolis, IN: Bobbs-Merrill, 1966: 113-116.

Hamilton, William. *The Quest for the Post-Historical Jesus*. New York, NY: Continuum, 1994.

Hardy, Daniel W. *God's Ways with the World. Thinking and Practising Christian Faith*. London: Continuum, 2005, 289.

Harries, Richard. *After the Devil. Christianity and Judaism in the Shadow of the Holocaust*. Oxford: Oxford University Press, 2003.

Hawkins, Ralph K. *A Heritage in Crisis. Where We've Been, Where We Are, and Where We're Going*. Lanham, MD: University Press of America, 2001.

Held, David. *Introduction to Critical Theory. Horkheimer to Habermas*. Berkeley, CA: University of California Press, 1980.

Heller, Sophia. *The Absence of Myth*. Albany, NY: State University of New York Press, 2006.

Hermans, Chris A. M. *Participatory Learning. Religious Education in a Globalizing Society*. Leiden: Brill, 2003.

Herrick, James A. *The Making of the New Spirituality. The Eclipse of Western Religious Tradition*. Downers Grove, IL: InterVarsity Press, 2003.

Hick, John. "Jesus and the World Religions". In: John Hick, ed. *The Myth of God Incarnate*. London: SCM Press, 1993: 167-185.

Hick, John. *The Metaphor of God Incarnate. Christology in a Pluralistic Age*, 2nd edn. Louisville, KY: Westminster John Knox Press, 2006.

Higgins, Gregory C. *The Tapestry of Christian Theology. Modern Minds on the Biblical Narrative*. Mahwah, NJ: Paulist Press, 2003.

Hill Fletcher, Jeannine. *Monopoly of Salvation? A Feminist Approach to Religious Pluralism*. London: Continuum, 2005.

Højsgaard, Morten T. "Cyber-religion: On the Cutting Edge between the Virtual and the Real". In: Morten T. Højsgaard & Margit Warburg, eds. *Religion and Cyberspace*. Oxford: Routledge, 2005: 50-64.

Horton, Michael S. *Lord and Servant. A Covenant Christology*. Louisville, KY: Westminster John Knox Press, 2005.

Horton, Michael. *The Gospel Commission. Recovering God's Strategy for Making Disciples*. Grand Rapids, MI: Baker.

Hryniewicz, Wacław. *The Challenge of Our Hope. Christian Faith in Dialogue*. Washington, DC: The Council for Research in Values and Philosophy, 2007.

Hungerford, Amy. *Postmodern Belief. American Literature and Religion since 1960*. Princeton, NJ: Princeton University Press, 2010.

Hunsberger, George R. *Lesslie Newbigin's Theology of Cultural Plurality. Bearing the Witness of the Spirit*. Grand Rapids, MI: Eerdmans, 1998.

Hunt, Anne. *What Are They Saying about the Trinity?* Mahwah, NJ: Paulist Press, 1998, 45.

Idinopulos, Thomas A. *Betrayal of Spirit. Jew-hatred, the Holocaust, and Christianity*. Aurora, CO: Davies Group, 2007.

Irr, Caren. "One-Dimensional Symptoms: What Marcuse Offers a Critical Theory of Law". In: Jeffrey T. Nealon & Caren Irr, eds. *Rethinking the*

Frankfurt School. Alternative Legacies of Cultural Critique. Albany, NY: State University of New York Press, 2002: 169-186.

Jasper, David. *The Sacred Desert. Religion, Art, and Culture*. Oxford: Wiley-Blackwell, 2004.

Jeanrond, Werner G. "Rahner's Theological Method and a Theology of Love". In: Pádraic Conway and Fáinche Ryan, eds. *Karl Rahner. Theologian for the Twenty-First Century*, vol. III: *Studies in Theology, Society, and Culture*. Bern: Peter Lang, 2010: 103-120.

Johann, SJ, Robert O. "Modern Atheism". In: Ralph M. McInemy, ed. *New Themes in Christian Philosophy*. Notre Dame, IN: University of Notre Dame Press, 1968: 348-369.

Jorgenson, Allen G. *The Appeal to Experience in the Christologies of Friedrich Schleiermacher and Karl Rahner*. New York, NY: Peter Lang, 2007.

Juschka, Darlene M. *Feminism in the Study of Religion. A Reader*. London: Continuum, 2001.

Kania, Walter. *Healthy Religion. A Psychological Guide to a Mature Faith*. Bloomington, IN: AuthorHouse, 2009.

Kärkkäinen, Veli-Matti. *An Introduction to the Theology of Religions. Biblical, Historical, and Contemporary Perspectives*. Downers Grove, IL: InterVarsity Press, 2003.

Kasper, Walter. *Jesus the Christ*. Mahwah, NJ: Paulist Press, 1976.

McManus, OP, Kathleen A. *Unbroken Communion. The Place and Meaning of Suffering in the Theology of Edward Schillebeeckx*. Lanham, MD: Rowman & Littlefield, 2003.

Kearney, Richard. *Modern Movements in European Philosophy. Phenomenology, Critical Theory, Structuralism*, 2nd edn. Manchester: Manchester University Press, 1994.

Kee, Alistair. "Death of God". In: Gordon S. Wakefield, ed. *The Westminster Dictionary of Christian Spirituality*. Philadelphia, PA: Westminster, 1983: 105-106.

Kellner, Douglas. *Herbert Marcuse and the Crisis of Marxism*. Berkeley, CA: University of California Press, 1984.

Kennedy, Philip, OP. *Schillebeeckx*. Collegeville, MN: Liturgical Press, 1993.

Kennedy, Philip. *A Modern Introduction to Theology. New Questions for Old Beliefs*. London: I.B. Tauris, 2006.

Korstvedt, Benjamin M. *Listening for Utopia in Ernst Bloch's Musical Philosophy*. Cambridge: Cambridge University Press, 2010.

Küng, Hans. *On Being a Christian*, trans. Edward Quinn (New York, NY: Pocket Books, 1976.

Lakeland, Paul. *The Liberation of the Laity. In Search of an Accountable Church*. London: Continuum, 2004.

Lambert, Frank. *Religion in American Politics. A Short History*. Princeton, NJ: Princeton University Press, 2008.

Lee, Keekok. *The Natural and the Artefactual. The Implications of Deep Science and Deep Technology for Environmental Philosophy*. Lanham, MD: Lexington Books, 1999.

Leffler II, William J., and Paul H. Jones. *The Structure of Religion. Judaism and Christianity*. Lanham, MD: University Press of America, 2005.
Lehmann, David. *Democracy and Development in Latin America. Economics, Politics, and Religion in the Post-War Period*. Philadelphia, PA: Temple University Press, 1990.
Lennan, Richard. *The Ecclesiology of Karl Rahner*. Oxford: Oxford University Press, 2002.
Levering, Matthew W. *Sacrifice and Community. Jewish Offering and Christian Eucharist*. Oxford: Blackwell, 2005.
Levitas, Ruth. *The Concept of Utopia*. Bern: Peter Lang, 1990.
Liebersohn, Harry. *Religion and Industrial Society. The Protestant Social Congress in Wilhelmine Germany*. Philadelphia, PA: The American Philosophical Society, 1986.
Lines, Dennis. *Spirituality in Counseling and Psychotherapy*. London: Sage, 2006.
Lints, Richard. *Progressive and Conservative Religious Ideologies. The Tumultuous Decade of the 1960s*. Farnham: Ashgate, 2010.
Lippy, Charles H. *Pluralism Comes of Age. American Religious Culture in the Twentieth Century*. Armonk, NY: M.E. Sharpe, 2002.
Luke, Timothy W. *Ecocritique. Contesting the Politics of Nature, Economy, and Culture*. Minneapolis, MN: University of Minnesota Press, 1997.
Mackey, James P. *The Critique of Theological Reason*. Cambridge: Cambridge University Press, 2000.
Magno, Joseph A. & Victor LaMotte. *The Christian, the Atheist, and Freedom*. New York, NY: Precedent, 1973.
Mancuso, Vito. "La religione civile che manca all'Italia". In: *La Repubblica*, 13 gennaio 2009. Accessed online as http://ricerca.repubblica.it /repubblica/ archivio/repubblica/2009/01/13/r2-la-religione-civile-che-manca.html, on March 14, 2011.
Manning, Russell R. *Theology at the End of Culture. Paul Tillich's Theology of Culture and Art*. Leuven: Peeters, 2005.
Marcuse, Herbert. *One-Dimensional Man. Studies in the Ideology of Advanced Industrial Society*. Boston, MA: Beacon Press, 1964.
Margolin, Victor. *The Politics of the Artificial. Essays on Design and Design Studies*. Chicago, IL: University of Chicago Press, 2002.
Marquardt, Friedrich-Wilhelm. *Auf einem Weg ins Lehrhaus. Leben und Denken mit Israel*. Frankfurt am Main: Otto Lembeck, 2009.
Martinez, Gaspar. *Confronting the Mystery of God. Political, Liberation, and Public Theologies*. London: Continuum, 2001.
Marty, Martin E. *Modern American Religion*, vol. III: Under God, Indivisible: 1941-1960. Chicago, IL: University of Chicago Press, 1996.
Mbogu, Nicholas I. *Christology and Religious Pluralism. A Review of John Hick's Theocentric Model of Christology and the Emergence of African Inculturation Christologies*. Berlin: LIT Verlag, 2006.
McAuliffe, Patricia. *Fundamental Ethics. A Liberationist Approach*. Washington, DC: Georgetown University Press, 1993.
McCabe, Herbert. *God Matters*. London: Continuum, 2005.
McCullough, Lisa. "Historical Introduction". In: Lisa McCullough & Brian Schroeder, eds. *Thinking through the Death of God. A Critical Companion to*

Thomas J.J. Altizer. Albany, NY: State University of New York Press, 2004: xv-xxviii.

McGreden, Lyn. *Luminous Moments. The Contemporary Sacred.* Hindmarsh, SA: ATF Press, 2010.

Meredith, Lawrence. *Life before Death. A Spiritual Journey of Mind and Body.* Atlanta, GA: Humanic Trade Group, 2000.

Merrigan, Terrence. "Postmodernity and Sacramentality. Two Challenges to Speaking about God". In: Lieven Boeve & John C. Ries, eds. *Sacramental Presence in a Postmodern Context.* Leuven: Peeters, 2001: 106-111.

Merrigan, Terrence. "The Historical Jesus in the Pluralist Theology of Religions". In: Terrence Merrigan & Jacques Haers, eds. *The Myriad Christ. Plurality and the Quest for Unity in Contemporary Theology.* Leuven: Peeters, 2000: 61-82.

Michener, Ronald T. *Engaging Deconstructive Theology.* Aldershot: Ashgate, 2007.

Miles, Grahame. *Science and Religious Experience. Are They Similar Forms of Knowledge?* Eastbourne: Sussex Academic Press, 2007.

Miles, Todd. *A God of Many Understandings? The Gospel and Theology of Religions.* Nashville, TN: B&H Publishing Group, 2010.

Miller, Ron, and Laura Bernstein. *Healing the Jewish-Christian Rift. Growing Beyond Our Wounded History.* Woodstock, VT: SkyLight Paths, 2006.

Moisio, Olli-Pekka, and Juha Suoranta, "Hope and Education in the Era of Globalization". In: Klas Roth & Ilan Gur-Zeév, eds. *Education in the Era of Globalization.* Dordrecht: Springer, 2007: 231-246.

Molnar, Paul D. *Incarnation and Resurrection. Toward a Contemporary Understanding.* Grand Rapids, MI: Eerdmans, 2007.

Molnar, Thomas. *Theists and Atheists. A Typology of Non-Belief.* The Hague: Mouton, 1980.

Monroe, Ann. *The Word. Imagining the Gospel in Modern America.* Louisville, KY: Westminster John Knox Press, 2000.

Monsma, Stephen V., Clifford Christians, Eugene R. Dykema, Arie Leegwater, *Responsible Technology*, ed. Stephen V. Monsma. Grand Rapids, MI: Eerdmans, 1986.

Moorhead, James H. *World without End. Mainstream American Protestant Visions of the Last Things, 1880-1925.* Bloomington, IN: Indiana University Press, 1999.

Moylan, Tom. "Bloch against Bloch: The Theological Reception of *Das Prinzip Hoffnung* and the Liberation of the Utopian Function". In: Jamie O. Daniel and Tom Moylan, eds. *Not Yet. Reconsidering Ernst Bloch.* London: Verso, 1997: 96-121.

Muller, Richard A. *The Study of Theology. From Biblical Interpretation to Contemporary Formulation.* Grand Rapids, MI: Zondervan, 1991.

Munt, Sally R. "Queer Spiritual Spaces". In: Kath Browne, Sally R. Munt &Andrew K.T. Yip, eds. *Queer Spiritual Spaces. Sexuality and Sacred Places.* Farnham: Ashgate, 2010: 1-34.

Murakami, Tatsuo. "Asking the Question of the Origin of Religion in the Age of Globalization". In Jennifer I.M. Reid, ed. *Religion and Global Culture.*

New Terrain in the Study of Religion and the Work of Charles H. Long. Lanham, MD: Lexington Books, 2003: 7-26.

Murphy, Richard. *Theorizing the Avant-Garde. Modernism, Expressionism, and the Problem of Postmodernity.* Cambridge: Cambridge University Press, 1998.

Murphy, Tim. *Nietzsche, Metaphor, Religion.* Albany, NY: State University of New York Press, 2001.

Nasr, Sayyed H. *The Need for a Sacred Science.* Albany, NY: State University of New York Press, 1993.

Negri, Antonio. *The Labor of Job. The Biblical Text as a Parable of Human Labor*, translated by Matteo Mandarini, foreword by Michael Hardt, commentary by Roland Boer. Durham, NC: Duke University Press, 2009.

Nelson-Pallmeyer, Jack. *Jesus against Christianity. Reclaiming the Missing Jesus.* Harrisburg, PA: Trinity Press International/Continuum, 2001.

Netland, Harold A. *Dissonant Voices. Religious Pluralism and the Question of Truth.* Vancouver, BC: Regent College Publishing, 1991.

Norris, Thomas J. *The Trinity. Life of God, Hope for Humanity: towards a Theology of Communion.* Hyde Park, NY: New City Press, 2009.

O'Boyle, Aidan. *Towards a Contemporary Wisdom Christology. Some Catholic Christologies in German, English, and French, 1965–1995.* Rome: Editrice Pontificia Università Gregoriana, 2001.

O'Donnell, John J. *Karl Rahner. Life in the Spirit.* Rome: Editrice Pontificia Università Gregoriana, 2004.

Ochs, Peter. "Judaism and Christian Theology". In: David F. Ford, ed. *The Modern Theologians. An Introduction to the Christian Theology in the Twentieth Century*, 2nd edn. Oxford: Blackwell, 2004: 607-625.

Ogden, Steven G. *The Presence of God in the World. A Contribution to Postmodern Christology based on the Theologies of Paul Tillich and Karl Rahner.* Bern: Peter Lang, 2007.

Oladipo, Caleb O. *The Will to Arise. Theological and Political Themes in African Christianity and the Renewal of Faith and Identity.* New York, NY: Peter Lang, 2006.

Olson, Carl. *Religious Studies. The Key Concepts.* Oxford: Routledge, 2011.

O'Meara, Janet M. "Salvation. Living Communion with God". In: Mary C. Hilkert and Robert J. Schreiter, eds. *The Praxis of the Reign of God. An Introduction to the Theology of Edward Schillebeeckx*, 2nd edn. Bronx, NY: Fordham University Press, 2002: 98-116.

Ong, Walter J., SJ. *The Presence of the Word. Some Prolegomena for Cultural and Religious History.* New Haven, CT: Yale University Press, 1967/Binghamton, NY: Global Publications, 2000.

Orosz, Gábor V. "Human Dignity and Genetics in a Postsecular Age: Habermas' Ideas Concerning Pre-Implantation Genetic Diagnosis and Enhancement in the Context of Theological Tradition Hermeneutic Age". In: Péter Losonczi, &Aakash Singh, eds. *Discoursing the Post-Secular. Essays on the Habermasian Post-Secular Turn.* Vienna: LIT Verlag, 2010: 167-178.

Padgett, Alan G. "Advice for Religious Historians: On the Myth of a Purely Historical Jesus". In: Stephen T. Davis, Daniel Kendall &Gerald O'Collins, eds. *The Resurrection. An Interdisciplinary Symposium on the Resurrection of Jesus.* Oxford: Oxford University Press, 1998: 287-307.

Padgett, Alan G. *Science and the Study of God. A Mutuality Model for Theology and Science*. Grand Rapids, MI: Eerdmans, 2003.

Pailin, David A. *God and the Process of Reality. Foundations of a Credible Theism*. London: Taylor & Francis, 1989.

Parliament, Andrea L. *Secular Hope. What the Religious Right Really Wants and Why Liberal Democrats Should Support Them*. Bloomington, IN: iUniverse, 2010.

Perry, Tim S. *Radical Difference. A Defense of Hendrik Kraemer's Theology of Religions*. Waterloo, ON: Wilfrid Laurier University Press, 2001.

Petrolle, Jean E. *Religious without Belief. Contemporary Allegory and the Search for Postmodern Faith*. Albany, NY: State University of New York Press, 2008.

Piazza, Michael S. *Holy Homosexuals. The Truth about Being Gay or Lesbian and Christian*, revised edition. Dallas, TX: Sources of Hope, 1997.

Pipolo, Tony. "*Winter Light* and *The Silence*". In: Mary L. Bandy and Antonio Monda, eds. *The Hidden God. Film and Faith*. New York, NY: The Museum of Modern Art, 2003: 114-120.

Placher, William C. *The Domestication of Transcendence. How Modern Thinking about God Went Wrong*. Louisville, KY: Westminster John Knox Press, 1996.

Podmore, Simon D. *Kierkegaard and the Self before God. Anatomy of the Abyss*. Bloomington, IN: Indiana University Press, 2011.

Prickett, Stephen. *Narrative, Religion, and Science. Fundamentalism versus Irony, 1700-1999*. Cambridge: Cambridge University Press, 2002.

Propp, Steven H. *And with All Your Mind. A Novel about Evangelical Theology*. Bloomington, IN: iUniverse, 2010.

Protherough, Robert, and John Pick. *Managing Britannia. Culture and Management in Modern Britain*. Exeter: Imprint Academic, 2002.

Quinney, Laura. *William Blake on Self and Soul*. Cambridge, MA: Harvard University Press, 2009.

Raadschelders, Jos C.N. *Government. A Public Administration Perspective*. Armonk, NY: M.E. Sharpe, 2003.

Rahner, Karl. *Foundations of Christian Faith. An Introduction to the Idea of Christianity*. New York, NY: Crossroad, 1978/2005.

Rahner, Karl. *Theological Investigations*, vol. V. Baltimore, MD: Helicon Press, 1966.

Reitz, Charles. *Art, Alienation, and the Humanities. A Critical Engagement with Herbert Marcuse*. Albany, NY: State University of New York Press, 2000.

Rennie, Bryan S. *Reconstructing Eliade. Making Sense of Religion*. Albany, NY: State University of New York Press, 1996.

Robbins, Jill. *Altered Reading. Levinas and Literature*. Chicago, IL: Chicago University Press, 1999.

Ross, James F. *Portraying Analogy*. Cambridge: Cambridge University Press, 1981.

Rubenstein, Mary-Jane. "The Unbearable Withness of Being: On the Essentialist Blind Spot of Anti-ontotheology". In: Creston Davis, John Milbank & Slavoj Žižek, eds. *Theology and the Political. The New Debate*. Durham, NC: Duke University Press, 2005: 340-349.

Saliba, John A. *"Homo Religiosus" in Mircea Eliade. An Anthropological Evaluation.* Leiden: Brill, 1976.

Sardar, Ziauddin. *Postmodernism and the Other. The New Imperialism of Western Culture.* London: Pluto Press, 1998.

Schaeffer, Frank. *Patience with God. Faith for People Who Don't Like Religion or Atheism.* Cambridge, MA: Da Capo Press/Perseus Books, 2009.

Schillebeeckx, Edward. *World and Church*, trans. N. D. Smith. London and Sydney: Sheed & Ward, 1971.

Schmidt, David J. "Circles-Hermeneutic and Otherwise: On Various Sense of the Future as "Not Yet'." In: David Wood, ed. *Writing the Future.* London: Taylor & Francis, 1990: 67-80.

Schreiter, CPPS, Robert J. "Edward Schillebeeckx". In: David F. Ford, ed. *The Modern Theologians. An Introduction to Christian Theology in the Twentieth Century.* Oxford: Blackwell, 2004: 152-161.

Schüssler Fiorenza, Francis. "Systematic Theology. Task and Methods". In: Francis Schüssler Fiorenza & John P. Gavin, eds. *Systematic Theology. Roman Catholic Perspectives*, vol. I. Minneapolis, MN: Augsburg Fortress, 1991: 1-88.

Schuurman, Egbert. *Faith and Hope in Technology*, trans. John Vriend. Toronto, ON: Clements Publishing, 2003.

Schwarz, Hans. *Theology in a Global Context. The Last Two Hundred Years.* Grand Rapids, MI: Eerdmans, 2005.

Schwarzschild, Stephen. "The Lure of Immanence – The Crisis in Contemporary Religious Thought". In: Manachem M. Kellner, ed. *The Pursuit of the Ideal. Jewish Writings of Steven Schwarzschild.* Albany, NY: State University of New York Press, 1990: 61-82.

Sellers, Susan. *Myth and Fairy Tale in a Contemporary Women's Fiction.* New York, NY: Palgrave Macmillan, 2001.

Shakman Hurd, Elizabeth. *The Politics of Secularism in International Relations.* Princeton, NJ: Princeton University Press, 2008.

Sloan, Douglas. *Faith and Knowledge. Mainline Protestantism and American Higher Education.* Louisville, KY: Westminster John Knox Press, 1994.

Smith, Christian. "Secularizing American Higher Education: The Case of Early American Sociology". In: Christian Smith, ed. *The Secular Revolution. Power, Interests, and Conflict in the Secularization of American Public Life.* Berkeley and Los Angeles, CA: University of California Press, 2003: 97-159.

Smith, Jonathan Z. *Map Is Not Territory. Studies in the History of Religions.* Chicago, IL: University of Chicago Press, 1993.

Spivey, Ted R. *Flannery O'Connor. The Woman, the Thinker, the Visionary.* Macon, GA: Mercer University Press, 1997.

Spong, John Shelby. *Eternal Life: A New Vision. Beyond Religion, Beyond Theism, Beyond Heaven and Hell.* New York, NY: HarperOne/HarperCollins, 2009.

Spong, John Shelby. *Rescuing the Bible from Fundamentalism. A Bishop Rethinks the Meaning of Scripture.* New York, NY: HarperOne/HarperCollins, 1992.

Stackhouse, Max L. "Christian Ethics, Practical Theology, and Public Theology in a Global Era". In: Michael Welker &Friedrich Schweitzer, eds. *Reconsidering the Boundaries between Theological Disciplines. Zur Neubestimmung der Grenzen zwischen den theologischen Disziplinen.* Münster: LIT Verlag, 2005: 99-112.

Stander, Simon. "The Commodity". In: Paul Zarembka, ed. *Why Capitalism Survives Crises. The Shock Absorbers*. Bingley: JAI Press/Emerald Group Publishing, 2009: 71-90.

Starkloff, SJ, Carl J. "Renewing the Sacred Loop". In: Vine Deloria Jr., ed. *A Sender of Words. Essays in Memory of John G. Neihardt*. Salt Lake City, UT: Howe Brothers, 1984: 159-172.

Stelzer, Mark. "A New Ecclesial Reality and a New Way of Doing Theology. Heralding a New Pentecost". In: Peter C. Phan & Diana Hayes, eds. *Many Faces, One Church. Cultural Diversity and the American Catholic Experience*. Lanham, MD: Rowman & Littlefield, 2005: 13-26.

Stirk, Peter M. R. *Critical Theory, Politics, and Society. An Introduction*. London: Continuum, 2005.

Summerell, Orrin F. "Introduction: When God Is Not Deity". In: Orrin F. Summerell, ed. *The Otherness of God*. Charlottesville, VA: The University Press of Virginia, 1998: 1-13.

Parsons, Susan F. "Watch and Pray. A Reflection on the Meaning of *Ut*". In: Francesca A. Murphy and Christopher Asprey, eds. *Ecumenism Today. Universal Church in the 21st Century*. Aldershot: Ashgate, 2008: 81-92.

Taylor, Mark C. *After God*. Chicago: The University of Chicago Press, 2007.

Taylor, Mark C. *Erring. A Postmodern A/Theology*. Chicago, IL: University of Chicago Press, 1987.

Whalen, Teresa. *The Authentic Doctrine of the Eucharist*. Kansas City, MO: Sheed and Ward, 1993), 135-136.

Thomas, Abraham V. *Christians in Secular India*. Cranbury, NJ: Associated University Presses, 1974.

Thomas, George M. *Revivalism and Cultural Change. Christianity, Nation Building, and the Market in the Nineteenth-Century United States*. Chicago, IL: University of Chicago Press, 1997.

Thomas, L. Eugene. "The Way of the Religious Renouncer: Power Through Nothingness". In: L. Eugene Thomas & Susan A. Eisenhandler, eds. *Aging and the Religious Dimension*. Westport, CT: Auburn House/Greenwood Publishing, 1994: 51-64.

Torevell, David. *Liturgy and the Beauty of the Unknown. Another Place*. Aldershot: Ashgate, 2007.

Torgerson, Mark A. *An Architecture of Immanence. Architecture for Worship and Ministry Today*. Grand Rapids, MI: Eerdmans, 2007.

Tóth, Cvetka. "The Hermeneutics of Utopia and of Hope in the Bible". In: Jože Krašovec, ed. *The Interpretation of the Bible. The International Symposium in Slovenia*. Sheffield: Sheffield Academic Press, 1998: 1619-1634.

Tracy, David. *Blessed Rage for Order. The New Pluralism in Theology*. Chicago, IL: University of Chicago Press, 1975.

Turner, Denys. "Religion: Illusions and Liberation". In: Terrell Carver, ed. *The Cambridge Companion to Marx*. Cambridge: Cambridge University Press: 310-338.

Ustorf, Werner. *Robinson Crusoe Tries Again. Missiology and European Constructions of "Self" and "Other" in a Global World 1789–2010*. Göttingen: Vandenhoeck & Ruprecht, 2010.

Vahanian, Gabriel. *The Death of God. The Culture of Our Post-Christian Era*. New York, NY: George Braziller, 1967.

Van Buren, Paul. *Discerning the Way. A Theology of Jewish-Christian Reality*. New York, NY: Seabury Press, 1980.

Van Buren, Paul. *The Secular Meaning of the Gospel based on an Analysis of Its Language*. New York, NY: Macmillan, 1966.

Vass, George. *A Pattern of Doctrines 1. God and Christ*, vol. III: Understanding Karl Rahner. London: Continuum, 1996.

Vatter, Miguel. "Introduction: Crediting God with Sovereignty". In: Robert Gooding-Williams, ed. *Crediting God. Sovereignty and Religion in the Age of Global Capitalism*. Bronx, NY: Fordham University Press, 2011: 1-28.

Verolini, Roberto. "The Soul and Its Destiny: Readings and Dialogues on Science, Philosophy, and Religion – a Meeting with Vito Mancuso and Orlando Franceschelli". In: Anna-Teresa Tymieniecka, ed. *Analecta Husserliana. The Yearbook of Phenomenological Research*, vol. IC: *Existence, Historical Fabulation, Destiny*. Dordrecht: Springer, 2009: 431-450.

Vickeri, Philip L. "The End of *Missio Dei* – Secularization, Religions, and the Theology of Mission". In: Volker Küster, ed. *Mission Revisited. Between Mission History and Intercultural Theology*. Münster: Lit Verlag, 2010: 27-44.

Wallis, James H. *Post-Holocaust Christianity. Paul van Buren's Theology of the Jewish-Christian Reality*. Lanham, MD: University Press of America, 1997.

Ward, Graham. "Postmodern Theology". In: David Ford, ed. *The Modern Theologians. An Introduction to Christian Theology since 1918*, third edition. Oxford: Blackwell, 2005: 322-338.

Ward, Ian. *Shakespeare and the Legal Imagination*. Cambridge: Cambridge University Press, 1999.

Weaver-Zercher, David L. "Theologies". In: Philip Goff and Paul Harvey, eds. *Themes in Religion and American Culture*. Chapel Hill, NC: The University of North Carolina Press, 2004: 5-38.

Webb, Val. *Like Catching Water in a Net. Human Attempts to Describe the Divine*. London: Continuum, 2007.

Wedderburn, Alexander J. M. *Jesus and the Historians*. Tübingen: Mohr-Siebeck, 2010.

Wiese, Christian. "'God's Adventure with the World' and 'Sanctity of Life': Theological Speculations and Ethical Reflections in Jonas's Philosophy after Auschwitz". In: Hava Tirosh-Samuelson & Christian Wiese, eds. *The Legacy of Hans Jonas. Judaism and the Phenomenon of Life*. Leiden: Brill, 2008: 419-460.

Wiley, Tatha. *Thinking of Christ. Proclamation, Explanation, Meaning*. London: Continuum, 2003.

Wilhelm, Robert. *Return to Soul. An Invitation to View the Soul*. Lincoln, NE: Writer's Showcase/iUniverse, 2002.

Wilkinson, John. "Introduction". In: Jacques Ellul, *The Meaning of the City*, trans. Dennis Pardee. Grand Rapids, MI: Eerdmans, 1993: vii-xvi.

Winquist, Charles W. "Theology, Symbolism, and Language in the Thought of Langdon Gilkey". In: Jeff B. Pool & Kyle A. Pasewark, eds. *The Theology of Langdon B. Gilkey. Systematic and Critical Studies*. Macon, GA: Mercer University Press, 1999: 259-273.

Woodhead, Linda, and Paul Heelas, *Religion in Modern Times. An Interpretative Theology*. Oxford: Blackwell, 2000.

Woodhead, Linda. "Theology: The Trouble It's In". In: Gavin Hyman, ed. *New Directions in Philosophical Theology. Essays in Honour of Don Cupitt*. Aldershot: Ashgate, 2004: 173-186.

Yü, Chün-Fang. "Chinese Religions on Population, Consumption, and Ecology". In: Harold Coward and Daniel C. Maguire, eds. *Visions of a New Earth. Religious Perspectives on Population, Consumption, and Ecology*. Albany, NY: State University of New York Press, 2000: 161-174.

Zaccaria, Francesco. *Participation and Beliefs in Popular Religiosity. An Empirical-Theological Exploration among Italian Catholics*. Leiden: Brill, 2010.

Index of Subjects

Absence   5, 56, 80-81, 85, 173-174, 182-183
Alienation   12, 33, 150-151, 179
Alteration   8, 89-90
Anthropology   2, 37, 89-90, 158, 160-161
Atheism   5, 7, 14, 57-58, 79, 87, 96, 99-101, 103, 147-148, 174, 184
Autonomy   7, 10, 78, 106-107, 134
Awareness   6, 9, 13-14, 16, 23, 28, 33, 40-42, 46, 56, 66-67, 69-71, 79, 85, 89-90, 96, 109, 117-119, 131, 141, 143-144, 146, 148, 171, 179-180, 182
Being   1, 3-4, 6-12, 14-18, 20, 22-23, 25-29, 31-42, 44, 46, 48-51, 53-58, 60, 62, 66-76, 78, 80, 82, 84-87, 89-91, 93-94, 97, 99-100, 102-103, 105-108, 110-111, 115, 118, 122-128, 130-134, 136, 138, 140, 144-150, 152-157, 160-164, 166-175, 177-182, 184-186
Belief   2-4, 6, 8, 22, 26-33, 37-39, 43, 46-48, 56, 59, 61-62, 65-67, 72, 79-83, 91, 93-94, 96, 98-100, 106-108, 116, 118, 120, 123, 126, 130, 133, 135-137, 139-140, 147-149, 155, 157-158, 161, 163-164, 166, 170, 172-173, 176, 183
Capitalism   2, 26, 49, 131, 176
Christ   4-9, 34-39, 42, 60-65, 67, 85, 89-92, 101-102, 104, 106-111, 131, 133, 157, 160-163, 166-167, 169, 172-174, 176-177, 180-181
Christianity   3, 5-11, 34-36, 38, 57-65, 73-75, 79-83, 86, 89-104, 114-115, 117-118, 125, 129-133, 135, 141, 152, 154, 157, 161-162, 164, 166, 168-178, 180-181, 184, 186
Christology   3-6, 8-9, 34-35, 37-39, 54, 56-57, 60-61, 63-64, 83-85, 89-90, 92, 146, 150, 160-161, 165, 172-173, 181
Church   5-6, 10-11, 13, 16, 53-59, 61-62, 64-65, 75, 107-111, 114, 116, 124, 129-132, 134-135, 139, 151, 165-167, 175-176, 181, 183-185
Communism   2, 26-27, 74, 114, 162-163
Consciousness   5-6, 10, 28, 40-42, 48-51, 58, 63-64, 67, 82, 94, 127-128, 135, 149, 152-153, 155, 162-163, 166, 171, 175-176, 178-180, 185
Creator   26, 53-54, 145, 168
Crisis   5, 31, 50, 172
Criticism   7, 9, 22, 57-59, 70-71, 98-99, 119, 121, 134, 183, 185
Culture   10, 13, 17, 28, 30, 41, 46-47, 70, 87-88, 91, 93-95, 105-107, 109, 132, 136, 159, 163-164, 172, 177-178, 183
Customs   2, 26-28, 46, 117, 158-159

Index of Subjects

Death   4, 7, 9, 45, 64, 71-73, 78-82, 85, 87, 89-97, 100-103, 106, 117, 122, 125, 136, 143, 148-149, 169-175, 185
Death-of-God   1, 9, 78-82, 85, 87, 89-97, 100-103, 106, 125, 143, 169-175
Democracy   2, 26-28, 111, 124, 159-160
Demystification   2, 10, 29, 50, 159
Demythologization   3, 34-38, 134, 160
Desacralization   2, 4, 25-28, 33, 43-46, 50, 57, 59, 115-116, 158, 162, 164-165, 178
Disappearance   13, 80-81, 143, 171, 181, 183-184
Distance   9, 60-61, 63, 65, 67
Divinity   1, 3, 9-10, 12, 14, 36, 38-39, 60, 65-66, 87-88, 90, 98-100, 102-105, 107, 118, 130, 134, 141-142, 144-145, 149, 153-154, 157, 161, 166, 174-175, 180-181, 185
Emancipation   10, 106-107, 134
Equalization   10, 52, 66, 106-108
Ethics   11, 14, 58, 72, 118-120, 134, 140, 184-186
Example   3, 6, 67, 75, 83, 145, 162-163, 179
Existence   1-9, 12-17, 22-23, 25, 27-29, 31-33, 35-42, 44-48, 50, 52-56, 59, 61, 64, 68, 70, 72-73, 79, 85-88, 90-93, 97, 99-100, 102, 105, 108, 118, 122-130, 131, 135-137, 140, 144, 146-156, 158-159, 161-164, 166, 168-169, 171-174, 178, 180, 182, 184-186
Expectation   6, 10-11, 72, 132-133, 144-145, 157, 165, 168, 184
Fiction   8, 85, 137, 170
Flesh   9, 38, 69-70, 98, 161, 166, 173-174
Freedom   3, 5, 7, 11, 27, 31-32, 48, 65-66, 70-71, 109-112, 119-120, 149, 155, 163-165, 180, 185
Future   2, 5-6, 15-23, 43, 45, 73-74, 76, 90, 144-145, 157-158, 160, 164-168, 178, 180
Goodness   14, 82-83, 91-92, 119, 147, 155, 185-186
Gospel   6-8, 63, 68-69, 85, 96, 99-101, 103, 121, 127, 170, 174
Guilt   9, 99-102
Hermeneutics   101-102, 158
History   1, 4, 6, 8, 11, 13, 15, 17, 19-23, 25-26, 28-32, 34, 36, 39-40, 43, 46-49, 51, 53, 57, 61-62, 64-65, 68, 72-74, 77-78, 80, 85, 94, 97, 99-102, 106, 114-118, 121, 124, 128, 130, 132-133, 138, 141-142, 144-146, 149, 153, 155, 157-158, 162-163, 165, 170-171, 174-175, 178-179
Hope   2, 6-7, 14, 16-24, 26, 73-76, 91-92, 95, 105, 109, 112-113, 122, 124, 132, 135-136, 145, 148-149, 152, 154, 157-158, 165-166, 168-169, 172, 184
Humanity   2-7, 9, 11-14, 17-19, 21-23, 29-30, 35-39, 45-48, 53, 57-58, 60, 62, 64-66, 71-76, 88, 90-92, 98-107, 109, 111, 118, 121, 123-126, 128, 130, 133-134, 138, 141-142, 145, 147, 149, 151-154, 157, 159, 161, 163-166, 168-169, 172-176, 178, 180-181, 184-186
Ideal   2, 5, 26-27, 30, 45, 48, 62, 130, 143, 157-158, 173
Identity   14, 40, 153-154, 179-181
Ideology   13, 26, 112, 117-118
Incarnation   3-4, 14, 35-39, 42, 62, 82, 98, 100-101, 150-152, 160-161, 166, 174, 181
Industrialization   2-3, 25-28, 45, 82, 158-160

Interpretation 4, 13, 47, 70, 73, 90, 118, 133, 157-158, 163, 169, 180-181
Islam 8, 81-83
Jesus 3-4, 6-9, 14, 34, 37-39, 42, 56, 60-67, 71-73, 75-76, 78, 80-81, 83-85, 89, 96-101, 125, 130, 150, 152, 160-162, 166-168, 170-171, 174, 179-180, 186
Judaism 8, 69, 75-76, 81-83, 114, 141-142, 145, 162, 174
Justice 14, 31, 62, 99, 107, 110-111, 147-149, 154-155, 184-186
Laicization 10, 149
Language 7-8, 29, 65, 71, 77-83, 89, 98, 117, 133, 136, 153, 160, 168, 171, 178
Liberalism 1-2, 26-28, 84, 143, 159-160, 167
Life 1, 5, 7, 11, 14-15, 18, 20, 23, 25-29, 33, 44-47, 50, 55, 58-59, 62-64, 67-69, 71-76, 78, 82, 85, 88-90, 93, 96-97, 99-101, 104, 107-108, 110, 112, 122-123, 125-137, 139-140, 144, 146, 148-150, 154-155, 158-160, 163-165, 168-169, 173-174, 176-177, 179-180, 185-186
Literature 8, 140, 183
Logos 6, 14, 37-38, 65, 67, 150, 152, 160-161, 180
Macrocosm 10, 41, 107
Marxism 4, 16-17, 22, 31, 74, 116-117, 162-163
Materiality 4, 9, 11, 30, 36, 39, 40-42, 46-50, 66-68, 87, 113, 118, 125, 127, 136, 143, 145, 149-152, 155, 161, 175, 181, 184-185
Matter 3-4, 9, 11-12, 15, 17-19, 21-22, 31-32, 35-41, 52, 63-64, 66, 69-70, 74, 76, 78, 84, 87-88, 98-100, 102, 107, 112, 116, 128, 135, 140, 142, 147, 150-153, 156, 161-162, 166, 173-174, 178, 185-186
Maturity 11, 119
Meaning 4, 7-9, 12-14, 17-18, 21-23, 31, 43, 45, 47-53, 55-56, 58-59, 62, 64, 68-69, 71-76, 78, 81, 83, 92-93, 98-99, 101-102, 107-109, 118-119, 122-125, 127-128, 131, 133, 135-138, 140, 144-146, 150-154, 161-175, 177, 179, 183
Metaphor 8, 61, 80-82, 84-85, 100-101, 150
Metaphysics 3, 7, 11, 20, 22, 28-29, 31-33, 38, 68, 75, 158-159, 168
Microcosm 10, 41, 107
Modernity 2, 43-45, 84, 105
Monotheism 80, 172
Morality 7, 11, 108, 110-111, 118, 129, 134, 147, 171, 176, 186
Ontology 7, 37, 80-83, 109, 152, 156, 171
Otherworldliness 8, 20, 22, 34, 93, 172-173
Past 2, 4, 9-11, 15-17, 25, 27, 29, 31, 33, 43, 45-46, 48, 52, 57-59, 66, 92, 94, 106, 108, 111, 116, 121, 125, 139, 144-146, 158-159, 163-164, 177, 179
Philosophy 1-3, 15, 17, 23, 28, 30, 60, 65, 68, 82, 87, 97, 106, 109, 140, 147, 159, 176-177, 181
Pluralism 7, 11, 60, 64, 69, 74-75, 91, 94, 118-120
Polytheism 8, 79
Present 1-3, 5-6, 8-10, 12-13, 15-23, 25, 35, 40, 42, 50, 53, 55-60, 63, 66-67, 70, 72, 78, 81-82, 84-85, 90-94, 97, 102, 104, 113-115, 117, 130, 139-143, 152, 155-157, 160-161, 165-165, 168, 174, 177, 179, 182-186
Profane 4, 8, 44-46, 88-89, 102, 129, 131, 133, 135, 137, 164

Index of Subjects

Progress   2-5, 10-11, 17, 19, 27, 29, 32, 40, 48, 57, 74, 82, 91-92, 100-101, 105, 109, 114-117, 125-126, 133, 139, 144, 158-159, 177

Quality   11, 18, 26, 32, 66, 83, 119, 154-155, 176

Radicalism   1, 77, 93, 156

Reason   3, 11, 30-33, 44-46, 49-50, 57-58, 71, 81, 104, 124, 132, 136, 144-145, 148, 157-159, 166-167

Reform   27, 111, 141

Relationship   14, 28, 40, 42, 52, 54-56, 78, 107, 113, 125-126, 146, 150-155, 161-162, 168, 180

Relevance   8, 59, 66, 76, 93, 99, 144-145, 153, 167, 184

Religion   1-6, 8-14, 20, 27-28, 30, 34, 38, 44-51, 53, 55-58, 60-67, 72, 75-79, 81-89, 93-99, 101-102, 104, 106-108, 110-119, 121-149, 151, 153-158, 162-179, 181-184, 186

Responsibility   6, 11, 69, 71, 74, 107, 119-120, 178

Revolution   7, 15, 27, 104, 129-131, 141

Sacred   4, 8, 11, 15, 43-51, 59, 88-89, 93-95, 102, 108, 112, 114-115, 129, 131, 133, 135, 137, 139, 142, 175, 180-182

Salvation   53-53, 57, 63-64, 66-67, 73, 101, 107, 131, 162, 164, 166-167

Science   3, 5, 10, 12, 31-33, 38, 48-49, 53-54, 57-59, 77-78, 82, 84, 105-109, 111, 114, 116-117, 130, 134-135, 140, 159, 164, 182

Self-communication   4, 40-42, 161-162

Self-transcendence   4, 36, 40-42, 161-162

Silence   5, 22, 80-82, 165, 173

Sin   9, 73, 99-102, 134, 163

Society   3, 5-15, 17, 19, 26-29, 32-33, 41, 44-45, 49-56, 58-59, 63-64, 66, 69, 71, 74, 77-79, 82, 85, 91-99, 103, 105-119, 121-124, 128-136, 138-140, 147, 149, 152-154, 156, 158-160, 162, 164-165, 167, 169-179, 183-184, 186

Space   4, 15, 18, 23, 39-40, 47, 86, 94, 170, 184

Spirit   3, 9, 14, 36-41, 50, 65, 69-70, 98-100, 102, 106-108, 125, 141, 153, 160-162, 173-175

Spiritualization   6, 68-70

Supernatural   1, 7-9, 11-12, 21, 62, 64, 80-81, 88-93, 99-102, 124-125, 131, 133, 135-137, 156, 166, 169, 173, 179, 181-182

Technology   3, 5, 10, 16, 31, 33, 35, 38, 45, 53-54, 58-59, 77-78, 96, 105-107, 109, 114, 116, 135, 140, 159, 164, 184

Teleology   2, 21-22

Theism   5, 14, 20, 54, 57, 68, 122, 184

Time   4, 9, 13, 18, 22-23, 25, 31-32, 39-40, 47, 49, 57, 78, 86, 88, 94-95, 101, 107, 110, 112, 119, 128, 130-132, 140-141, 144-145, 148, 153, 161-165, 168, 170-171, 176

Traditionalism   1, 10, 35, 89-91, 114, 167, 169

Transcendence   3-4, 9, 12, 20-22, 24, 30, 32, 36, 40-42, 47, 62, 64, 66, 68, 90, 97, 100, 102, 124-125, 141-144, 146, 149-152, 156-157, 160-162, 164, 172-175, 179, 182

Trinity   14, 125, 147-148, 152-155

Universe   1, 4, 11, 30, 38-39, 41-42, 49, 68, 93, 107, 112-113, 123, 136, 149-150, 156, 160, 168, 179, 184

Word (of God)   9, 21, 38, 52-53, 63, 65-66, 71, 76, 78-82, 92,

102, 107, 109, 124, 127, 171, 175, 177-178

World   2-10, 12-23, 25, 27, 29-30, 33-48, 50-77, 79-102, 104-114, 116-119, 121, 123-143, 145-146, 149-158, 160-186

www.ingramcontent.com/pod-product-compliance
Lightning Source LLC
Chambersburg PA
CBHW052042300426
44117CB00012B/1930